# 'TRANSFORMING' CHILDREN'S SERVICES?

Social Work, Neoliberalism and the 'Modern' World

**Also by Paul Michael Garrett:**

*Remaking Social Work with Children and Families: A Critical Discussion on the 'Modernisation' of Social Care* (2003)
*Social Work and Irish People in Britain: Historical and Contemporary Responses to Irish Children and Families* (2004)

# 'TRANSFORMING' CHILDREN'S SERVICES?

## Social Work, Neoliberalism and the 'Modern' World

*Paul Michael Garrett*

 Open University Press

Open University Press
McGraw-Hill Education
McGraw-Hill House
Shoppenhangers Road
Maidenhead
Berkshire
England
SL6 2QL

email: enquiries@openup.co.uk
world wide web: www.openup.co.uk

and Two Penn Plaza, New York, NY 10121–2289, USA

First published 2009

A catalogue record of this book is available from the British Library

ISBN13: 978-0-33-523425-7 (pb)   978-0-33-523424-0 (hb)
ISBN10: 0335234259 (pb)   0335234240 (hb)

Library of Congress Cataloging-in-Publication Data
CIP data applied for

Typeset by RefineCatch Limited, Bungay, Suffolk
Printed in the UK by Bell and Bain Ltd, Glasgow

**Mixed Sources**
Product group from well-managed
forests and other controlled sources
www.fsc.org  Cert no. TT-COC-002769
© 1996 Forest Stewardship Council

FSC

The *McGraw·Hill* Companies

This book is for Lisa Arthurworrey

# Contents

# Acknowledgements

I am entirely responsible for the contents of this book, particularly its short-comings. There are, however, a few people I would like to thank.

Brenda Clare, Elizabeth Fernandez (both in Australia) Nora Duckett, Eileen Munro (both in England) and two anonymous readers provided helpful guidance and suggestions when I initially submitted the proposal for the book. Furthermore, staff at McGraw-Hill/Open University were also very helpful, efficient and responded promptly to my queries.

I am also grateful to students and colleagues within the School of Political Science and Sociology, at the National University of Ireland in Galway: within the staff group Allyn Fives was a reliable source of advice. On the editorial collective of *Critical Social Policy*, Gerry Mooney was constantly supportive. My more recent involvement with the editorial board of the *European Journal of Social Work* also led me to reflect further on some of the themes I was trying to develop in the book.

Finally, simply to acknowledge some people who kept on throwing beams of light into, sometimes, dark corners: John and Mary Cunningham, Sarah Clancy, Katerina Erlebachova, Su-ming Khoo, Kenneth Madden, Paddy McDonagh (who provided the book's eclectic jazz soundtrack), Maureen McGrath, Christina O'Rourke, Vera Orschel, Henrike Rau, Gabi Zebrowska, all at Charlie Byrne's Bookshop.

Paul Michael Garrett
Galway, May 2009

# List of main abbreviations

ACPO – The Association of Chief Police Officers
ADSS – The Association of Directors of Social Services
AF – Assessment Framework for Children in Need and their Families
ASBO – Anti-Social Behaviour Order
BASW – The British Association of Social Workers
CAF/eCAF – Common Assessment Framework/Electronic Common Assessment Framework
CAR – Core Assessment Record
CfC – *Change for Children* programme
CPd – ContactPoint database
CS – Connexions Service
DCSF – Department for Children, Schools and Families
DfEE – Department for Education and Employment
DfES – Department for Education and Skills
DFP – Dundee Family Project
DoH – Department of Health
ECM – *Every Child Matters*
GPS – Global Positioning Systems
ICO – Information Commissioner's Office
ICS – Integrated Children's System
ICT – information and communications technologies
IFSPs – intensive family support projects: more recently referred to as family intervention projects (FIPs)
IRT – Identification, Referral and Tracking
JAR – Joint Area Review
JCHR – House of Lords and House of Commons Joint Committee on Human Rights
LP – Lead Professional
NCH – National Children's Home
PIU – Performance and Innovation Unit
RFID – radio frequency identification
SETF – Social Exclusion Task Force
SWP – Social Work Practices
YOTs – Youth Offending Teams

# 1 Introduction

In England, the Children Act 2004, initially heralded by *Every Child Matters* (ECM), reflects the government's project to reshape Children's Services.[1] At present, therefore, a range of policy initiatives flowing from this legislation is beginning to impact on the ways in which services are organized and provided. In this context, two factors are striking: first, the government's commitment to what has been referred to as the 'transformational reform agenda' within the sector (DfES 2006a: 2): second, an apparent wariness on the part of many practitioners about the direction of these 'reforms'. In spring 2006, for example, well-attended conferences took place in Nottingham and Liverpool, which illuminated social workers' concern. The former event set out to 'affirm' the social work 'value base' and the latter was intent on retaining a social work commitment to promoting 'social justice' in a field where work is increasingly being 'shaped by managerialism, by the fragmentation of services, and by restrictions and lack of resources'. In short, the message from these conferences was that many practitioners felt under threat from a New Labour administration seemingly tough on social work and tough on the values of social work.

While not implying that such conferences and related fora are entirely orientated to the past, *'Transforming' Children's Services* is underpinned by an understanding that sentimental appeals, which beckon a return to a 'golden age', fail to promote an adequate analysis. At the same time, it is recognized that, for example, New Labour's *Every Child Matters: Change for Children* programme (CfC) may include potentially positive currents. For example, the aspiration, for some merely rhetorical, to rid services for children of the stigma with which they are often associated. Perhaps more fundamentally, while committed to the promotion of a new 'democratic professionalism' (Davis and Garrett 2004), this book is founded on the idea that no profession, or set of working practices, can remain static and undisturbed in disturbing times. However, the book is also rooted in an understanding that any trace of progressive elements detectable in the endeavour to 'transform' Children's Services has been located within a neoliberal framework which is likely to constrain, nullify, or at best render ephemeral the more potentially positive components.

I am not, of course, assuming the bogus 'posture of a motionless specta-tor' (Bourdieu 2000: 22) because in the field of higher education, throughout Europe, the workforce is also subjected to – and resists – neoliberal *remaking* practices which are not entirely dissimilar to those at the core of the 'trans-formational reform agenda' within Children's Services (see also Mautner 2005). However, this contribution will be firmly rooted in a commitment to encouraging close, critical and sceptical reading of texts (central to agenda of 'transformation') which purport to be authoritative and which seek, albeit often implicitly, to 'shutdown' alternative readings, reflections and practices.[2] That is, although avoiding becoming a vapid or 'ritualized critique of New Labour policies' (Pithouse 2007: 2), the book's focal aspiration is to assist stu-dents (and other readers) to evolve practices of reading and reflection which are wary, inquisitive, hesitant and reluctant to rush to judgement about the 'success' of neoliberal inflected 'transformation'.

## Spinning the 'transformation': New Labour's way with words

Even prior to the publication of the Laming Report into the death of Victoria Climbié and the appearance of ECM an earlier book concluded by tentatively identifying six significant developments having an impact on the evolution of Children's Services (Garrett 2003a):

- the emergence of new structures and new professions
- increasing direction from the centre
- the managerialist fixation with 'targets' and 'performance' and the increasing use of corporate management consultants to plot pathways for faltering services or even to takeover particular services
- the complex, far from uni-directional character of New Labour's 'mod-ernization' of Children's Services: for all the emphasis on the 'modern' and the benefits of information and communications technology (ICT), the government's project could be interpreted as rather backward-looking given some of its preoccupations and favoured policy 'solutions'
- the introduction of a new social work degree and, more specifically, the emphasis on 'practical social work' with children and families
- the gradual criminalization of child welfare discourses and the emergence of a new fixation with electronic surveillance.

Subsequently, I and other writers have explored particular facets of these and related questions (see, for example, Parton 2006a; Webb 2006; McLaughlin, K. 2008; White et al. 2008). These six areas of 'transformation' remain significant, but what new factors can, perhaps, be added to the analysis? What are some of the new elements which can be detected? Such questions have, moreover, a fresh resonance given the death of 'Baby P' in August 2007 and the contro-versy which then followed, the culmination of the related criminal case, in late-2008.[3]

More generally, *'Transforming' Children's Services* can be located alongside critical approaches to social policy. The book also draws on social theory and seeks to question and be gently disruptive of narratives which merely amplify and promote the New Labour vision of services for children and families in a 'modern world': a vision characterized by a vocabulary and ideology apt to circle around a cluster of focal or pivotal words: keywords such as 'modernization', 'globalization', 'knowledge economy', 'benefit dependency', 'leadership', 'empowerment', 'social exclusion', and so on.

Although this is not a book which seeks to provide a discourse analysis, the argument implicit throughout is that those interested in the evolution of social policy, or situated within Children's Services (maybe as service providers, students and associated academics), might begin to think more deeply and more politically about how the promoters of 'transformation' *put language to work*. More specifically, how do government ministers (and other primary definers) persuade, cajole, and enlist support from a diverse range of professional fields for policies which can be seen interpreted, in a number of ways, as deeply retrogressive? (Boltanski and Chiapello 2005)? What, moreover, is the context for the 'transformation' of Children's Services? Why are particular measures being introduced (or evolving) now rather than at some other time? What is the broader political, economic and social context? What are the core ideas underpinning 'transformation'? Are there are 'common-sense' assumptions which are left unchallenged, not interrogated? Are there positions which are silenced or not heard from? What role is being fulfilled by 'experts', particularly academics? How are professional roles being delineated anew?

At this juncture, at least three points appear significant in terms of how the 'change' agenda is being defined and mapped. First, the shallowness of some of New Labour's policy documents is striking (for example, DfES 2006b). This is particularly the case if these contemporary documents are contrasted with Labour-inspired documents from the past, concentrating on 'reforming' social work and associated services, which were reasoned and detailed (Committee on Local Authority and Allied Personal Services 1968). In contrast, the New Labour documents are written in a manner which often appears largely promotional and lacking in detailed evidence to substantiate the claim that policy must shift in a particular direction (see Fairclough 2000). For some, this depthlessness and superficiality can be interpreted as a feature of 'the cultural logic of late capitalism' – postmodernism – and this can, perhaps, be related to the use of populist, frequently emotive, slogans which are incessantly deployed in order to 'brand' and 'market' particular initiatives and to blur, or render porous, the distinction between the public and private sectors. As Anthony Barnett has astutely observed, New Labour understands 'that the *way a policy is projected is an essential part of the policy*, much in the way that the design of a consumer durable is today part of the product itself' (Barnett 2000: 88, emphasis added). In this work of projection, and the associated emphasis on text, talk and imagery, the government has been heavily influenced by the approach of the US administrations also intent on promoting a neoliberal 'change agenda'. Thus, the 'Every Child Matters' slogan implicitly references the controversial 'No Child Left Behind' programme instigated by Bush (Goldstein 2004). Similarly, 'Sure Start' can be viewed as sharing discursive kinship with the earlier US 'Head Start' endeavour. Furthermore, this symbolic technique, and the branding of particular programmes of governance, seeks to mask the deeply ideological content of much of the 'transformational reform agenda.'

Second, 'reforms' are frequently triggered prior to the culmination of the evaluation of 'pilot' projects (see, for example, France and Crow 2005; Tunstill et al. 2005): in terms of the setting up of Children's Trusts, the government even appeared to have 'ignored the results of its own pilot study' (Audit Commission, 2008). Moreover, the discursive re-fashioning of 'pilots' as 'trailblazers' illustrates aspects of this dynamic; the latter suggestive of adventurous, brash, unrelenting momentum, and the former suggestive of a more tentative, sceptical and scientific orientation. Third, it is recognized that New Labour (and the interlocking departments embarked on the 'transformation' of Children's Services) are not monolithic and within these organizational fields and within the fields associated with those which New Labour is apt to dub 'partners', struggles have and will take place resulting in resistance, compromises and trade-offs. Indeed, one of the intentions of the branding strategy is to render 'whole', coherent and seamless what is – unavoidably – contradictory, unfinished, messy, resisted (see Clarke 2004). Moreover, the coalition seeking 'change' (both inside New Labour and among the cadre of senior civil servants responsible for formulating policy) is always unstable, with elements being jettisoned and new 'partners' for 'change' recruited. In this context, the question of *which* government department is expected to 'take the lead' in respect of particular policies can also be significant because of different discursive and historical traditions, different cultures and different tensions.

Related to this, particularly in the context of New Labour's plans for 'workforce reform', it should not be assumed that policy initiatives that have the highest visibility will also have the greatest empirical impact or practical significance. Thus, a new 'configuration does not finally and fully emerge until it is formed in the minds and habits of those who work the system. Until these personnel have formed a settled habitus appropriate to the field, enabling them to cope with its demands and to produce it "as a matter of course", the process of change remains partial and incomplete' (Garland 2001: 21–2). Nonetheless, it remains clear that New Labour is truly intent on transforming Children's Services – a sector still largely staffed by women workers – and it is committed to promoting changes which have meshed, it will be argued, with the politics of neoliberalism (see also Children's Workforce Development Council 2008: 8). Indeed, one of the core ideas in this book is that grasping some of the key elements characterizing neoliberalism furnishes a set of coordinates which might enables us to better understand the character of the 'transformations' taking place.

## Children's Services and 'modern' times

Although neoliberalism – the 'N' word – is rarely mentioned, the 'transformation' of Children's Services as been embedded in dominant neoliberal ideas about the direction, or shape, of modernity (Foley and Rixon 2008). Such ideas are also related to policy innovations which seek to produce practitioners who are 'modern' and able to respond to the demands of the 'modern world'. Tony Blair (Labour Leader 1994–2007 and Prime Minister 1997–2007), in one of his later speeches, in March 2007, referred to the 'demands of the modern labour market'. Within this market, today's 'employer's need employees who are creative, good at communicating, not cogs in the great machine but individual turners of the wheel' (Blair 2007). More generally, the 'modern world' [was for Blair] one of 'flux and adjustment, a kind of permanent revolution in the way we work . . . It won't change. It will intensify' (Blair 2007).[4] The theme was, moreover, returned to by the Department of Work and Pensions, in the summer of 2008, when – in the course of laying out plans to introduce workfare – it was claimed the 'objective' was a 'social revolution' (Department for Work and Pensions 2008a: 12, 75).

This overarching narrative, as can be seen, is apt to contain references to what are perceived as the attributes and assets, shortcomings and deficits which individual members of the workforce (including as we shall see the children's workforce) are likely to bring with them into the arena of 'reform' or 'modernization'. For example, those objecting to changes to the nature of jobs and service provision are apt to be characterized as 'traditional', or 'conservative' (Taylor-Gooby 2000). Similarly, those troubled by the implementation of 'modern, active welfare', pursued by an 'empowering state' are likely to be caricatured as opposed to breaking the 'cycle of benefit dependency' (Hutton 2006; see also Purnell 2008). In short, those opposed to neoliberal 'reforms' have tended – certainly until the evidence of neoliberalism's palpable failure became apparent in 2008 – to be positioned as anachronistic and 'anti-modern': people, in short, seemingly *out of time.*

Related to this point, the discourse of 'modernization' presents difficulties for those seeking to oppose specific policies because:

> modernisation is rhetorical in that it functions to persuade and motivate. It is an 'up' word that makes things sound exciting, progressive and positive. But it is also ideological in that this rhetorical usage helps to generate an appearance of structured and unified thinking beyond which is either nonsense or (by implication) out-dated thinking.
>
> (Finlayson 2003: 67)

In this context, it is not, of course, only the providers of public services who at risk being labelled as 'anti-modern'. The 'cultural nature of the predicament of the poor is often cast as a failure to "modernise" because of limitations reproduced and reinforced by themselves or because of their disadvantaged position within global economic processes' (Haylett 2001: 45). Chris Haylett (2001: 46) has articulated this perspective as follows:

> The argument goes like this: in debates about welfare reform there is no point dwelling on the things that can't be changed, namely ineluctable global forces or the economic hardware, so we must focus on the social and cultural accommodation of the economic, that is, on people and cultures or the software that can be changed.

Key ideas about what it is to be 'modern' and implicit characterizations of 'modern' times, are not, however, apt to be interrogated in any detail in, for example, the (largely promotional) policy documents focused on the 'reform' or 'modernization' of public services (see also Fairclough 2000). Similarly, much of the literature associated with social work and related spheres of activity related to Children's Services is apt to omit discussion on this still important theme (see also Garrett 2009). In contrast, this book is underpinned by an understanding that the government's 'modernization' project should be scrutinized because what

> the apparently neutral language of a 'modernising process' masks are highly political decisions concerning the extension of the market into more areas of social life. The presentation of modernisation as a technocratic exercise, above ideological imperatives, is particularly important to New Labour. Unable to openly advocate the free market quite as aggressively as the Conservatives, New Labour have found in modernisation the vehicle for extending neoliberalism.
>
> (Leggett 2005: 157)

Indeed, questions related to the direction, or trajectory, of 'modernity', are – as the above extract suggests – much debated and highly contested within social theory and sociology. Moreover, some of the foundational theories and ideas which underpin the 'transformation' of Children's Services and other areas of the public services in England have been debated, in some detail, in journals associated with social work (see, for example, the exchanges featured in Ferguson 2001; 2003; Garrett 2003b). This is not to argue that ideas and theories derived from social theory and sociology are driving the 'reform' agenda, but it is difficult to understand the 'transformation' of Children's Services without being mindful of the way in which more abstract theorizing is impacting in 'applied' domains. Indeed, as John Clarke and his colleagues have argued, there are 'strong links' between dominant and mainstream sociology of modernity and the 'politics of public service reform in the UK' (Clarke et al. 2007: 13).

## Chapter map

The book does not aspire to comprehensiveness or to provide readers with an all-inclusive picture of the 'transformation' of Children's Services, the 'landscape' of which is now said to encompass a range of interconnected components which include: Education, Health, Youth, Justice and Crime Prevention, Sports and Culture, Early Years, Social Family and Community Support (DCSF 2008a: 18; 10; see also DCSF 2007). However, the chief focus in what follows, is on those areas related to social work with children and their families and on some of the changes to policy and practice having an impact on this field of activity.

The book seeks, therefore, to provide an invitation to readers to query the direction which some of the 'reforms' and 'transformations' are taking. Each chapter can be read in isolation, but together they form a structured argument which illuminates how the 'transformation' of services for children as been refracted through a neoliberal prism. Divided into nine chapters, it seeks to be challenging (even argumentative), but also a lucid and accessible resource. In order to encourage critical thinking and debate on some of the key themes referred to, a series of 'Reflection and talk boxes' also feature at the end of each chapter. The aim of this device (which can be skipped, of course, if it is not to the taste of particular readers) is particularly to assist students to critically reflect (individually and in class/seminar and fieldwork/workplace discussions) on key facets of the 'transformation' of Children's Services. Furthermore, each 'Reflection and talk box' seeks to aid students to ponder how this 'transformation' agenda is impacting on their own sense of being, for example, a social worker working in Children's Services. How are students, on the cusp of entering working in Children's Services, being formed and constructed as 'professionals'? More specifically, what are being constructed as the focal concerns and themes? How might some of the areas explored in the book relate to the experience of fieldwork placements in particular specialist settings? How, more broadly, can students evolve into critical thinkers committed to social change and orientated *against* neoliberal ways of *seeing* and *doing*?

Importantly, while the book is focused on England, the danger of conceptual and geographical insularity is acknowledged. Indeed, an implicit and recurring argument is that an investigation of Children's Services in England needs to be conceptually adventurous and spatially expansive. In terms of the latter dimension, although the book does not provide a sustained comparative analysis, it is recognized that an international perspective or, more appropriately perhaps, international awareness is vital. The author, for example, is located outside England and lives – often it appears mostly among hardworking and low-waged Eastern European workers – on Europe's western edge in Galway in the Republic of Ireland. Chapter 2 refers to a sociologist from France who did much of his earlier empirical research in North Africa. An Italian Marxist (dead for over 70 years) also – metaphorically – ambles in and out of the same and other chapters. Periodically the focus briefly switches to the USA and it is suggested that ideas relating to practice with children and families there may be influencing the 'transformation' of Children's Services in England. Furthermore, the book – inevitably – includes discussion on the inquiry into child welfare professionals' responses to an Ivorian child who, despite the actions of an asylum-seeking taxi-driver intent on getting her to hospital, died in London.

Indeed, in terms of this international dimension, the transformation of Children's Services in England will be similar to 'reform' programmes initiated and progressed elsewhere. Thus, readers of this book, located outside England, are likely to detect resemblances. That is, it is likely that 'reform' endeavours operative in other jurisdictions may seem similar (perhaps in terms of the broad, overarching themes and 'reform' narratives, perhaps in terms of particular 'new' mechanisms of intervention) because the scope, reach and parameters are also likely to have been calibrated in line with a narrow neoliberal 'common sense'. However, every programme of 'transformation' for Children's Services will look and *feel* different within different national and perhaps even regional settings. The forms of resistance and accommodation which 'reforms' generate will also be different. Often, therefore, readers in, say, North America and Australasia, may need to 'make the connections' for themselves and, in this context, it will be necessary to taper some of the topics featured in the reflection and talk areas to fit local, particular conditions.

Chapter 2, therefore, focuses on neoliberalism. This is a form of capitalism, whose proponents are somewhat more defensive, of course, since the commencement of the global economic crisis in 2008, which can be associated with a number of defining characteristics. Importantly, neoliberalism lays an emphasis on commodifying aspects of life, previously regarded as beyond the market, and seeks to inject competition into all domains. In this way, neoliberalism can, perhaps, be perceived as a reinvigorated, more spatially expansive and mobile capitalism: yet, as the collapse of the investment banking and related sectors in 2008 revealed, it remains an economic system which is still vulnerable, still fragile, still beset by recurrent crises. Neoliberals are also apt to be confronted, across a range of fronts, with inchoate, multiple and diverse forms of recalcitrance and resistance. Moreover, the neoliberal agenda is, in part, characterized by a constant and unrelenting aspiration to achieve hegemony – to construct and consolidate a 'coalition of the willing' – for 'radical' 'reforms' and 'transformations' which are, in general terms, deeply troubling and damaging to human welfare. More emphatically, this entire book can be read as an inquiry into how the drive to establish and maintain hegemony for neoliberal ideas has, thus far, been constructed and assembled within one particular field of operations, Children's Services.

Chapter 3 moving away from more abstract considerations broadly outlines New Labour's 'transformational reform agenda': The *Change for Children* (CfC) programme. In terms of the promotion of the CfC programme, the government has maintained that one of the key aims is to create a 'modern' children's workforce. In this context, therefore, this chapter will outline the main practice components associated with CfC initiative: the tripartite system comprising of a national database for children, ContactPoint (CPd),[5] the Common Assessment Framework (CAF/eCAF) and a new Lead Professional (LP) role. It is also suggested that developments in the USA appear to have influenced New Labour despite this dimension being omitted in most English accounts of the 'transformation' of Children's Services. Nonetheless, 'reforms' in the USA *do* appear to have had an impact in England: for example, the policy aspiration to make Children's Services more 'businesslike' and 'outcomes' oriented. This is reflected by, for example, influential 'reforms' introduced in states such as Vermont.

The Climbié Inquiry has, of course, frequently furnished a substantial part of the discursive and rhetorical basis for New Labour's 'transformation' programme and Chapter 4 sets out to critically examine neglected aspects of the immensely influential Laming Report. A 'hegemonically successful' public inquiry report is one that is 'wholly or largely uncritically accepted as providing a comprehensive and accurate account of the events it purports to describe, which is seen to be fair in its assessment of culpability and the allocation of blame, and which makes seemingly appropriate recommendations' (Brown 2003: 96). Some criticisms of the omissions in the Laming Report are now beginning to emerge, with Cooper (2005), for example, pointing to its 'untold stories', 'thin stories', 'radically incomplete' accounts and willingness to present narratives which concentrate on 'surface' as opposed to 'depth' readings of key vital aspects of the 'case'. Nevertheless, it is still reasonable to maintain that, on account of the largely favourable responses it has generated, the report *has* achieved hegemony within the discourse on child protection and, more broadly, Children's Services, within England. Certainly it is clear that Laming and his team produced a report and set of recommendations which have largely won the backing and support of politicians and a diverse range of professional groups.

Although it was not the intention of the Laming Inquiry, the report it produced also provides a series of devastating snapshots of the impact of the neoliberal policies on a part of the public sector in England. Nevertheless, while welcoming the detail that the Laming Report furnishes on the some of the events surrounding Victoria's death and his commitment to wholesale reform of Children's Services, it will be maintained that the report is problematic because the interpretation provided – on, for example, questions of child welfare practice, 'race' and diversity – is flawed. Moreover, it entirely failed to locate professional responses to Victoria in a context which embraces New Labour's more general approach to 'race', asylum seekers and refugees.

The Laming Report has also provided a basis for New Labour to argue that 'modern' services for children needed to make more extensive use of information and communication technologies, the 'privileged technology of neoliberalism' (Harvey 2005: 159). This is reflected, of course, in the plan to introduce the database on 11 million children, and this is examined in Chapter 5. The chapter traces the evolution of ContactPoint after examining ideas on the 'surveillance state' or 'surveillance society'. Furthermore, it is maintained that the increasing use of ICT could, perhaps, be prompting what I termed, some years ago, an 'Electronic Turn', perhaps more appropriately 'e-Turn', in social work and related areas of practice with the day-to-day tasks of practitioners, in a 'transformed' Children's Services, becoming more and more reliant on and structured by specific corporate software programmes (Garrett 2005). Indeed, this is an issue which has emerged once again in the context of the debate surrounding practitioner responses to 'Baby P': more specifically, it has been argued that social workers are having to spend far too much time completing the various elements associated with the Integrated Children's System (ICS) and that this is diverting them from direct work with families (UNISON 2008a).

Rather contentiously, in May 2008, it was argued that the 'slow death of Tony Blair's flagship measure' against 'anti-social behaviour' – the Anti-Social Behaviour Order (ASBO) – was 'confirmed' by figures showing that the total number of these orders fell from 4123 in 2005 to 2706 in 2006 ('Asbos in their death throes as number issued drops by a third', *Guardian*, 9 May 2008: 6). Chapter 6, however, looks, in more detail at 'ASBO politics' and examines how such politics have contributed to the 'transformation' of Children's Services. More specifically, the focus will be on how senior New Labour politicians have played specific and distinctive roles in creating an 'ASBO politics' which has, for example, endeavoured to deflect the work of child welfare practitioners. On a related theme, Chapter 7 suggests, despite all the references to 'innovation', that the government has been apt to look to the past for inspiration. Perhaps, more generally, neoliberal 'modernization', despite the aura of 'radicalism' and sheen of newness, can be viewed as a film running backwards. For example, the 'problem family' has been re-excavated and located at the centre of the drive against 'anti-social behaviour'. Connected to this is a commitment, announced at the launch of the Respect Action Plan, to put in place a network of 'intensive family support projects' (IFSPs) or so-called 'sinbins'. The schemes, moreover, have uncomfortably close resemblances, in their steering perceptions and modalities of operation, with schemes pursued elsewhere in Europe in the 1930s.

Chapter 8 focuses on the government's proposals for the 'reform' of services for children in public care, or 'looked after', particularly the controversial proposal to set up Social Work Practices (SWP). These changes have been mapped out by a Green Paper, *Care Matters: Transforming the Lives of Children and Young People in Care* (published in October 2006), a subsequent working group report and *Care Matters: Time for Change*, a White Paper (published in June 2007). This was followed by the publication of the Children and Young Persons' Bill which went on to receive Royal Assent on 13 November 2008. The British Association of Social Workers (BASW) (2007) has reported that the SWP proposal had been 'fiercely debated' within the organization and a pro-SWP policy was narrowly adopted at its Annual General Meeting in May 2007. In this chapter it is, however, argued that SWP is a highly retrograde policy departure and that the envisaged structures herald the privatization of a major area of social work with children and families. Indeed, the plan fits comfortably within the pervasive neoliberal approach to 'transformation'. As Ronaldo Munck (2005: 65) has maintained for neoliberalism 'the market is not only the most efficient way to allocate resources but also the optimum context to achieve human freedom'. This notion rhetorically underpins the endeavour to create SWP and provides an illustration – or even 'case study' – which shows how primary definers seek to define the 'transformation' agenda and to try to win support and hegemony for a particular set of neoliberal ideas and approaches. In this context, particular attention needs to be accorded to how the drive to install these new organizational forms is being orchestrated. The final and concluding chapter draws together some of the themes addressed in the book and comments on political and related responses to the death of 'Baby P'.

The next chapter, therefore, focuses on an interpretation of modernity which emphasizes the significance of neoliberalism: a form of seemingly rejuvenated capitalism which appears, it is maintained, to have provided the main impetus and ideology for the 'transformation' of services for children and their families – for example, what we might call 'transformation talk' is soaked and saturated (in often complex, complicated and contradictory ways) in neoliberal 'common sense'. Nevertheless, this 'modernization' project is far from unidirectional and, as this book suggests, it is likely to produce alternative and competing visions of what it is to be 'modern'.

**Reflection and talk box 1**

If you are a student currently on a course leading to a professional qualification which will enable you to work in Children's Services (for
example, a social work course) try to look at examples of curricula from
the past: perhaps ask your lecturer to show you the curriculum which
they may have studied. How does it differ from your current curriculum?
What is now omitted? Are there differing emphases? How, for example,
does it engage with questions related to social class, gender, 'race' and
ethnicity?

# 2 Theorizing neoliberal 'transformation'

During the Climbié Inquiry a trade union representative advised Lord Laming about the 'conveyor belt social work' provided in the local authority where she worked. Here a largely business 'ethos' – influenced by the 'new public management' – seemed to concentrate on 'seeing the cases through the system and meeting targets, meeting the statistics, getting them through the system' (Secretary of State of Health and the Secretary of State for the Home Department 2003: 112; see also Care Standards Tribunal 2008: para. 58). Laming himself was happy to refer to the users of services as 'customers' (Secretary of State of Health and the Secretary of State for the Home Department 2003: 198) and it is apparent that 'innovations' which had been introduced mimicked the private sector and undermined practitioners' ability to respond to children and families in need of assistance. For example, in one of the London authorities said to have failed Victoria, the corporate structure had been revised and a witness to the inquiry reported that this 'did away with everything which I think you would recognise as traditional local government'. The same witness also stated that 'at one point there were nine different business units in children's social work and they were all semiautonomous operating without traditional line manager responsibilities'. This resulted in 'lots of separate managers, really, doing their own thing' (Secretary of State of Health and the Secretary of State for the Home Department 2003: 80).

However, a good deal of contemporary theorizing fails to adequately grasp the nature of the work within contemporary Children's Services. For example, it has been asserted that 'post traditional social work' should be 'understood and evaluated essentially as a methodology of life planning' aiding individuals in 'colonising the future' (Ferguson 2001: 51). Nonetheless, it could be countered that this notion does not recognize the fact that individual social workers and other child welfare professionals provide services inside welfare bureaucracies which are shaped by constraining, economic and political forces. The suggestion in what follows, therefore, is that alternative conceptual approaches which recognize the centrality of capitalism are better equipped to define and understand some of the key, often underlying and implicit, dynamics impacting on the 'transformation' of Children's Services. More specifically, it is argued that conceptualizations of neoliberalism provide a 'lens' through which to view the themes covered in the rest of the book.

During the final decade of the twentieth century, opposition to 'neoliberalism' became the rallying call for a wide and disparate conglomeration of 'anti-capitalist' groups.[1] More recently, what the historian Eric Hobsbawm (2008: 28) has termed the 'most serious crisis of the capitalist system since 1929–33', has prompted those critical of neoliberalism to become emboldened. Some commentators, examining the crisis in a more historical and structural manner, have also argued that fundamental economic transitions are, perhaps, now under way:

> Since the 1930s the non-communist world has experienced two shifts in international economic norms and rules substantial enough to be called 'regime change'. They were separated by an interval of roughly thirty years: the first regime, characterized by Keynesianism and governed by international Bretton Woods arrangements, lasted from 1945 to 1975; the second began after the crisis of 2007–08. The latter regime, known variously as neoliberalism, the Washington Consensus or the globalization consensus, centred on the notion that all governments should liberalize, privatize, deregulate – prescriptions that have been dominant at the level of global of economic policy as to constitute, in John Stuart Mill's phrase, 'the deep slumber of decided opinion'.
>
> (Wade 2008: 5)

Following the economic shocks of the past year, and another approximately thirty years on from the last major shift, we may, therefore, be witnessing a third financial 'regime change' (Wade 2008: 6). How, though, should neoliberalism be understood and interpreted? This question still seems important in a book addressing 'transformation' within a field of welfare – specifically within Children's Services – because, despite passing references to 'neoliberalism', it is a question rarely posed or addressed in sufficient detail in most accounts which purport to provide an authoritative mapping of the CfC programme. Given this lacunae, authors such as David Harvey and Stuart Hall, merit referring to at some length because they are two of the most helpful and lucid guides in aiding an understanding of neoliberalism. Drawing on their work and that of others, it is argued that that those seeking to grasp the meaning of neoliberalism should be attentive to at least seven key elements: how we might define neoliberalism in relation to the 'embedded liberalism' it seeks to supplant or displace; the role of the state within neoliberalism; actually existing neoliberalism and how this is often at variance with the theory and rhetoric; the concept of 'accumulation by dispossession' which illuminates how neoliberalism seeks to redistribute in favour of the rich; the centrality of precariousness and 'flexibility'; the renewed and retrogressive faith in incarceration; and finally, there is a need to be alert to neoliberalism's 'national articulations' and how it operates differently in different places.

In an English context, for example, ideas connected to the 'Third Way' have influenced attempts to 'modernize' and 'transform' social work and related professions. Giddens (1998: 64) argues that the 'overall aim of third way politics should be to help citizens pilot their way through the major revolutions of our time, globalization, transformations in personal life and our relationship to nature'. However, in what follows, it is maintained that the 'Third Way' provides a good example of a variant of neoliberal ideology despite the fact that its promoters (such as, of course, Giddens) rhetorically construct their theorization on an apparent renunciation, even denunciation, of neoliberalism (Garrett 2008a).

Finally, it is suggested that the task of embedding neoliberalism is far from easy and that it is likely to encounter oppositional tendencies, forces and currents. New Labour's 'way with words' and the emphasis on how the transformation of Children's Services is discursively constructed is, therefore, vitally important as it attempts to win 'hearts and minds' for a particular version of social and economic change. Here it will be argued that Pierre Bourdieu and Antonio Gramsci provide valuable insights and might inform our understanding.

## Defining neoliberalism

Neoliberalism can best be comprehended as succeeding 'embedded liberalism' which was dominant in most of the industrial west during the period stretching from the end of the Second World War until the late-1970s (see also Hall et al. 1978; Hall and Jacques 1989). During this period 'market processes and entrepreneurial and corporate activities were surrounded by a web of social and political constraints and a regulatory environment that sometimes restrained . . . economic and industrial strategy' (Harvey 2005: 11). In contrast, the neoliberal project has endeavoured to 'disembed capital from these constraints' (Harvey 2005: 11). Thus, to different degrees, depending on the specific cultural and national context, neoliberalism has been intent on the comprehensive displacement of 'embedded liberalism'. In this way processes of neoliberalization have tried to 'strip away the protective coverings that embedded liberalism allowed and occasionally nurtured' (Harvey 2005: 168). Related to this is, of course, is the fact that neoliberalism seeks to inject a fresh and reinvigorated emphasis on 'competition' at all levels of society, including those areas of life and social interaction which were previously perceived as *beyond* the reach of competition and commodification.

Furthermore, this should be seen as a process that has

> entailed much 'creative destruction', not only of prior institutional frameworks and powers (even challenging traditional forms of state sovereignty) but also divisions of labour, social relations, welfare provisions, technological mixes, ways of life and thought, reproductive activities, attachments to the land and habits of the heart.
>
> (Harvey 2005: 3; see also Klein 2007; Thompson 2008)

Thus, the aim has been to try to install a new 'common sense' (Hall 1993) and seek to ensure that people begin to *think* and *act* in a manner which is conducive to neoliberalism and to prompt a cultural shift – even, perhaps, to 'change the soul'. More generally and in terms of its bedrock philosophy, neoliberalism holds that 'the social good will be maximized by maximizing the reach and frequency of market transactions, and it seeks to bring all human action into the domain of the market' (Harvey 2005: 3). In this regard, it should be viewed as a

> a theory of political economic practices that proposes that human well-being can best be advanced by liberating individual entrepreneurial freedom characterized by strong private property rights, free markets, and free trade. *The role of the state is to create and preserve an institutional framework appropriate to such practices.*
>
> (Harvey 2005: 2, emphasis added)

## Remaking the state

The comment which Harvey makes on the role of the state is important because a rather crude and misguided perspective might maintain that neoliberalization heralds a relentless and irrepressible 'rolling back' of the state with the 'market' and 'market mechanisms' being *entirely* left to 'takeover' society. However, he and others make clear that, within the neoliberal paradigm, the state continues to play an active role in that it creates and preserves an 'institutional framework' for capital (Brenner and Theodore 2002; Munck 2005). This has entailed the introduction of new forms of regulation and governance with 'new market-orientated rules and policies to facilitate the development of the "new" capitalism' (Munck 2005: 63). Indeed, since a new (or second) phase of global neoliberalism began in the 1990s, there has been more of a commitment on the part of governments to *roll out* new policies rather than *roll back* the state (Munck 2005: 63). That is, there is currently much more of an emphasis on 'positive' or 'proactive' interventions and, in England, this has been evident, not only in terms of specific macroeconomic interventions, but also in discourses and practices focused on promoting 'social inclusion' and 'prevention' in relation to children and families. This remodelled state has, therefore, been apparent in the numerous initiatives seeking to 'activate' the unemployed (or 'jobseekers'). This drive to ensure that the unemployed 'do the right thing' (Home Office 2008: 106) has, since 1997, resulted in a whole series of measures being used by the state to coerce the unemployed into work. Indeed, current plans – essentially pivoting on introducing a 'workfare' regime – will include 'full-time work in return for benefits' for those unemployed for two years or, indeed, 'at any stage' (Home Office 2008: 19, 43).

More generally, of course, the state must continue to guarantee

> the quality and integrity of money. It must also set up those military, defence, police and legal structures and functions required to secure private property rights and to guarantee, by force if need be, the proper functioning of markets. Furthermore, if markets do not exist (in areas such as land, water, education, health care, social security, or environmental pollutions) then they must be created, by state action if necessary.
>
> (Harvey 2005: 2)

This activity is rooted in the core function of the neoliberal state which is to furnish an 'apparatus whose fundamental mission [is to] facilitate conditions for profitable capital accumulation on the part of both domestic and foreign capital' (Harvey, 2005: 7). Moreover, despite the 'anti-big government' rhetoric, often associated with neoliberalism, there has been little diminution in the actual size of governments in the west. Indeed 'big government' has not gone away even in a world supposedly governed by neoliberal rules. This is because capitalism 'can no more do without the state today that it could do in the Keynesian period' (Harman 2008: 97; see also Jacques 2008); a fact which was, of course, illustrated during the current economic crisis. The key point is that processes of neoliberalization seek to retool, reconfigure, radically change and remake the state, its role and core functions.[2]

However, the neoliberal state remains a complex (and at times contradictory) ensemble – variegated and dispersed – which also includes spaces, of course, for potential opposition. As Bourdieu reminds us, it is simply not convincing to baldly claim it 'is an instrument in the hands of the ruling class. The state is certainly not completely neutral, completely independent of the dominant forces in society, but the older it is and the greater the social advances it has incorporated the more autonomous it is. It is a battlefield' (Bourdieu 2001: 34).[3]

## Actually existing neoliberalism

As some of the above comments indicate, there is a need to be cautious and to try and distinguish between 'neoliberalism as a system of thought and actually existing neoliberalism' (Munck 2005: 60; see also Harvey 2005: 21). Brenner and Theodore (2002: 5), for example, have argued that there is a:

> rather blatant disjuncture between the ideology of neoliberalism and its everyday political operations and political effects. One the one hand, while neoliberalism aspires to create a 'utopia' of free markets liberated from all forms of state interference, it has in practice entailed a dramatic intensification of coercive, disciplinary forms of state interference in order to impose market rules on all aspects of social life. On the other hand, whereas neoliberal ideology implies that self-regulating markets will generate an optimal allocation of investments and resources, neoliberal political practice, has generated pervasive market failures, new forms of market polarization, and a dramatic intensification of uneven development.

There is certainly a 'disjuncture' or discrepancy between the theory and rhetoric of neoliberalism and the pragmatics of neoliberalism. Related to this point, as mentioned earlier, it is clear that the state has not, been driven back in the way desired by influential ideologues such as Friedrich Hayek (Klein 2007). Perhaps, in this sense, we are also 'dealing here less with a coherently bounded "ism" or "end-state" than with a process . . . neoliberalization' (Brenner and Theodore 2002: 6). This is partly because neoliberals are rarely presented with a bare landscape on which to operate. Where this occurs (after, for example, natural disasters, in post-war and post-invasion scenarios) this can give rise to, what Melanie Klein (2007) refers to as, neoliberal inspired 'disaster capitalism'. More frequently, however, neoliberal 'transformation' projects are, what has been referred to as, 'path-dependent' (Brenner and Theodore 2002: 3) and are even apt to falter because they are forced to engage with – and even compromise with – ingrained cultural legacies and expectations, ways of *seeing* and *doing* which are averse to neoliberal 'common sense' (Forgacs 1988).

Actually existing neoliberalism is also liable to generate resistance across a range of social and professional fields and it must, therefore, seek, as Bourdieu has observed, to erode or circumscribe the autonomy of such 'fields'. As Pileggi and Patton (2003: 318) maintain, when working in a neoliberal context, 'practitioners of a field become liable to two masters: the practices and norms of the discipline and the practices and norms of the market'. Given this tension, this competition for the allegiance of, for example, practitioners located within public services, individual workers are confronted with a choice as to which 'master' to follow. The field of social work, for instance, because of its value base – reflected in humanistic 'codes of ethics' – may be at odds with the neoliberal notion that services for children in care should be privatized and become a source of capital accumulation (see also Chapter 8). This, in turn, may prompt resistance and opposition and counter strategies of 'modernization' and 'transformation'.

## Accumulation by dispossession

Irrespective of the precise character of actually existing neoliberalism, in specific places at specific times, it remains a philosophy and series of practices which universally aspires to restore class power (Dumenil and Levy 2004).[4] This involves vast transfers of income to the richest groups in society. However, it is also apparent that the 'neoliberal revolution has had a much more devastating effect on the countries of the East' (Harvey 2005: 64). The demise of the USSR and the subsequent introduction of neoliberal economics to such states, often by means of so-called 'economic shock therapy' and a wholesale assault on public health provision, have caused death and hardship on a mass scale (Klein 2007). For example, it was reported by the United Nations (UN) that since the early 1990s, in the Russian Federation, there 'has been a marked increase in male mortality over and above the historical trend' and the number of additional deaths during 1992–2001 is estimated at an astonishing 2.5–3 million. As a UN report remarked, in the 'absence of war, famine, or health epidemics there is no historical precedent for the scale of loss' (United Nations Development Programme 2005: 23). A fledging social work profession has, moreover, had to respond to this widespread immiseration (Iarskaia-Smirnova and Romanoz 2002). However, redistribution in favour of the rich as also taken place in the West:

> Between 1980 and 1999, the richest 1 per cent pf the UK population increased its share of national income from around 6 per cent to 13 per cent. In 2002, this 1 per cent owned approximately 25 per cent of the UK's marketable wealth. In contrast, 50 per cent of the population shared only 6 per cent of the total wealth. Excluding housing from these estimates, and inequality increases even further. In 2000, 50 per cent

of families had £600 or less in savings, and 25 per cent were more than £200 in debt.

(Rutherford 2005: 10; see also 'Poverty gap has not narrowed under New Labour', *Guardian*, 3 April 2008: 13)

In the USA, so often a template for New Labour, a similar picture emerges with the distribution of income as unequal as it was before the Great Depression with the 'richest 10 per cent of Americans' owning 70 per cent of the country's wealth' (Irwin 2008: 121).

Central here has been what Harvey refers to as 'accumulation by dispossession' which he perceives as the 'continuation and proliferation of accumulation practices which Marx had treated as "primitive" or "original" during the rise of capitalism' (Harvey 2005: 159; see also Garrett 2009). Thus, some of the characteristics of this 'accumulation by dispossession' dynamic include the corporatization, commodification, and privatization of hitherto public assets' and the opening up of 'new fields for capital accumulation in domains hitherto regarded as off-limits to the calculus of profitability' (Harvey 2005: 160). Indeed, it is argued, in Chapter 8, that this is a clearly evident in Children's Services in terms of the plans to set up 'social work practices' for children in public care or 'looked after'. Moreover, the state 'once neoliberalized, becomes a prime agent of retributive policies, reversing the flow from the upper classes that had occurred during the era of embedded liberalism. It does this in the first instance through the pursuit of privatization schemes and cutbacks in those state expenditures that support the social wage' (Harvey 2005: 163).

## Precariousness and flexibility

One interpretation of neoliberalism suggests that one of its key defining characteristics is that it seeks to inject new forms of insecurity into people's working lives. This new insecurity, impinging on the lives of many of those engaging with Children's Services, is frequently discussed in terms of the notion of 'precariousness', or 'precaricity', and this is reflected in, for example, the growth of short-term contracts and insecure patterns of employment; perhaps especially in the growth of 'agency' working where staff have few employment rights, 'enjoy' low pay and – on occasions – even have difficulty in trying to determine their identity of their employer.[5] Given this trend, activated by neoliberalization, 'the figure of the "disposable worker" emerges as prototypical upon the world stage' (Harvey 2005: 169). Related to this, in terms of work practices, neoliberalism favours 'flexibility' and is 'hostile to all forms of social solidarity that puts restraints on capital accumulation' (Harvey 2005: 75).

Importantly, precariousness also extends beyond work and into the sphere of welfare. For example, neoliberal theory maintains that 'unemployment is always voluntary. Labour, the argument goes, has a "reserve price" below which it prefers not to work. Unemployment arises because the reserve price is too high' (Harvey 2005: 53). In this context, it is apt to be maintained that this 'reserve price' is partly set by welfare benefits (within the neoliberal lexicon ordinarily referred to disparagingly as 'handouts'). Indeed, a good deal of the 'welfare reform', undertaken in both the USA and England, has been founded on this notion. Related to the same perspective has been the aspiration to 'transfer all responsibility for wellbeing back to the individual' (Harvey 2005: 76). Meanwhile, as 'the state withdraws from welfare provision and diminishes its role in arenas such as health care, public education, and social services . . . it leaves larger and larger segments of the population exposed to impoverishment' (Harvey 2005: 76).

## Lockdown

Another element – perhaps often overlooked – which can be regarded as central to neoliberalism's mode of social regulation is the 'new punitiveness' (Pratt et al. 2005). This is reflected in the evolution of penal policy and, more broadly, the tendency to locate particular sections of the population (those regarded as ambiguously 'troublesome' and ambiguously 'out of place') within enclosures which may not in the ordinary sense of the word be 'prisons' but which remain zones of varying degrees of confinement, monitoring and supervision (see also Butler 2004). What is more, as is stressed in Chapter 5, there is the connected aspiration to use technology for surveillance purposes to 'track' the troublesome 'in the community' (see also Nellis 2005).

Neoliberalism's renewed and retrogressive faith in the efficacy of the actual prison was stated in a report from the Prime Minister's Strategy Unit (2007: 3), where it was reported that the 'prison estate has been expanded to almost 80,000 and the sentence lengths for all serious offences are now longer than [when New Labour entered government] in 1997'. Prison reform campaigners have also illuminated the rise in prison suicides and acts of self-harm during the same period: in 2007, for example, 92 men, women and children killed themselves in prisons in England and Wales; a 37 per cent increase on the previous year (Howard League for Penal Reform 2008).

This new ideological and material investment in the prison is, moreover, a global trend (Garland 2001; Ladipo 2001; Wacquant 2002). The USA, for example, can be perceived as having moved toward 'mass incarceration with – in 2005 – a prison population of 2.1 million, with 1 in 75 of all men in prison (Pratt et al. 2005: xi). This development also contains a racialized component in that it is, of course, black men who are disproportionately incarcerated. Women, moreover, are now the 'fastest growing population of prisoners in . . . Canada, USA, Britain and Australia' (Pollack 2008). Specifically, in England, and despite the branding of the English 'reform' of Children's Services 'Every Child Matters', there are more children locked up than in most other countries in the European Union (EU). For example, for every 100,000 children in the population, 23 are locked up in England, compared to 6 in France and 2 in Spain ('Minister blamed for "scandal" of too many children in custody', *Guardian*, 14 February 2007). Furthermore, within places of confinement there is, perhaps, a growing recognition that children are being subjected to a panoply of violent measures aimed at 'restraining' them and promoting compliance with the various incarceration regimes. Indeed, it was announced – the very month that there was a public outcry about the fatal harm caused to

'Baby P' – that a review of 'restraint' in juvenile secure settings had reached the conclusion that it may be 'appropriate' for the state, and its agents – to 'use pain compliance techniques' on children ('Jails get go-ahead to continue to use pain to control children', *Guardian*, 16 December 2008: 13).

The expansion of the penal estate should, perhaps, also lead to a reappraisal of overly simplistic readings of neoliberalism, mentioned earlier, which highlight the 'roll back' of the state because prison expansion relies on a strong, interventionist state.[6] Although the private sector is fulfilling a larger role in the penal sector, the doctrine of 'small government' and the policy of downsizing public employment has 'not applied to penal confinement' (Wacquant 2005: 9). Indeed, the tremendous increase of numbers in prison should be perceived as the hidden face of the neoliberal model and the necessary counterpart – and new sensibility – underpinning the 'restructuring' of welfare. Moreover, this was apparent in an 'independent report' published by the Department for Work and Pensions, in late 2008, which – in setting out a vision for 'a radically reformed welfare system between now and 2015' – casually referred to some benefit recipients, 'found to be playing the system', as 'repeat *offenders*' (Gregg 2008: 5, 8, 15, emphasis added). This criminalizing approach might also be perceived as encompassing plans to introduce 'voice risk analysis technology' to test whether housing benefit claimants are providing false information ('Lie detector tests to catch benefit cheats', *Guardian*, 9 December 2008: 1). Moreover, ensuring actual criminals wear 'vests of shame' – bright orange bibs – when they are undertaking 'community' punishments emanate from the same neoliberal perspective ('Straw launches high-visibility community punishment', *Guardian*, 2 December 2008: 6).

In this sense, therefore, it seems entirely legitimate to refer to the '*penalisation of poverty* designed to manage the effects of neo-liberal policies at the lower end of the social structure of advanced societies' (Wacquant 2001: 401, original emphasis). Indeed, for Bauman (2000a: 216), somewhat more floridly:

> [S]tate governments are allotted the role of little else than oversized police precincts; the quantity and quality of the policeman on the beat, efficiency displayed in sweeping the streets clean of beggars, pesterers and pilferers, and the tightness of the jail walls loom large among the factors of investors' confidence, and so are among the items calculated when the decisions to invest or cut the losses and run are made. To excel in the job of precinct policeman the best (perhaps the only) thing state governments may do to is to cajole the nomadic capital into investing in its subjects' welfare.

Furthermore, and related to the earlier point about the emergence of quasi-prisons and other types of enclosure and 'supervision', it is now possible to detect a 'whole variety of paralegal forms of confinement ... including pre-emptive or preventive detention prior to a crime being committed' (Rose 2000: 335). These are targeted at, for example, *potential* paedophiles and *potential* terrorists – 'monstrous individuals', the 'incorrigibly anti-social' and others representatives of a 'new human kind' (Rose 2000: 333). As Rose (2000: 331) has observed:

[O]utside the circuits of inclusion – in 'marginalized' spaces . . . exists an array of micro-circuits, micro-cultures of non-citizens, failed citizens, anti-citizens, comprised of those who are unable or unwilling to enterprise their lives or manage their own risk, incapable of exercising responsible self-government . . . It is in relation to these zones of exclusion that new strategies of risk management are directed.

These remarks might also inform our understanding of 'anti-social behaviour' and 'anti-social families' destined for the so-called 'sinbins' and this theme is returned to later in the book. These are quasi-penal settings in which families – more specifically, perhaps, those which the government's Respect website refers to unambiguously as the 'worst families' (Home Office, 2007) – are, in effect, interned, placed under a form of 'lockdown' and subjected to a range of curfews and other restrictions. New places of coercion and confinement (other 'residential options') are also being considered in related areas of intervention rhetorically committed to combating the 'social exclusion' of children and families (see, for example, Guillari and Shaw 2005). Perhaps also, these developments can be analytically conjoined to a series of not entirely dissimilar 'transformations' relating to 'detention' and 'detainees' which are becoming more and more central in the context of 'national security' in England and elsewhere (Neocleous 2007).

## The 'double shuffle': doing neoliberalism the New Labour way

The global imposition of neoliberalism has 'been highly uneven, both socially and geographically, and its institutional forms and socio-political consequences have varied significantly' (Brenner and Theodore, 2002: ix). Consequently, when seeking to examine developments in England it remains important to recognize that neoliberalism, rather like McDonald's, comes to speak the 'local language'. This 'implies thinking about neoliberalism in ways that foreground "unevenness", rather than a fluid spread across a flat landscape' (Clarke 2004: 94). This perspective is analytically essential because it acknowledges that 'reforms', such as those introduced by New Labour in terms of interventions in the lives of children and families, are '*not only* neoliberal. They are . . . the effect of specific national articulations' and may even encompass ostensibly progressive elements (Clarke 2004: 95, original emphasis).

In this context, perhaps, Stuart Hall (2003) has been one of most lucid commentators providing interpretations on the specific character of New Labour administrations in England. More specifically, he identifies the national articulation of neoliberalism as being ushered in by means of what he refers to as a complex 'double shuffle':

New Labour is confusing in the signals it gives off . . . It constantly speaks in a forked tongue. It *combines* economic liberalism with a commitment to 'active government'. More significantly, its grim alignment with the broad interest and values of corporate capital and power – the neo-liberal, which is the *leading position* in its political repertoire – is paralleled by another *subaltern* programme, of a more social-democratic kind, running alongside. This is what people invoke when they insist, defensively, that New Labour is not, after all, 'neo-liberal'. The fact is that New Labour is a hybrid regime, composed of two strands. However, one strand – the neo-liberal – is the dominant position. The other strand – the social democratic – is subordinate. What's more, its hybrid character is not simply a static formation: it is the *process* which combines the two elements which matters. The process is 'transformist'. The latter always remains subordinate to and dependent on the former, and *is constantly being 'transformed' into* the former, dominant one.

(Hall 2003: 19, original emphases; see also Gilbert 2004)

However, this is not to maintain, of course, that a neoliberal project – itself far from politically unified – can be, imposed, without resistance, onto the entire social formation (Clarke 2004; 2005).

## Embedding neoliberalism: Giddens and the 'Third Way'

Prior to looking at how New Labour has endeavoured to 'win hearts and minds' and for its plan to 'transform' Children's Services, it is important to briefly have regard to the 'Third Way' because this has tended – certainly during the period of the Blair administrations – to provide an intellectual foundation or narrative for New Labour. Indeed, it can be viewed as the dominant discourse through which restructuring has proceeded and 'through which the meanings of welfare, work and Labour are being remade' (Haylett 2001: 44; see also Cammack 2004; Leggett 2005). Maybe over-simplistically, it could be suggested that the Giddens's abstract theorization, reflected in the idea that we have now entered a 'post-traditional order'/'post-traditional society', gives rise to a policy which is reflected in 'Third Way'/'neoprogressive' politics. Certainly New Labour's 'modernizing' economic and political project has tended to be promoted as a 'Third Way' or (to a lesser extent) 'neoprogressivism' (Giddens 2003) and here, of course, Giddens has been the key figure within the New Labour intelligentsia. Moreover, even if his ideas, preoccupations and prejudices have not always resulted in specific changes and 'reforms' to welfare programmes and practices, they have, to some extent, provided the atmosphere or 'mood music' for New Labour 'modernization'.[7]

More fundamentally, it could also be argued that the 'Third Way' is a neoliberal way; perhaps more accurately a specific and national articulation of neoliberalism. As Paul Cammack (2004: 165) has maintained, it can be interpreted as reflecting the 'second phrase' of neoliberalism 'which moves on from initial "shock treatment", aimed at dismantling structures hostile to the operation of markets, to the construction for the longer term of enduring institutions which will sustain markets and capitalist disciplines into the future'. In this sense, therefore, Giddens's interventions can, perhaps, be perceived as aspiring to maintain, shore up and further embed neoliberalism (see, for example, Giddens 2008). Moreover, within this political frame of reference, every proposed regressive measure is predictably promoted as a 'radical' 'reform'. For Giddens, 'no one any longer has any alternatives to capitalism – the arguments that remain concern how far, and in what ways, capitalism should be governed and regulated' (Giddens 1998: 43–4). Furthermore, it is apparent that his way forward, his proclivity to 'predict the unpredictable', chimes with rhetoric of neoliberalism (Giddens 2003: 32). This is also apparent in his aspiration to make 'government and state agencies transparent, *customer orientated* and quick on their feet' (Giddens 2001: 6, emphasis added; see also Needham 2004). Similarly, his opposition to public service workers is detectable in influential ideas he promulgates, such as that of 'producer capture', and the notion, not underpinned with specific evidential examples, that public service workers 'form vested interest groups if they act in bad faith – if they use an appeal to public goods and values to advance or protect their own interests' (Giddens 2003: 20).[8]

Although Giddens himself – perhaps now realizing a certain weariness about the 'Third Way' 'brand' on the part of a sceptical or cynical public – is now less likely to use the phrase, his neoliberal politics are still to the fore in *Over to You, Mr Brown: How Labour Can Win Again*, one of his most recent books in which he maps out a programme for the Brown administration (Giddens 2007). Significantly also, a good deal of his 'programme' is still in tune with New Labour policy-making and the way in which business culture is apt to be lauded and mimicked (see also Garrett 2008a).[9] Moreover, in line with neoliberal orthodoxy, Giddens continues to promote labour market policies which prompt workers to be 'flexible' while conferring greater freedom to capital. Movement in this direction can, within the area of social welfare provision, be associated with the evolution of what has been termed 'strenuous welfare' and the 'range of new, "business-focused", "entrepreneurial" managerial powers over welfare workers' (Law and Mooney 2007: 34).

According to Bourdieu and Wacquant (2001: 5), Giddens, 'the globe trotting apostle of the "Third Way" ' is a 'planetary prototype' of the 'consultant to the prince'. More generally, Bourdieu criticized the role that some intellectuals fulfilled in promoting so-called 'modernization':

> [B]y associating efficiency and modernity with private enterprise, and archaism and inefficiency with the public sector, they seek to substitute the relationship with the customer, supposedly more egalitarian and more effective, for the relation to the user; finally, they identify 'modernization' with the transfer into the private sector of the public services with the profit potential and with eliminating or bringing into line subordinate staff in the public services, held responsible for inefficiency and every 'rigidity'.
>
> (Bourdieu, in Bourdieu et al. 2002: 182–3)

How, therefore, is the task of winning support for, winning 'hearts and minds' for, such plans undertaken?

## Winning 'hearts and minds'

The final part of the chapter suggests that part of the strategy entails, as observed by Bourdieu, identifying the processes of neoliberalization as mere – albeit necessary and adventurous – 'modernization'. More theoretically, it is suggested that the concept of 'hegemony', mainly associated with Antonio

Gramsci, provides potentially helpful insights into how the 'transformation' of Children's Services, and other areas of public provision, is discursively constructed.

### Bourdieu: 'modernization', 'conservative revolution' and 'resistance'

For Bourdieu, the key political and social struggle of the contemporary period which we inhabit was to be waged against the 'scourge' of neoliberalism which has come to 'be seen as an inevitability' (Bourdieu 2001: vii, 30). However, he recognized that often because of political 'spin' the true intent of the neoliberal project was disguised, even seeking to appear as 'new', 'modern' and 'radical'.

> It is characteristic of *conservative revolutions* . . . that they present restorations as revolutions . . . [This new form of conservative revolution] ratifies and glorifies the reign of what are called the financial markets, in other words the return of the kind of radical capitalism, with no other law than the return of maximum profit, an unfettered capitalism without any disguise, but rationalized, pushed to the limits of its economic efficacy . . .
>
> (Bourdieu 2001: 35, original emphasis)

Against 'narrow, short-term economics' what is needed, asserted Bourdieu (2001: 40), is 'an economics of happiness'. Moreover, we are now witnessing the 'destruction of the economic and social bases of the most precious gains of humanity' (Bourdieu 2001: 37). It is vital, therefore, that the 'critical efforts of intellectuals [and] trade unions . . . should be applied as a matter of priority against the withering away of the state' (Bourdieu 2001: 40). Unlike voguish social theorists, such as Ulrich Beck (2000), for whom trade unions are to be derided and ridiculed as 'zombie categories', Bourdieu recognized the vital role they fulfil within social democracies.

He also continued to view it as crucial to combat the 'myth of globalization' (see, particularly, Bourdieu 2001: 28–9). A 'myth' which is, of course, frequently central to the New Labour 'project' in England (Garrett 2003a: ch. 5). Indeed, today it is

> accepted with resignation as the inevitable outcome of national evolution. [However, an] empirical analysis of the trajectory of the advanced economies . . . suggests, in contrast, that 'globalization' is not a new phase of capitalism, but a 'rhetoric' invoked by governments in order to justify their voluntary surrender to the financial markets'. [In reality, however, it is] *domestic political decisions* [that are] tipping the balance of class forces in favours of the owners of capital.
>
> (Bourdieu and Wacquant 2001: 4, original emphasis)

Specifically in relation to Children's Services, Bourdieu viewed social workers as 'agents of the state' who are 'shot through with the contradictions of the state' (Bourdieu, in Bourdieu et al. 2002: 184). There are, moreover, a number of examples, particularly in the collection *The Weight of the World*, where he tries to highlight the 'real institutional dilemmas haunting "street-level" bureaucrats' (Stabile and Morooka 2003: 337). He also recognizes the fact that many social workers, and those undertaking similar work, should 'feel abandoned, if not disowned outright, in their efforts to deal with the material and moral suffering that is the only certain consequence' of rampant neoliberalism (Bourdieu, in Bourdieu et al. 2002: 183). Here, one of the chief problems is that social workers 'must unceasingly fight on two fronts: against those they want to help and who are often too demoralized to take a hand in their own interests, let alone the interests of the collectivity; on the other hand, against administrations and bureaucrats divided and enclosed in separate universes' (Bourdieu et al. 2002: 190).

Bourdieu was also constantly alert to the problems encountered by individual social workers, encased in public sector bureaucracies during a period of neoliberal inspired, or inflected, 'transformation'. He noted, for example, the 'antinomy between the logic of social work, which is not without a certain prophetic militancy or inspired benevolence, and that of bureaucracy, with its discipline and its prudence' (Bourdieu et al. 2002: 190). Here, a key paradox is that 'the rigidity of bureaucratic institutions is such, that . . . they can only function, with more or less difficulty, thanks to the initiative, the inventiveness, if not the charisma of those functionaries who are the least imprisoned in their function. If bureaucracy were left to its own logic . . . then bureaucracy would paralyse itself'. Moreover, this type of contradiction 'opens up a margin of manoeuvre, initiative and freedom which can be used by those who, in breaking with bureaucratic routines and regulations, defend bureaucracy against itself' (Bourdieu, in Bourdieu et al. 2002: 191).

## Gramsci: hegemony and 'keywords' in 'transformation' projects

As Bourdieu's interpretation – or recoding – of 'modernization' as 'conservative revolution' makes plain, the struggle against neoliberalism is, in part, a struggle over meaning. In this sense, the work of Antonio Gramsci remains important: more specifically, his ideas on 'hegemony'.[10] This is a term and concept which has 'a long history before Gramsci. Derived from hegemon, literally meaning leader, and its Greek root . . . traditionally signifies some combination of authority, leadership and domination' (Ives 2004: 63). Hegemony also 'presupposes an active and practical involvement of the hegemonized groups, quite unlike the static, totalizing and passive subordination implied in the dominant ideology concept' (Forgacs 1988: 424). Furthermore, 'hegemonic power does not flow automatically from the economic position of the dominated group, rather it has to be constructed and negotiated' (Joseph 2006: 52).

According to Gramsci, a movement does not become hegemonic simply because it manages to manipulate 'passive masses into supporting it, nor because it manages to construct cross-class alliances at the level of elite politics' (Robinson 2006: 82). In short, there were, for Gramsci, no short cuts to achieving hegemony and so in order for a hegemonic project to be successful it had to address and respond to people's lived experience of the world. So, for example, particular visions for 'transformation', at societal level or focused on particular sectors (such as Children's Services) have to appeal to and try to 'win over' actual people 'endowed with dreams, desires, ambitions, hopes, doubts, and fears' (Harvey 2005: 167). That is, such visions, or templates for change, (as stressed in Chapter 8 which draws on the work of Boltanski and Chiapello) have to appeal to professional intuitions and instincts and to our values and desires. Moreover, if successful, this 'conceptual apparatus becomes so embedded in common sense as to be taken for granted and not open to question' (Harvey 2005: 5).

The concept of hegemony, therefore, lays emphasis on how rule is something which is constructed rather than given. In this context, therefore, Gramsci's theorization is suggestive of how those in Children's Services, for example, might seek to comprehend their own positions, within differing and specific national settings, during a period of contested and possibly fracturing neoliberal hegemony (Mooney and Law 2007). How do Children's Services function in the context of specific hegemonic orders in a specific time and place? What does this hegemony actually *look* and *feel* like in concrete historical contexts, and how might it be overcome? Specifically in an English context, and influenced by Gramscian approaches, John Clarke (2004: 4–5) has tried to map some of the changes taking place in relation to 'welfare' regimes which house Children's Services and related fields. Analytically, this perspective encourages us to have regard to 'multiple and potentially divergent or opposed projects or designs for the future . . . even if there are dominant forces and voices' (Clarke 2004: 5). More fundamentally, this approach is rooted in an 'approach to institutions, arrangements and relationships as contradictory – containing antagonistic pressures, forces, interests and potentials (that may be contained, but also overflow their containment)' (Clarke 2004: 5).

Perhaps also, thinking about how hegemony works, might lead to reflection on the extent to which those involved in educating students for future roles within Children's Services are embedded in, what Gramsci referred to as, the 'fortresses' and 'earthworks' of civil society. In this context, are educators complicit shapers (under the guise of aiding professional formation) of demeanours which are conducive to hegemonic projects which maintain current market-dominated and commodified relationships and forms of practice which (often despite 'empowerment' talk) further diminish, stigmatize and exploit those who have recourse to services? Such questioning might, moreover, direct attention to the use of language used within micro-engagements with the users of Children's Services.

Those situated within Children's Services and the educational pathways governing entry to such fields of activity might, therefore, begin to think more deeply and more politically about how language *works* within discourses and encounters (Hawkins et al. 2001; Beckett 2003; Gregory and Holloway 2005; Heffernan 2006; McLaughlin, H. 2008). Thus, it might be inquired, what might particular words 'assume about a social totality or infrastructure, or the presumed characteristics of social actors' (Barrett 1992: 202)? This reflective activity is *not* an exercise in what is often caricatured as 'political correctness', but would be a much deeper interrogation of how power relations operate through language. Even more specifically, such an orientation might prompt an investigation of how keywords and phrases can continually – but often imperceptibly – contribute to the solidifying of neoliberal hegemonic order. As

Nancy Fraser and Linda Gordon (1997: 122) have argued, there is a need to acknowledge that 'terms that are used to describe social life are also active forces in shaping it'. Thus, 'particular words and expressions often become focal . . . functioning as keywords, sites at which the meaning of social experience is negotiated and contested. Keywords typically carry unspoken assumptions and connotations that can powerfully influence the discourses they permeate'. This interpretation – entirely in tune with Gramsci's approach – leads, therefore, to their attempt to develop a 'critical political semantics' (Fraser and Gordon 1997: 123): a practice rooted in a project to 'defamiliarize taken-for-granted beliefs in order to render them susceptible to critique and to illuminate present-day conflicts' (Fraser and Gordon 1997: 122). Conversely, failure to operate in this way could be highly problematic for those located within social work and other areas of Children's Services because 'unreflective' use of keywords 'serve to enshrine certain interpretations of social life as authoritative and to delegitimate or obscure others, generally to the advantage of other groups in society and to the disadvantage of subordinate ones' (Fraser and Gordon 1997: 123).

In England, for example, a range of these keywords – or what might also be termed 'welfare words' – can be identified: as will be observed in the next chapter, 'flexibility' is one such word within the discourse of the *Every Child Matters* programme seeking to 'reform' the Children's Services workforce (Chief Secretary to the Treasury 2003). Indeed, it could be argued that 'flexibility' is apt to be discursively deployed as part of an encompassing screen discourse which seeks to render personal and organizational uncertainty as 'child-centred' and a venture into a deeper 'professionalism'. Furthermore, a range of other 'welfare words' and phrases, which merit investigation and contestation, include 'anti-social behaviour' (which is examined in Chapter 6). Similar examination could take place in terms of a other words which are central to the 'transformation' agenda for Children's Services; for example, 'customer' (Needham 2004), 'empowerment' (Bairstow 1994/95), 'problem families' (Welshman 1999a), 'social exclusion' (Levitas 1996), 'therapy' (Furedi 2004), 'underclass' (Macnicol 1987), 'welfare dependency' (Fraser and Gordon 1997) and, of course, many more.

However, it also needs to be emphasized that a Gramscian approach is *not* one which is *entirely* preoccupied with words, and discursive struggle. Vitally, for him, such an approach needed to be aligned with a commitment to a more orthodox politics and a search for alternative bases (within, for example, trade unions, political parties and professional associations) from which to forge counter-hegemonic strategies (Mooney and Law 2007).

## Conclusion

This chapter has maintained that it is vital to try to reach some understanding of neoliberalism and its key elements if the 'transformation' of Children's Services is to be understood and resisted. This is because neoliberalism has furnished what we might refer to as the 'back-story' for some of the key changes which are now taking place. In this context, the state is not simply 'rolled back' and people left entirely abandoned and subject to the whims of an unregulated market. Rather, the state is being reconstituted or remade. In this sense, the 'neoliberal state as *disorganiser* of old forms of welfare and social collectivity' (Coleman and Sim 2005: 105, emphasis added)

Those providing and those receiving services are, of course, unlikely to quietly accept some of the more troubling dimensions of the essentially neoliberal 'change agenda'. For example, people – be they the providers of Children's Services or users (and these categories are, moreover, fluid) – are apt to 'find ways of surviving, negotiating, accommodating, refusing and resisting' and do not merely 'act like automatons envisaged in the governmental plans and strategies of the powerful' (Clarke 2005: 459). Indeed, the next few years – as the neoliberal crisis is likely to deepen – are also likely to bring to the fore many of these modes of obstruction, many of which will be implicitly grounded in an alternative and more progressive understanding of what it is to be 'modern'.

The next chapter, moving from 'wide angle' to 'close-up', will focus on planned changes to practice within Children's Services. More specifically, the aim is to identify the three main practitioner components of the *Every Child Matters: Change for Children* programme. These are ContactPoint, the Common Assessment Framework and the role of the lead professional. This tripartite system is central to the government's drive to create a 'modern' children's workforce. It will be suggested, however, that the notion of practitioner 'flexibility' – a core motif within the CfC enterprise – gels with the neoliberal vision of working lives. It is also maintained that there may be an American dimension, once again chiefly neoliberal in character, to the programme, although this is rarely acknowledged in most accounts of the 'transformations' under way within Children's Services.

**Reflection and talk box 2**

Reconsider some of the characteristics of neoliberalism mentioned earlier and think and talk about the following:

Does it shed light on your experience as someone who may be working in or about to begin working in Children's Services?

In what areas, in your work, are you able to detect what has been referred to as 'accumulation by dispossession'?

Can you identify ways in which neoliberalism is 'playing out' in a specific way in your particular professional, local or national setting?

What are the main 'hegemonic' forces which are dominant in terms of the 'transformation' of children's and related services in your national setting? How have these forces achieved the position of dominance? How is it maintained?

In your work, can you identifying particular recurring or emerging patterns of 'precariousness' or 'precaricity'?

How does incarceration and imprisonment impact on the work of those in Children's Services?

What are the keywords – or 'welfare words' – around which the 'change agenda' is being organized?

If you are a professional practitioner working in Children's Services, examine your specific Code of Ethics. What tensions are there in terms of the values in the document and the wider forces of neoliberalism impacting on you and your work?

In his book *The Progressive Manifesto*, Giddens (2003: 6) observed that 'ideological breakout demands *new* concepts and *new* policy perspectives. We must continue to *think radically*, but radicalism means being *open* to *fresh* ideas, not *relapsing* back into the *traditional leftism* of the past' (emphasis added). Here, how is he constructing his case to 'win hearts and minds' and trying to deflate criticism?

On account of the global economic crisis, the neoliberal project is now clearly vulnerable, but how can it be opposed in your particular setting? Where might it be possible to forge alliances, in and beyond the sector, to help 'transform' Children's Services in a way which seeks to counter neoliberal ways of *thinking* about and *doing* work in the sector?

# 3 The 'transformational reform agenda': the *Change for Children* programme

The first part of the chapter is mostly descriptive and focuses on the main practice-based components of the *Change for Children* programme originally trailed in the *Every Child Matters* (Chief Secretary to the Treasury 2003):[1] the CPd, referred to in ECM as a local electronic 'information hub containing all the children living in the area other basic details' (Chief Secretary to the Treasury 2003: 53–5); the Common Assessment Framework; and the plan to create a 'Lead Professional' (LP) role. This is followed by a look at, more general, 'workforce reform' within Children's Services and the idea that practitioners need to have a 'common' vision.

The second part of the chapter draws on the perspective of Pierre Bourdieu and Loic Wacquant on the role which the USA fulfils in terms of the international transference in ideas associated with welfare and other discourses. It is argued that approaches to 'modernizing' services for children and their families in the USA – more specifically, the policy aspiration to make these services more 'businesslike' and 'outcomes' oriented – *may* have had an impact on 'transformation' strategies in England. This is reflected by, for example, seemingly influential 'reforms' introduced in the New England state of Vermont. It is also maintained that a renewed emphasis on 'prevention' in Children's Services in England is, in part, likely to have been prompted by policy and practice developments in the USA.

## Launching the 'transformational reform agenda'

This is 'the beginning of a long journey, which will present challenges for us all, but from which we must not flinch' avowed a combative Chief Secretary to the Treasury, in the introduction to ECM, in September 2003 (Chief Secretary to the Treasury 2003: 4). This consultation document can be viewed as part of the wider 'modernization' drive which began soon after the first New Labour administration took up office (Newman 2001). However, ECM was also presented as a response to the Laming Report, which inquired into the circumstances surrounding the death of Victoria Climbié, and to the deaths of other children who were in contact with social work and associated services. In this context, it was maintained that the 'common threads which led in each case to a failure to intervene early enough were poor co-ordination; a failure to share information; the absence of anyone with a strong sense of accountability; and frontline workers trying to cope with staff vacancies, poor management and lack of effective training' (Chief Secretary to the Treasury 2003: 5). Embedded in the New Labour policy trope focused on combating 'social exclusion', ECM identified five key 'outcomes' which, it was maintained, were central for all children. Indeed, it was later to be elaborated, more emphatically, that 'children and young people have told us' that these five outcomes were the 'key to wellbeing in childhood and later life' (DfES 2004: 4). These were referred to as being healthy, staying safe, enjoying and achieving, making a positive contribution, and economic well-being.

To deliver the outcomes, a number of policy 'challenges' had to be dealt with and these were identified as a need for: better prevention; a stronger focus on parenting and families; earlier intervention; the 'weak accountability and poor integration' of existing services; and workforce reform (Chief Secretary to the Treasury 2003: ch. 1). Related to this approach, in September 2004, the government published the National Service Framework (NSF) for Children, Young People and Maternity Services which set out 'new standards . . . designed to generate a step change in the quality of children's health services' (DoH 2004). This was to be implemented over a ten-year period and was devised to contribute to the achievement of the five outcomes. The Children Act 2004 secured Royal Assent on 15 November 2004 but the Act was only the 'legislative spine' on which the New Labour administration wanted to 'build our reforms' (DfES 2004: 5). With the publication of CfC, in December 2004, therefore, the five outcomes gave rise to 25 'specific aims'. Moreover, a new tripartite system would, it was maintained, assist in the promotion of these aims.

## The tripartite system to facilitate better 'outcomes'

As observed, ECM set out the government's plans to promote 'early intervention and effective protection' and it was in this context that the new tripartite system for the children's workforce was formulated. This is comprised of (what was to become) the ContactPoint database, the Common Assessment Framework and Lead Professional. In what follows, therefore, each of these will be outlined.

### The ContactPoint database (CPd)

In terms of the plans for the CPd, the idea of using technology to promote more 'joined up' services for children had been proposed even prior to the publication of the Laming Report and ECM. Indeed, it was stated, in early 2002, that the government was of the view that better use could be made of technology in 'identifying and supporting children at risk of social exclusion' (PIU 2002: 108–9). Furthermore, the faltering Integrated Children's System (ICS) which aims to electronically manage a immense amount of personalized, detailed information on 'looked after' children and children 'in need' has been evolving for a number of years (see Calder 2004; Bell 2008; Cleaver et al. 2008; UNISON 2008a).

Significantly, however, the practical moves to introduce change and to improve the 'identification, referral and tracking of vulnerable children' were *not* initially situated within a discourse focused on combating 'social exclusion' or promoting 'well-being': they were focused on tackling crime. Initially, '6 local authorities in urban areas (Bolton, Knowsley, Kensington and Chelsea, Lewisham, Camden and Sheffield) which were involved in the Government's Street Crime Initiative were chosen as Trailblazers' (DfES 2005a: 7): four other groups were subsequently added (Telford and Wrekin and Shropshire; Leicester, Leicestershire and Rutland; East and West Sussex; Gateshead and Newcastle). Nine of these were to then go on to develop 'IT applications akin to [what was referred to at the time as] an Index' and three – East Sussex, Lewisham and Sheffield – were reported, in 2005, to 'have successfully rolled out their Indexes' (DfES 2005a: 8).

The CPd was to prove particularly controversial and gave rise to opposition in Parliament (House of Lords and House of Commons Joint Committee on Human Rights (JCHR), 2004) and elsewhere (Cushman 2004; Dowty 2004). These criticisms – which are examined in more detail in Chapter 5 – centred on fears that the human rights, specifically the right to privacy, of children and their parents would be infringed and that the database idea could result in highly subjective notions about what might constitute a 'concern' about a child and the quality of parenting which was available to them. Important here was, for example, the suggestion – at this stage – that a 'flag of concern' could be inserted within a child's database field.

Subsequently, the government has been anxious to erase the Orwellian 'database' tag which dominated discussion on the idea in Parliament and, at present, the less sinister ContactPoint, is the preferred designation. Some 'trailblazer' authorities have also tried to customize their systems in order, perhaps, to try and soften criticism. In one London borough, for example, the system is merely the 'Lewisham Information Sharing and Assessment' – or just plain LISA (DfES 2005b). More generally, the government has been intent on emphasizing the role of the 'trailblazers' in, it is claimed, ironing out practical and legal difficulties in relation to the scheme. Indeed, their 'experience has demonstrated benefits in service effectiveness and efficiency' (DfES 2005c: 1; see also Ruddy 2004). In 2005, following a (rather lukewarm) evaluation by Cleaver et al. (2004), it was announced by Beverley Hughes, the Minister for Children, Young People and Families, that the one-off implementation cost for the scheme would be '£224 million over the next three years' (Hughes 2005: 7). Moreover, operating costs (after this) are expected to be £41 million per year (Hughes 2005: 7). However, we are advised that in 'financial terms the benefits of reducing the time currently used unproductively by practitioners trying to contact each other could equate to around £88m per year. This will free up more time for practitioners to concentrate on delivering services' (DfES 2005d: 2).

Section 12 of the Children Act 2004 gives the Secretary of State the power to make regulations and issue guidance in terms of the detailed operation of the datebases. It is stated that no assessment or case information will be featured and it will not replace child protection registers. However, it remains the plan that all children in England (aged up to 18) will have data kept on them. In some instances data will be maintained post-18 if a person is thought to have 'multiple needs' and they give consent to their database entries being retained. There will be a central system with data partitioned into 150 parts, one relating to each local authority in England. Testing and piloting began in 2007 and the database was originally scheduled for a national 'roll out by the end of 2008' (DfES 2005d: 1). Importantly, though, and as discussed in Chapter 5, the government has made no substantial concessions to critics of the scheme. However, the original plan to insert 'flags of concern', mooted in ECM, was abandoned. Instead there is to be a 'a *facility* for practitioners to indicate that they wish to be contacted in relation to a child because they have information to share, are currently taking action, or have undertaken an assessment (DfES 2005c: 1, emphasis added). This would seem to refer to practitioners' being electronically alerted that a CAF/eCAF has been completed.

## The Common Assessment Framework (CAF/eCAF)

A draft 'common assessment framework' was developed in late 2004 and it was published in revised form in 2005. According to its associated literature, the CAF/eCAF is 'a new, more standardised approach to assessing children's needs for services. It is for children with additional needs, i.e., those at risk of poor outcomes' (DfES 2005e: 1). The three stated aims of the CAF/eCAF are to: support earlier intervention; improve multi-agency working by, for example, '*embedding a common language* of assessment'; reduce 'bureaucracy for families' (DfES 2005e: 1, emphasis added). In this context, two elements, both constructed as electronic templates, are important: a three-page 'simple pre-assessment checklist' and a standard 14-page CAF/eCAF form (DfES 2005e: 1).

The CAF/eCAF will not replace many other assessment schedules used in the various agencies, such as the Assessment of Children in Need and their Families documentation, but the government wants the CAF/eCAF to 'become the main assessment tool to support inter-agency referral and multi-agency working' (DfES 2005e: 2). In this way, it is 'likely to be of most help' when there is 'reason to think that a child is not making the progress they should be at their age but it is not clear what the underlying causes are or what would help; the child is likely to need the support of another agency' (DfES 2005e: 3). Importantly, though, the guidance documentation is clear that the completion of a CAF will *not* automatically generate resources. Indeed, since 'resources for services are finite, doing a common assessment cannot guarantee that services (especially those involving another agency) will be delivered' (DfES 2005e: 4).

Thematically, the CAF/eCAF is organized into three 'themes or domains' (DfES 2005e: 8). These prompt the completer of the documentation to focus on: the development of the baby, child or young person; the parents and carers; the family and environment. Each of these areas is then subdivided to take into account factors identified as relevant by the creators of the immensely influential 'looking after children' materials and assessment framework for children and need and their families (Parker et al. 1991; Ward 1995; Department of Health, Department for Education and Employment, Home Office 2000). In addition, the CAF/eCAF is a 'tool to support practice' and it is not meant to be 'used mechanistically or when it adds little value' (DfES 2005e: 8).

Significantly and reflecting what has been termed social work 'Electronic' or 'e-Turn' (Garrett 2005), in summer 2007, it was announced that the implementation of this form would be based on a single national information technology (IT) system and would tend, henceforth, to be referred to as the eCAF. As Sue White and her colleagues have maintained, although this schedule has 'received little criticism or attention ... dilemmas about sharing information and consent' relating to the deployment of the CPd, also apply to CAF/eCAF (White et al. 2008: 3). Moreover, the Department of Health is now also intent on developing a CAF/eCAF for adults (Social Exclusion Task Force 2008: 15).

### The Lead Professional (LP)

The LP is the vital third element in the 'modern' tripartite practice component to the 'transformational reform agenda' and the governments maintain that sections 10 (duty to co-operate) and 11 (duty to safeguard welfare) of the Children Act 2004 provide the legal basis for the implementation of this fulcrum role. The LP task is to:

> act as a single point of contact that children, young people and their families can trust, and who is able to support them in making choices and in navigating their way through the system; ensure that children and families get appropriate interventions when needed, which are well planned, regularly reviewed and effectively delivered; reduce overlap and inconsistency from other practitioners.
>
> (DfES, 2005f: 1)

This role, although discursively positioned within the 'modernizing' endeavour to transform Children's Services recalls, in many respects, the role envisaged for social workers in the Seebohm report in the late 1960s (Committee on Local Authority and Allied Personal Services 1968). However, here the policy aspiration appears, in part, to be one of *replacing* the professionally qualified social worker given that, following the initial and core assessment phases, any 'relevant practitioner' (for example, a personal adviser, member of school support staff or housing support staff) can become a LP for a child 'in need'. Social workers will, it seems, mainly be left to act as the LP for children who are 'looked after' or/and have their names on the child protection register (DfES 2006c: 10, annex A). Significantly also, a 'budget-holding' LP was piloted in 15 local authorities during 2006–08 (DfES 2006d: 9). In this context, the LP acts as the 'single account holder' enabled to 'commission services from a wide range of providers – statutory, private and voluntary' (DfES 2006d: 9). If this role becomes institutionalized and more widespread, following the piloting, it is not difficult to see how it might facilitate the greater incursion of 'for profit' Children's Services into what has been mainly a public and voluntary sector domain. Indeed, this type of incursion, as is made plain in Chapter 8, is going to become more substantial given related plans to set up 'independent' Social Work Practices.

The more encompassing emphasis which is now being placed on 'transforming' the Children's Services' workforce is also important. This aspect of the CfC programme stresses that a 'skilled and effective workforce' has to exhibit malleability because to 'work effectively on an inter-agency basis professional and support staff need a strong commitment to flexible working' (DfES 2004: 17). We are advised that this is because delivering 'more integrated services requires new ways of working and significant culture change for staff used to working within narrower professional and service-based boundaries' (DfES 2004: 17). This also relates, of course, to New Labour's promotion of 'joined up government' and the emphasis placed on 'joined up working' (see, for example, Ling 2002; Allen 2003). Associated with this discourse, the 'old' structures of health and social services – perhaps perceived as moribund 'zombie' institutions (Beck 2000) – have been presented as encased in bureaucratic 'silo' structures which were no longer amenable to 'modern' and 'flexible' ways of working.[2]

The next part of the chapter, therefore, focuses on this 'workforce' reform dimension to the 'transformational reform agenda' (DfES 2006a). Here, the CfC programme can also be interpreted as being influenced and inflected by New Labour's neoliberalism and, it is argued, that the emphasis given to notions pivoting on 'flexibility' – also referred to in Chapter 2 – is significant and revealing.

### 'Imagine you are in a foreign country'

'Transformations' having an impact on Children's Services and related fields can, of course, be associated with much broader changes having an impact across 'workscapes' in the early years of the twenty-first century (see Felstead et al. 2005). Moreover, the types of 'reform' envisaged are not, of course, restricted to England, but are part of more global, often neoliberal inspired, changes to the character of the 'care' work provided by public services. In this context, Donna Baines (2004a; 2004b), for example, has provided informative accounts of developments in Canada.

Perhaps the 'transformations' which New Labour is promoting appear, in some respects, to gel with Zygmunt Bauman's notion that we are now living in a period of 'liquid modernity', a new, fluid and in 'many ways, novel, phase in the history of modernity' (Bauman 2000b: see also Ferguson 2004). Thus, for Bauman (2000b: 149) – in part related to the 'advent of light, free-floating capitalism' – modernity is now 'de-regulated', 'liquefied', 'flowing', 'dispersed', and 'scattered'. This is a 'world of universal flexibility' and work is one of the key domains of life where this is detectable (Bauman 2000b: 149). Unlike in the past – a period of 'heavy capitalism' – the work in which people are involved in today 'can no longer offer the secure axis around which to wrap and fix self-definitions, identities and life-projects' (Bauman 2000b: 146, 139).

The discussion in the previous chapter on neoliberalism and its core characteristics sheds a more illuminating light on workforce changes within Children's Services than does Bauman's impishly pessimistic, yet popular, social theory. Nonetheless, his description of what work is beginning to *look* like is partly persuasive and perhaps illuminates the shift from the so-called 'Seebohm factories' (Simpkin 1983), ushered-in in the late 1960s and early 1970s, and the Children's Services 'workscapes' being envisaged early in a new century. More fundamentally, the complex changes proposed for the *work* in, for example, social work, can only be properly interpreted if situated alongside similar changes which are taking place in other sectors for, as confided in the government literature on 'transformation', handling 'periods of change and uncertainty is becoming increasingly common for practitioners in all organisations' (DfES 2006b: 13).

The complexity of New Labour's uneasy relationship with social work also needs to be stressed. The introduction of a new degree, bursaries and setting up of a General Social Care Council (GSCC) perhaps suggests that policy-making is far from unidirectional and hardly provides evidence of a desire to simply liquidate social work. Across a wider canvas, social work is also said to be experiencing a 'boom' and can be perceived as a 'growth industry even in countries that ideologically would rather do without it' (Lorenz 2005: 97). Nonetheless, in England, New Labour can, perhaps, still be viewed as committed to breaking up social work as *a discrete field of activity and values*. This is hinted at in the attempts to alter the profession's ideological shape and to render it more 'practical' and less theoretical (DoH 2002). Possibly related to this, the GSCC is now provided with 'unprecedented powers to regulate and decide on' the appropriateness of social workers' 'non-work life' (McLaughlin 2007: 13).

In terms of the some of the focal preoccupations of this book, the attempt to create more 'flexible' social work within fluid 'multi-agency' institutional paradigms is a crucial development. It is, however, important to perceive this hankering for 'flexibility' as part of the overt neoliberal project referred to, at length, in the previous chapter. Indeed, this promotion of 'flexibility' is a recurring motif throughout the CfC policy documents. More specifically, the authors of these documents are intent on locating work with children and families in an *infinitely* 'flexible' and elastic milieu:

> It is common shorthand to describe people's roles within a multi-agency service in relation to their professional background – for example 'the social worker', 'the mental health worker' or the 'health visitor'. This can certainly be helpful for getting a quick overview of what the service can offer . . . However, if you are trying to break down barriers and understand the individual skills that people can bring to bear in support of individual children and their families, it is not always the most helpful way for colleagues to think about each other.
>
> (DfES 2006b: 14)

Individuals are informed that in the envisaged

> multi-agency service where people come from a range of different agencies, you are likely to find that your terms and conditions are different from those of your colleagues. Some may be paid more, some less. Some may be on term-time-only contracts, others may have to work through the year. Some will have more annual leave, others less.
>
> (DfES 2006b: 16)

Problems such as this, it is conceded somewhat blandly, have no 'easy short-term solution' (DfES 2006b: 16). However, it is maintained that, for example, making use of 'performance appraisal' systems might help; so also could speaking to the 'manager/coordinator about how you feel' (DfES 2006a: 16). Indeed, the point that the manager is pivotal here is frequently reiterated: so, for example, if 'you have a concern about your terms and conditions, the best starting point is to speak to your manager' (DfES 2006b: 17). Both the British Association of Social Workers and UNISON were asked to participate in the 'Options for Excellence' review of the social care workforce, established in July 2005, but there are scant references to these organizations fulfilling a *meaningful* role within much of the 'transformational reform agenda' literature (see DfES 2006e). On account of this omission, the impression remains that the key workplace relationship is, in line with neoliberalism, that involving the *atomized* individual worker and their sovereign manager/employer.

## The 'common' vision

Ultimately, it would seem, the onus is on the individual worker to *change* and *adapt*: 'Remember you may have to work with resistance – and sometimes this resistance will be your own . . . Being open and patient and keeping sight of the *common vision* of your service can help to get you through it' (DfES 2006b: 13, emphasis added). Indeed, 'common vision', 'common assessment' and 'common core' (of skills) are significant keywords, located within the CfC programme, which indicate that an attempt is being made to forge a particular type of hegemony over, through and within, a 'transformed' service.

It is, for instance, maintained that 'the key starting point in developing a shared understanding is for all service members to sign up to a common vision for your work with children and young people' (DfES 2006b: 8). Furthermore, if 'you do not know what the vision or goals are for your service, speak to your manager' (DfES 2006b: 10). Much of this is derived from the corporate sector and can be perceived, in part, as predictably facile. However, the promotion of 'common' visions, a 'common core' of skills for the children's workforce with a 'common' glossary (DfES 2005g; 2005h) can also be interpreted as implicitly ideological and potentially damaging. For example, the emphasis on the 'common' can be interpreted as a censoring mechanism which seeks to subjugate and suppress dissenting vocabularies and visions regarded as potentially subversive of the 'common' hegemonic endeavour: perhaps, for example, vocabularies which include *uncommon* words which, nonetheless, reflect people's experiences (for example, 'exploitation', 'capital', 'power', 'inequality', and so on). That is to say, ideas pivoting on the promotion of a 'common language' can be perceived as containing centralizing and disciplinary elements. Indeed, this aspect has even been conceded by the Dartington Research Unit, influential English supporters for developing a 'common language' in Children's Services. For example, Axford et al. (2006: 174) recognize that the 'objective of smooth, speedy and inter-disciplinary decision-making may seem to parents and children to be a "ganging up" of agencies against them, with matters substantially agreed between professionals before a joint meeting'.

This emphasis on the centrally devised, 'common' approach has, perhaps, many potentially adverse implications for those having recourse to Children's Services. Important here, for example, is the fact that the associated 'tools' are apt to be soaked and saturated with market-based ideological pre-suppositions, including a fixation with the conduct, motivation and attitude of children and young people (Garrett 2003a). More fundamentally, this is rooted in a neoliberal workfarist ethic and is reflected in the CAF/eCAF's concern about, for example, where a child or young person is 'developing enterprising behaviour' and is 'ready for employment' (DfES 2005e). Furthermore, there would seem to be many disadvantages for those working in the children's workforce with such centrally devised forms and e-templates and they are apt to be resisted because they are 'perceived as exerting control over hitherto fairly autonomous areas and suspected of being a cost-cutting device' (Axford et al. 2006: 172). More generally, 'tools' such as the CAF/eCAF (and similar materials largely derived from the 'Looking After Children' system and the Framework for the Assessment of Children in Need and their Families) can be interpreted as seeking to structure the interaction with the users of services and put in place new thematic and temporal frameworks for that interaction (Knight and Caveney 1998; Garrett 2003a; White et al. 2008).

One of the main messages conveyed in the CfC literature, however, is that individual members of the children's workforce must be tenacious and hold true to the 'common vision' because the 'benefits' of a 'multi-agency service' include 'high levels of job satisfaction compared with their previous jobs' and – even more emphatically – a '*sense of liberation* from bureaucratic or cultural constraints' (DfES 2006b: 3, emphasis added). One way to imagine the pathway to this 'liberation' is as a move to another place: 'Imagine you are working in a foreign country, experiencing a new culture. You have to begin to understand what is acceptable behaviour and the written and unwritten rules of personal engagement' (DfES 2006b: 7). The notion that the 'transformed' Children's Services can deliver 'liberation' is examined in greater detail in Chapter 8. In what follows, however, it is argued that the neoliberal practices of another country – an *actual* place, the USA – are appearing to have an impact of the evolution of Children's Services in England. In this context, two themes, central to the development of policy in the USA, have been important: the attempt to entirely reshape services along 'business' lines and the policy fixation with 'prevention'.

## Being 'modern' and being American

For many, it is a source of disquiet and vexation that the relationship between England and the USA is so close and intertwined in the area of international politics (Blair 2003; see also Johnson 2004). However, the impact of policies, partly derived from the USA, has, of course, also been significant in terms of New Labour's *domestic* plans and policies for welfare (King and Wickham-Jones 1999; Neocleous 1999; Walker 1999; Deacon 2000; Swanson 2000; Peck 2001; Newburn 2002; Sargent 2003; Prideaux 2005). Even though New Labour's various New Deals and related reforms have fallen short 'of the US models of enforcement associated with the 1996 "end of welfare" ', the inspiration for its reforms has 'emerged from 20 years of US anti-welfare politics' (Clarke 2005: 448). This has been revealed in policy-making rhetoric by, for example, the government's keenness to craft a 'modern welfare state', getting people off benefits, giving them 'a hand up not a handout' (Blair 1999: 13; see also Hutton 2006; Purnell 2008).

Perhaps more fundamentally, as John Gray (2003: 18) has asserted, the former Prime Minister believed there was 'only one way of being modern and it is American'. This fascination with American practices and values is not, however, restricted to the former head of government: Gordon Brown, the successor to Blair, is similarly heavily influenced by what he perceives as the dynamism of the US economy. Indeed, for him, the 'success of the American economic experience teaches us that the lifeblood of a market economy is the continuous injection of new competition' (Brown 2006). Similar views are apt to be echoed within other tiers of the New Labour administration and this is personified in the biographies of key figures associated with the 'transformation' project: for example, Ed Balls, the current Secretary of State for Children, Schools and Families has spent time in the John F. Kennedy School of Government at Harvard. However, this preoccupation with the neoliberalizing 'modernizing' route which the USA has taken is not solely detectable in the career paths of individuals because it is also reflected, to some extent, in changes taking place with Children's Services and in related fields. This policy transfer dimension is complex, but also pervasive and structural. It is, moreover, a development which may seem somewhat surprising – even deeply paradoxical – because Children's Services in the USA remain 'generally poor by comparison with those in the UK' (Little et al. 2003: 208). With 28 million Americans now surviving on food stamps, the scale of poverty faced by children and their families is also quite extraordinary (see also 'United States of America 2008: The Great Depression', *Independent*, 1 April 2008: 1–2). In New York City, for example, 1.7 million people – 25 per cent of all families with children – live beneath the federal poverty line; each night, moreover, 7000 families – with nearly 14,000 children – crowd into the city's night shelters (www.unitedwaynyc.org). Why, therefore, this fixation with American templates for 'reform'?

## Looking to the 'symbolic Mecca'?

Perhaps in the context, Bourdieu and Wacquant may provide a foundational framework to aid our understanding. For them, 'cultural imperialism' and the symbolic dominance of the USA have resulted in 'numerous topics directly issuing from ... the social particularity of the American society' being 'imposed, in apparently de-historicized form, upon the whole planet' (Bourdieu and Wacquant 1999: 41). Furthermore, this results in 'a sort of generalized and even spontaneous "Washington consensus", as one can readily observe in the sphere of economics, philanthropy or management training' (Bourdieu and Wacquant 2001: 4). Thus, notions derived from the discourse of welfare 'reform' in the USA are having an impact in England and elsewhere, and keywords, such as 'globalization', 'flexibility', 'governance', 'employability', 'underclass' and 'exclusion' can be interpreted as forming part of a 'new planetary vulgate' (Bourdieu and Wacquant 2001: 2), an interlinked matrix of 'screen discourses' (Bourdieu and Wacquant 2001: 4) from 'which the terms "capitalism", "class", "exploitation", "domination" and inequality" are conspicuous by their absence' (Bourdieu and Wacquant 2001: 2).[3] It is also important to recognize that the:

> international circulation of ideas . . . tends by its very logic, to conceal their original conditions of production and signification . . . [T]hese commonplaces, which the perpetual media repetition has gradually transformed into a universal common sense, succeed in making us forget that, in many cases, they do nothing but express, in a truncated and unrecognizable form (including to those who are promoting it), the complex and contested realities of a particular historical society, tacitly constituted into the model and measure of all things: the American society of the post-Fordist and post-Keynesian era, the world's only superpower and symbolic Mecca.
>
> (Bourdieu and Wacquant 2001: 3)

This process is, moreover, influenced by the 'driving role played by the major American philanthropic and research foundations' and 'great international think tanks, more or less directly plugged into the spheres of economic and political power' (Bourdieu and Wacquant 1999: 46, 50; see also Hogan and Murphey, 2002: ch. 10). Moreover, highly esteemed

> US research universities were and are the training grounds for many foreigners who take what they learn back to their countries of origin – the key figures in Chile's and Mexico's adaptation to neoliberalism were US-trained economists for example – as well as into international institutions such as the IMF, the World Bank, and the UN.
>
> (Harvey, 2005: 54)

Friedman (2000: 140) has argued that matters are a good deal more complex than Bourdieu and Wacquant maintain, given that the USA is not 'the sole locus of celebratory liberalism' and that some of 'strongest critiques' of neoliberalism are also from the US. Moreover, in spite of US military power, the world system has become decentralized in terms of capital accumulation, with significant regional poles of accumulation as well. However, perhaps the key point remains that Bourdieu and Wacquant were alert to – horrified by – the way in which capital is continuing to transform the USA and they were fearful that Europe risked being transformed in a similar way. This specifically relates to their concern about the impact of neoliberalism on the social and economically marginalized in contact with the social workers and associated professionals. For them, the ghettos of the USA were now 'abandoned sites that are fundamentally defined by an absence – basically that of the state and of everything that comes with it, police, schools, health care institutions, associations, etc.' (Bourdieu, in Bourdieu et al. 2002: 123). Indeed, in some US cities 'public authority has turned into a war machine against the poor' with social workers only able to see 'clients' in their offices (Wacquant, in Bourdieu et al. 2002: 137–8).

Perhaps the way in which this 'transfer' of ideas, plans, practices and vocabularies works is detectable is in terms of how elements of the CfC programme can be seen to have, in part, originated in the USA. Indeed, across a range of policies and practices, the similarity of recent New Labour 'reforms' is striking and provides a potentially rich area for future research: for example, in terms of responses to 'anti-social behaviour' (Garrett 2007c) and child adoption (Van de Flier Davis 1995; Sargent 2003). In these areas implemented policies are, of course, markedly different in the two jurisdictions, but the *ideological* foundation – the 'common sense' – which provides the policy orientation remains broadly similar and increasingly delimits the sphere of policy choices and 'transformation' strategies seemingly available. Certainly, a number of prominent English 'think tanks' close to New Labour, such as the Institute of Public Policy Research, have been keen to *remake* Children's Services in ways which are clearly influenced by US models (see, for example, Kendall and Harper 2002). Furthermore, the Association of Directors of Social Services (ADSS) (2002) has highlighted that 'outcome-based approaches' have had a seemingly beneficial impact on states such as Vermont. Shortly before the publication of the Laming Report, for example, it was reported that the ADSS had circulated a paper to Members of Parliament which called for reforms 'along the lines pioneered in Vermont' ('Move to improve child protection', *Guardian*, 2 September 2002). A short exploration of policy development in this small state is, therefore, instructive and enables us to examine some of the neoliberal ideological assumptions – rarely made explicit – in which the 'transformational reform agenda' within Children's Services, in England, is embedded.

## Venturing to Vermont

Certainly Con Hogan and David Murphey's *Outcomes: Reframing Responsibility for Well-being* (2002), which largely draws on the Vermont experience, appears to have influenced New Labour's policies for Children's Services. Their book, produced by a philanthropic organization, the Annie E. Casey Foundation, can be located alongside a range of ideas, fixations and policy shifts which were promoted not only by Clinton's 'New Democrats', but also by those (even) further to the political right. Here, a core principle is that 'big' government needs to be radically trimmed and denuded of its core 'welfare' role. In the 1990s this political project was often rhetorically underpinned by an assertion that 'government' needed to be 'reinvented' with the public sector being injected with a more 'entrepreneurial spirit', and a programme for change coalesced around a series of keywords and slogans which blared that governments should: 'steer rather than row'; 'empower rather than serve'; 'inject competition into service delivery'; 'fund outcomes, not inputs'; 'meet the needs of the customer, not the bureaucracy'; be committed to 'prevention rather than cure'; seek to 'leverage change through the market' (Osborne and Gaebler 1992; see also Hogan and Murphey 2002: 13, 33, 46). Significantly, a key aspect of this programme, in a US context, is – as argued in the previous chapter – to *remake* and *reconfigure* the state; also, to clawback some of the working-class gains accrued during the 40 years from 1935 to 1975; from Roosevelt's New Deal programmes to the 'War on Poverty' and 'Great Society' initiatives in the 1960s and 1970s (see also Abramovitz 2006). Moreover, during the Clinton administrations, the hegemony achieved by the 'New Democrats' within the Democratic Party following their routing of 'New Deal Democrats', made this neoliberal project more viable (Birnbaum 2004).

Hogan and Murphey's (2002: 3) 'new "physics" of social change' can, therefore, be understood as part of this transformation project and this is reflected in bland comments such as:

> More and more, we know that government can take us only so far . . . While government has a history and important role in assisting people, we are now realizing the extent to which people can contribute to their own well-being . . . We have become so conditioned to having government solve our problems that we have abrogated our community responsibilities. Through disuse, we have forgotten how to make a difference in the lives of our neighbors . . . If people in communities connect with each other around common purpose, they can do anything.
>
> (Hogan and Murphey 2002: 6, 45)

The approach which these authors and policy activists seek to champion is rooted in a 'taken-for-granted commonsense', a set of beliefs or neoliberal *doxa*, which seek to evade 'critical scrutiny' (Fraser 1997: 122–3). They are, for example, intent on 'getting people into jobs and out of the *cycle of dependency*' (Hogan and Murphey 2002: 91, emphasis added). Furthermore, they feel that the aspiration to 'End Welfare as We Know it' 'galvanized' change (Hogan and Murphey 2002: 10), welcome the 'welfare reform legislation of 1996' and assert, contrary to a number of other more complex readings, that the 'results were spectacular. Numbers of cash assistance recipients declined by nearly half. In some parts of the country, welfare caseloads dropped by more than 75 percent. Most former welfare recipients now have jobs' (Hogan and Murphey 2002: 78). More fundamentally, as a result of the changes, 'welfare reform' 'truly changed the nation's conversation with the poor' (Hogan and Murphey 2002: 79).[4]

Another striking characteristic of this approach adopted in Vermont, is that it appears to be mesmerized by 'business' and seeks to mimic and hegemonize a 'business' perspective and to apply this to 'human services' (Hogan and Murphey 2002: ch. 5). Even more fundamentally, the aim appears to be to progressively *transform* public services *into* business organizations. Business people are, we are advised, 'generally action orientated and positive about their work. And they are usually natural problem solvers. Consequently, the private sector may have much to teach the public sector about how to achieve outcomes' (Hogan and Murphey 2002: 32). Thus, there is a need to 'transfer some of that positive, focused energy of business to our work. Indeed, many of the conceptual approaches of the private sector could invigorate human services' (Hogan and Murphey 2002: 32). This thinking is used to apply notions focused on 'profit' to work within children's services.

> Different groups realize profit in different ways. Shareholders profit by receiving dividends or an increased return on their investment when they sell their shares. Customers profit by receiving higher quality products, more responsive service, and more competitive pricing. Employers profit by receiving higher compensation or bonuses, opportunities for profit sharing, better health care, and other benefits – all of which contribute to a higher standard of living. Profitability, rather than being exclusive to the business community, applies to all us.
>
> (Hogan and Murphey 2002: 32)

This business perspective 'offers some striking, yet under-developed, parallels to human service agencies. If the fundamental purpose of a business is to improve its profitability for shareholders, then the parallel purpose for human services is to improve the well-being of people and communities' (Hogan and Murphey 2002: 32). In short, 'we are all shareholders in the well-being of children and families, so any demonstrable improvement in well-being improves the lives of all' (Hogan and Murphey 2002: 33). Perhaps unsurprisingly, given this encompassing orientation, 'well-being' is 'the human services analog to business profitability. Certainly, well-being is a product of tangible short – and long – term assets minus current and longer term social liabilities, together with the intangible assets of people and communities' (Hogan and Murphey 2002: 38). Improving 'indicators and outcomes for children and families is the equivalent to improving a company's fiscal health. Well-being is the counterpart in the human services of profitability in the business world' (Hogan and Murphey 2002: 33). Consequently, indicators and outcomes are promoted – as in the English CfC programme – as the main mechanism for bringing about transformations. How, they inquire, 'do we motivate performance toward better results? Improved performance seldom results, for example, from funding based on inputs, whereas funding based on outcomes typically leads to management being "obsessive" about performance. Such is the power of outcomes' (Hogan and Murphey 2002: 75; see also Parker et al. 1991; Ward 1995).

As mentioned earlier, notions associated with a 'common vision', 'common assessment' and 'common core' (of skills) are significant keywords located within the CfC agenda in England. For Hogan and Murphey this is identified as a key aspect of the approach promoted in Vermont. We are advised, for example, that the 'spirit of working together toward common ends is at the center of business success' and this 'spirit' should be emulated by public sector professionals (Hogan and Murphey 2002: 33). In this context, a common language fulfils an important function. When 'multiple agencies commit to . . . outcomes, each benefits from a common purpose' (Hogan and Murphey 2002: 27). Indeed, 'simple, declarative statements of outcomes and indicators project an image that is much more closely allied with business's own approach' (Hogan and Murphey 2002: 33). Again learning from business, the authors' suggest that 'market techniques' could play a useful role in seeking to reframe 'responsibility for well-being outcomes'. Thus, brand 'names and corporate logos, styled to create a certain image' are important and 'Government agencies need to develop more direct parallels to this kind of marketing' (Hogan and Murphey 2002: 34; see also Needham 2004). Thus, the 'the right language is important' and the outcomes which are strived for should be 'Clear, Declarative Statements of Well-Being' (Hogan and Murphey 2002: 13). Furthermore, consistent 'with the notion of common purpose, outcomes are best stated in positive terms with strong emotional content . . . An effective goal statement is stronger when it connects to our deepest feelings' (Hogan and Murphey 2002: 14). Thus, 'emotionally laden language' is preferable and this is best deployed in the context of a 'mission' statement (Hogan and Murphey 2002: 17, 14). Moreover, policy-makers 'might try discussing human service goals with business representatives in terms of a targeted demographic, such as pregnant teens' (Hogan and Murphey 2002: 34). This, in turn, can assist in cutting costs since, in Vermont, it was discovered that 'for every young teen pregnancy avoided, we could assign an annual cost-offset of $20,500' (Hogan and Murphey 2002: 98).

As with 'reforms' and 'transformations' in England, it is also stressed that technology can also help to facilitate these changes given that physical 'proximity makes less and less difference, now that we have the ability to access and transfer information anywhere' (Hogan, and Murphey 2002: 100). There is also a commitment to 'what works' and 'evidenced-based' approaches (Hogan and Murphey 2002: 31, 65): related to this, is a certain wariness of the 'academic world', encumbered by 'guild values' and an apparent preference for 'skilled generalists' (Hogan and Murphey 2002: 68). This approach, promoted by Hogan and Murphey (2002: 14), which is not, of course, restricted to Vermont, also 'builds in a preference for prevention and early intervention'. Indeed, this 'preference' is mirrored in the 'transformational reform agenda' and is rhetorically located at the core of a range of New Labour initiatives.

## Prevention and 'prevention science'

Clearly, English child welfare discourses have had an interest in preventative measures for many years (see, for example, Committee on Local Authority and Allied Personal Services 1968: ch. 14). In a more abstract sense, 'prevention operates at 'a deep level of cultural order or common sense' (Freeman 1999: 233). Perhaps more fundamentally, prevention can be perceived as a quintessentially 'modern project . . . Preventive interventions are essentially acts of social engineering, predicated on the capacity of states and the integrity of scientific and professional expertise' (Freeman 1999: 234; see also Howe 1994).

However, the CfC programme reflects a renewed emphasis on prevention within Children's Services (Pithouse 2007). With former Prime Minister Blair, this endeavour to embed 'prevention' as the foundational theoretical and practice orientation for child welfare professionals was, moreover, frequently conflated with a range of disparate discourses which referred – as we see in Chapters 7 and 8 – to the fear of crime, 'anti-social behaviour', 'neighbours from hell' and (even more ambiguously) 'security'. Blair also constantly hinted at how technology can be deployed to surveil and profile the *potentially* criminal, 'anti-social' or merely wayward.

> The 'hardest to reach' families are often the ones we need to reach most. People know what it's like to live on the same estate as the family from hell. Imagine what it's like to be brought up in one. We need far earlier intervention with some of these families, who are often socially excluded and socially dysfunctional. That may mean before they offend; and certainly before they want such intervention. But in truth, we can identify such families virtually as their children are born. The power to intervene is another very tricky area; but again, on the basis of my experience, the normal processes and the programmes of help we have rightly introduced, won't do it.
>
> (Blair, 2006a)

More broadly, in terms of the English approach to 'prevention' in child welfare, it is possible to identify at least five prevention discourses which have had an impact, often maybe only implicitly, on policy-making 'talk' and practices. These discourses, never tidily separable, include one associated with the largely benign modernism of Labourism, perhaps more specifically Fabianism, which was committed to 'efficiency', 'planning' and trying to deploy rational mechanisms to achieve human betterment. Second, is a prevention discourse primarily focused on the financial cost of welfare and prisons with the stress laid on the need to intervene *early* to prevent more substantial costs at a *later* stage.[5] The third of these discourses is one preoccupied with social order and committed to rooting out 'risk', the *potentially* criminal, the 'dangerous' and the 'anti-social'. The fourth discourse is especially alert to how scientific developments, for example in relation to DNA and computer technologies, can aid 'prevention' strategies. Finally, although mostly ignored in mainstream accounts of child welfare, is a prevention discourse associated with the British Empire, colonial policing and, in a more contemporary sense, 'counter-insurgency' interventions. This fifth discourse is intent on managing 'problem' and 'risky' populations, and the emphasis of this preventative strategy is placed on 'intelligence gathering', the collating of information, 'targeting', 'screening' and 'pre-emptive' activity (see also Graham 2006).[6]

What remains the focal interest here, however, is the fact that the expansion, development and growth of prevention services for children and families in England also appears, in recent years, to have been influenced by ideas and projects emanating from the USA. This has been apparent in terms of the setting up of Sure Start (Glass 1999; Tunstill et al. 2005), which was, in part, modelled on the US Head Start and High/Scope programmes.[7] Other New Labour initiatives, such as On Track (Precht, 2003; Hine, 2005) and the Children's Fund Prevention Fund (Mason et al. 2005), reflect the impact of prevention discourses from across the Atlantic. All of these initiatives were, advise France and Utting (2005: 83), 'introduced with specific reference to evidence of effectiveness and cost-effectiveness largely drawn from America'.

Furthermore, the US Communities that Care (CtC) programme, devised in the US by Hawkins and Catalano in 1992, was subsequently introduced to the UK, in 1998, and there are now approximately 30 programmes (www.channing-bete.com; see also France and Crow 2005). In the USA there are over 500 programmes, and central to the CtC approach is the technocratic aspiration to produce immensely detailed 'risk profiles' of communities.[8] In this context, the CtC has, it appears, 'been working in partnership with the Metropolitan Police and Government Office in London to profile risk and protection factors across a number of boroughs' (France and Utting 2005: 83). The CtC in England was not formally instigated by the government because it was funded by the Joseph Rowntree Foundation. However, even 'projects that are independent of government design . . . rely on political goodwill to succeed and are consequently influenced by political interests and positioning' (France and Utting 2005: 85).

Similarly, the emergence, again primarily in the USA, of a new 'prevention science' appears to be influencing the direction of the 'transformational reform agenda' within Children's Services in England (Hawkins et al. 2002). In the USA, a Society for the Prevention Research has been formed to 'create a scientific, multi-disciplinary forum for prevention science' (in France and Utting 2005: 79) and its views are promulgated in, for example, the *Prevention Science Journal* (www.preventionresearch.org). This 'science' is accompanied by seemingly ambitious claims concerning its capacity to address a range of social problems, including educational underachievement, poor mental health, criminality and drug misuse, and the focus of the approach has 'chiefly been on the scope for early intervention with children and young people "at risk" of later problems, and so reaching them; whether individually, through schools or through communities' (France and Utting 2005: 79).

## Conclusion

Many of the key coordinates of the English CfC 'reform' process seem, in part, derived from the USA and the 'transformation' of services for children and families appears to be increasingly being reformulated in line with the lexicon and practices of the new 'symbolic Mecca'. However, 'European countries with a strong state tradition, either Catholic or social-democratic, are not headed towards a slavish duplication' of US models (Wacquant 2001: 406). It also clear that a range of policy changes – and the thematic preoccupations underpinning these – are rooted in Europe: for example, the New Labour focus on combating 'social exclusion' owes as much to Brussels and the policy agenda of the European Union as it does to the ruminations of those in Washington or Wisconsin (see Daly 2008).

More fundamentally, charting the spread of ideas is, of course, always difficult and, in England, the focus on 'outcomes' and the renewed interest in 'prevention' also draws on indigenous discourses and practices. Nonetheless, there is perhaps a need to be wary of the apparent omnipresence and omnipotence of 'made in the USA' models for social welfare. Indeed, frequently the apparent 'success' of such models can mislead because promoters, writing in an American idiom, are apt (while often being literally intent on 'selling' their 'product' or particular 'expertise') to drift into mere marketing and hyperbole. More generally, refining the perspective of Bourdieu and Wacquant, the 'transformational reform agenda' which CfC seeks to promote needs to be viewed and interpreted as a complex range of programmes (DfES 2006a: 2): it is not simply *imported* wholesale from the USA because this is not how policy transfers operate (Dolowitz et al. 2000; Jones and Newburn 2004; Muncie 2004; Pinkerton 2006). As Newburn and Sparks (2004: 7) observe, among 'the salutary discoveries of recent comparative research is that the terms and institutions that at first blush look strikingly similar (indeed often consciously adopted or adapted from an imported model) turn out on closer examinations to be distinct in interesting and meaningful ways'.

Importantly, the New Labour 'reform' of Children's Services is constructed in a cultural context which is clearly unlike that in the USA. In England, for example, there is a tradition of labourism and public sector trade unions which are likely to resist those elements within CfC which are focused on 'workforce reform'. In a more abstract sense, the symbolic 'targets' of 'reform', such as 'problem families' might also be interpreted as specific to an

English cultural milieu (Respect Task Force 2006: 21–4). New Labour's plans are, perhaps, most accurately perceived as the *product of multiple determinations located with a narrow neoliberal sphere of constrained choices*. Furthermore, in England the death of a specific child – Victoria Climbié – was to have consequences in terms of the national evolution of policy for Children's Services. This dimension – with a specific focus on questions of 'race' and space within neoliberal modernity – is, therefore, be examined in the following chapter.

---

**Reflection and talk box 3**

How is the 'Lead Professional' role likely to impact on children and their families?

Read White et al. (2008) and examine and discuss the CAF/eCAF document/template.

In a speech to the Children's Workforce Development Council, in March 2007, Beverley Hughes (2007: 8) maintained that professionals should 'define themselves first and foremost as working for children and families rather than as a health visitor, teacher or social worker . . . This isn't just semantics. It's an essential part of breaking down the boundaries between different services so that the child's needs come before the job description'. What is your view of this statement?

Are there any connections between Hughes's comments and the discussion on neoliberalism featured earlier in the book?

If you are presently training to undertake a particular role, within Children's Services, how do you think your job is likely to change? What are the advantages and disadvantages?

Do job descriptions aid users of Children's Services to fully comprehend the role of practitioners?

In what ways is Children's Services work becoming more 'flexible'? What are some of the drawbacks? What might some of the advantages be?

What is your opinion of the notion that there should be a 'common vision' within Children's Services?

Why is policy-making in England so frequently influenced by policy emanating from the USA? What are the advantages and disadvantages of this process? Does Bourdieu and Wacquant's 'symbolic Mecca' notion assist our understanding?

Why is 'prevention' so central to the 'transformational reform agenda'?

# 4 Neoliberal globalism, 'race' and place: reviewing the Laming Report on the death of Victoria Climbié

Adjo Victoria Climbié, known to child welfare professionals throughout her time in England as Anna Kouao, died in London in February 2000 after suffering neglect and violence from her aunt, Marie Therese Kouao and the aunt's partner, Carl Manning. In January 2001 they were convicted of the murder of the 9-year-old child and are currently serving sentences of life imprisonment. The Laming Report provides a lengthy exploration of the circumstances surrounding Victoria's death and highlights the failure of social work, health and police services to safeguard her and to respond in a competent way to the glaring and multiple concerns about the child's welfare during the 11 months she spent in England (Secretary of State for Health and the Secretary of State for the Home Department 2003).[1]

In November 2008, during the controversy relating to the death of 'Baby P', Herbert Laming was asked to prepare an urgent report of the progress made across the country to implement effective arrangements for safeguarding children (Laming, 2009; see also UNISON, 2008a): Mor Dioum, director of the Victoria Climbié Foundation, was also to maintain, rather contentiously, that the 'case is worse than Climbié' ('50 injuries, 60 visits – failures that led to the death of Baby P', *Guardian*, 12 November 2008: 4). However, it is the Laming Report, which was published in 2003, which remains the most substantial contribution to the government's decision to entirely reshape services for children in England and Wales (Chief Secretary to the Treasury 2003). Nevertheless, it is, perhaps, a little surprising that issues relating to 'race' and 'place', alluded to in 'Laming', have not been investigated, in any detail, despite the gradual emergence of contributions which are less inclined to accept uncritically all aspects of the report (see, for example, Chand 2003; Rustin 2004; Cooper 2005; Rustin 2005). In what follows, therefore, the aim is not to provide a definitive account of the Laming Report: it is simply an attempt to provide an alternative reading of key muted aspects and to prise open complex and difficult dimensions for additional reflection and comment. In short, the aim is to try to *stretch out* the Laming approach to 'race' and 'place'. Indeed, this spatial metaphor seems entirely apt because factors connected to place and movement seem, albeit often implicitly, so central.[2] Related to this, it is maintained that politically pervasive and dominant ideas on issues connected to immigration, asylum seekers and refugees *may* have had an impact on how Victoria and her aunt were responded to during the period they were in England.

## 'Working with diversity': Laming, 'race' and racism

The first occasion when Laming directly addresses the issue of 'race' is in two brief paragraphs in the report's Introduction:

> Understandably, the agencies with whom Victoria came into contact have asked the question: 'If Victoria had been a white child, would she have been treated any differently?' Having listened to the evidence before me, it is, even at this stage, impossible to answer this question with any confidence. Much has been made outside this Inquiry of the fact that two black people murdered Victoria, and a high proportion of the staff who had contact with her were also black. But to dismiss the possibility of racism on the basis of this superficial analysis of the circumstances is to misunderstand the destructive effect that racism has on our society and its institutions.
>
> (para. 1.62)

> As Neil Garnham QC put it so perceptively in his opening statement: 'Assumption based on race can be just as corrosive in its effect as blatant racism . . . racism can affect the way people conduct themselves in other ways. Fear of being accused of racism can stop people acting when otherwise they would. Assumptions that people of the same colour, but from different backgrounds, behave in similar ways can distort judgements'. He urged the Inquiry to 'keep its antennae finely tuned' to the possible effects of racial assumptions. This I have sought to do . . .
>
> (para. 1.63)

However, it is only in Chapter 16, toward the end of the lengthy report, that the issue of 'race' and 'racism' is revisited. This commences with a statement from Ratna Dutt, the director of the Race Equality Unit.

> There is some evidence to suggest that one of the consequences of an exclusive focus on 'culture' in work with black children and families, is [that] it leaves black and ethnic minority children in potentially dangerous situations, because the assessment has failed to address a child's fundamental care and protection needs.

In the rest of chapter 16 it is possible to identify three main points which Laming is intent on making. First, the idea that the views of practitioners, based on 'racial assumptions', may have had an impact on how Victoria was treated. Second, is the assertion that child welfare practitioners may have acted, or not acted, in a particular way because of fear of being accused of racism. Third, Laming is keen to promote the idea of 'safety first' in work with children and families. Below, therefore, each of these three areas are looked at in greater detail.

Laming confides that he found himself 'wondering whether a failure by a particular professional to take action to protect Victoria, may have been partly due to that professional losing sight of the fact that her needs were the same as those of any other seven-year-old girl, from whatever cultural background' (para. 16.2). This 'losing sight' of Victoria could, he speculates, have been connected to the 'effect of assumptions'. He continues:

> I do not for one moment suggest that the ill treatment of Victoria by Kouao and Manning was either condoned or deliberately ignored by those responsible for Victoria's case. However, it may be that assumptions made about Victoria and her situation diverted caring people from noting and acting upon signs of neglect or ill-treatment.
>
> (para 16.3)

In order to substantiate this speculative claim, Laming furnishes a trio of examples from the main body of his report (see para. 16.4). The first of these relates to the remarks of the Haringey social worker, Lisa Arthurworrey, who had commented that when she had heard of Victoria 'standing to attention' before Marie Therese Kouao and Carl Manning she 'concluded that this type of relationship was one that can be seen in many Afro-Caribbean families because respect and obedience are very important features of the Afro-Caribbean family script'. Victoria's parents had, however, made it clear that their daughter was not required to stand in this formal way when she was at home with them. The second instance concerned Pastor Pascal Orome who had told the Inquiry that he attributed, what her aunt perceived as, Victoria's troublesome behaviour to the fact that she had come 'freshly' from Africa. This of course was not the case – Victoria had been in Europe for almost a year by the time she came to his attention. Finally, on 'more than one occasion', medical practitioners who 'noticed marks on Victoria's body considered the possibility that children who have grown up in Africa may be expected to have more marks on their bodies than those who have been raised in Europe'. As a result, this assumption, 'regardless of whether it is valid or not, may prevent a full assessment of those marks being made'.

Laming's conclusion is that:

> The danger of making assumptions of this kind is clear. Cultural norms and models of behaviour can vary considerably between communities and even families. The concept of Afro-Caribbean behaviour referred to in Victoria's case illustrates the problem. The range of cultures and behavioural patterns it includes is so wide that it would be meaningless to make generalisations, and potentially damaging to an effective assessment of the needs of the child. The wisest course is to be humble when considering the extent of one's own knowledge about different 'cultures' and to take advice whenever it is available.
>
> (para 16.5)

Nonetheless, it is

> impossible to assess after the event the likelihood of a particular step being taken in Victoria's case if she had been a white child. There were so many instances of bad practice in this case that one simply cannot begin

to determine which of them may have been influenced by some form of prejudice, and which were due to incompetence or a lack of attention. However, it may well be that, at some point, the focus may have shifted from Victoria's fundamental needs because of misplaced assumptions about her cultural circumstances.

(para. 16.6)

Laming then moves on to address the notion that some of the professionals who came into contact with Victoria may have been hampered because they were concerned that an accusation of racism could have resulted if they had followed a particular course of action. Again, like with the 'assumptions' point, this returns to an idea first raised by Neil Garnham QC in one of the opening statements. Here, however, Laming is only able to furnish one instance where, he felt, this was a relevant factor. Thus, he refers to a remark made by Dr Mary Rossiter, a consultant at North Middlesex Hospital, who had informed the Inquiry: 'I was aware that as a white person I had to be sensitive to the feelings of people of all races and backgrounds, both clinically and with professionals. Maybe some social workers felt they knew more about black children than I did' (para. 16.8).

Finally, the Laming Report suggests that the Inquiry highlighted the fact that 'child safety comes first'. This is articulated in greater detail:

> The basic requirement that children are kept safe is universal and cuts across cultural boundaries. Every child living in this country is entitled to be given the protection of the law, regardless of his or her background. Cultural heritage is important to many people, but it cannot take precedence over standards of childcare embodied in law. Every organisation concerned with the welfare and protection of children should have mechanisms in place to ensure equal access to services of the same quality, and that each child, irrespective of colour or background, should be treated as an individual requiring appropriate care.
>
> (para. 16.10)

For Laming, there 'can be no excuse or justification for failing to take adequate steps to protect a vulnerable child, simply because that child's cultural background would make the necessary action somehow inappropriate' (para. 16.11). He seeks to underscore this point by referring to the comments of Dr Nnenna Cookey, a consultant paediatrician and participant in the seminars that comprised Phrase Two of the Inquiry. According to Laming, she 'put the matter very eloquently' (para. 16.11) and he 'entirely' agreed with her (para. 16.12) when she asserted:

> I do take huge issue with the emphasis that black families should be assessed by or given the opportunity to have a black social worker. For me that detracts from the whole process. A child is a child regardless of colour. I think the social and cultural differences or backgrounds . . . of these families is crucial and should be taken into account as part of a general assessment. But I think if we are not careful we'll lose the whole emphasis on the child's welfare. I think if we are not very careful we will send out the very wrong message that non-black social workers do not

have the capabilities, the standards and everything that goes with it to assess black families. That would be a mistake, that will be wrong, and I think it does fly in the face of lots of social workers who are *Caucasian*, or whatever . . . who are doing a very good job. I say that not because I want to be anti-establishment. *I do not do political correctness when it comes to children.* I really do think that these children may be further disadvantaged if we go down that track. I also feel that it means in some ways non-black social workers do not feel able to access the information they need regarding a child's cultural background.

(para. 16.11, emphases added)

Laming concludes that his was not an 'Inquiry into racism'. However, what 'cannot be ignored is that we live in a culturally diverse society and that *safeguards must be in place to ensure that skin colour does not influence either the assessment of need or the quality of services delivered. That is the challenge to us all*' (para. 16.13, emphasis added).

## 'I do not do political correctness': Laming on 'race'

How, therefore, should the Laming Inquiry be regarded in respect of its influential interventions on 'race', child welfare and, more specifically, safeguarding and protecting children? What is initially striking is the fact that, after such an exhaustive and detailed report, this section is a rather slender section: only two and half pages in a report of over 400 pages. This exploration of the area of 'race' and racism might also seem cursory given that the deaths of black female children and the failure of child welfare services has been a recurrent event in the history of 'child protection' in England over the past 20 years. Furthermore, the deaths of, for example, Jasmine Beckford, Kimberley Carlile and Tyra Henry all resulted in high-profile inquiries (London Borough of Brent 1985; London Borough of Greenwich 1987; London Borough of Lambeth 1987). However, no attempt is made to locate Victoria's death in the context of the deaths of these other black girls, nor is there any interest in trying to ascertain if there were any similarities in terms of how agencies or individual practitioners failed in their duty to protect these children. Furthermore, Laming's three key interventions (those on 'racial assumptions', 'white practitioners' 'fear of being accused of racism' and the idea of 'safety first') need to be interrogated.

The comments on 'racial assumptions' are sensible and reflect the best of theorization in this area (see, for example, Channer and Parton 1990). However, the idea that some of the (white) child welfare professionals who had contact with Victoria could have been influenced by a fear of being accused of racism is less sustainable in that, Rossiter aside, the evidence does not seem to unequivocally support the contention. However, it is Laming's idea of 'safety first' that is the most problematic and it is this which needs to be critically examined. Here, the recourse to the notion of 'political correctness' (his endorsement of Cookey's 'I do not do political correctness when it comes to children') can, perhaps, be interpreted as seeking to caricature and disparage the attempts of social workers, and associated professionals, to respond to complex issues relating to 'race', ethnicity, migration and cultural dislocation. Moreover, Cookey's slogan 'a child is a child regardless of colour' and use of odd, anachronistic language ('social workers who are Caucasian or whatever') hints at a nostalgic desire to return to times which were less *complicated*; times, indeed, when the so-called 'colour-blind' approach was the dominant (and damaging) approach to child welfare practice. This 'liberal, assimilationist' approach proceeds on the basis of 'treating everyone the same' and fails to recognize 'race' as a significant dimension requiring attention. Within this paradigm, it 'is assumed that all children and families are the same and hence should receive the same *professional* response and be subject to the same *objective* criteria for the purposes of assessment and intervention' (Channer and Parton 1990: 109, original emphases).

Furthermore, Laming appears to be arguing, in his assertion that 'safeguards must be put in place to ensure that skin colour does not influence the assessment of need' that a child's 'race' can be *partitioned off* from the core business of assessment. Whereas, a child's 'race', ethnicity and sense of communal belonging (and the perceived threats to it) is integral to their sense of self (and that of their caregivers) and, thus, is a key assessment issue. That is, it is not feasible or possible, to *do* the 'safety first' and then to mechanistically *add on* matters relating to 'race' and culture at some later stage.

More broadly, this attempt to partition off and, perhaps, to downgrade the significance of 'race' and ethnicity for children in contact with Children's Services was subsequently reflected in ECM, the government's plan for the reorganization of services for children which later became the Children Act 2004 (Chief Secretary to the Treasury 2003; see also Cunningham and Tomlinson 2005). This is not, of course, to argue that the Laming Report prompted this development, but it is to suggest that Laming's treatment of 'race' can be interpreted as mirroring a more encompassing and pervasive tendency, on the part of the neoliberal state, to shift the attention of professionals away from this area. This issue is, therefore, returned to later in the chapter. First, however, it is suggested that 'place' was a much more substantial element relating to Victoria's death than the Laming Report acknowledges and that this still, perhaps, needs to be more fully appreciated.

## A world shook up: neoliberal globalism and the Victoria Climbié tragedy

In England, social work, housing and related forms of social intervention provided by local authorities have been intent, since before the introduction of a 'reformed' poor law in 1834, on ensuring that those seeking aid are only dispensed help and assistance within particular spatial enclaves (see also Fekete 2001: 32). That is, there was and is a constant requirement, on the part of the capitalist state, to ensure that help (in cash or kind) should only be given if the provider is financially 'responsible' and this is partly determined by the applicant's geographical location or point of origin. This accounts, for example, for the perennial questions which the poor face about their 'place of residence' and 'local connection'. Should, moreover, the request for assistance be directed to another authority located elsewhere? Indeed, such questions have formed a focal part of the process of adjudicating on who is the truly 'deserving' and who is not. Furthermore, the 'policing of "desert" has increasingly become entwined with managing the boundaries of the nation as "scrounging" becomes configured around refugees, migrants and aliens' (Clarke 2004: 130).

Perhaps, in the past these issues related to the deserving/undeserving dichotomy were apt to focus on the location of the applicant *within* the national territory (see also Garrett 2000). However, as John Clarke's remarks imply, in a globalized world, one in which capital has become more mobile, this is rendered more complex. More specifically, given neoliberal imperatives, movement of labour – on an international scale – needs to be scrutinized much more intently. In European terms, for example, the introduction of a single market in the early 1990s, resulted in more 'open' and 'free' economic borders which promoted the fluidity of capital and trade. However, in this context 'the control of population movement (particularly for those individuals with a perceived low-economic or production value) was a central concern' (Malloch and Stanley 2005: 58). As a result, the 'liberal, free-flowing market was juxtaposed with an authoritarian . . . controlled approach to population movement' (Malloch and Stanley 2005: 58). The assessment of a migrants 'value' or potential 'value' within this frame of reference is, of course, central. In this context, it is, perhaps, hardly surprising that case notes completed on Marie Therese Kouao by a social worker in Ealing noted that she had 'no skills'. Moreover, whatever was done 'with this case, there will inevitably be a long-term financial implication for this department if she remains' (para. 4.86).

This approach illuminates the neoliberal sensibility which appears to have underpinned social work activity. However, on another level, the Climbié tragedy shows how many working within Children's Services in England are increasing likely to be involved, sometimes albeit briefly, with users of services who are uprooted and dislocated from their place of birth or 'normal' cultural milieu – migrants who are, either by will or compulsion, beyond their national borders. Reflecting these and related demographic shifts, it was revealed that, in 2001, 8.3 per cent (4.9 million) of the total population of the UK was born overseas. This is almost double the proportion in 1951 (4.2 per cent) (National Statistics 2004). Moreover, contemporary forms of migration are also apt to 'stretch' the family across space, creating 'global chains of care' (Hochschild, in Clarke 2004: 79). Indeed, Laming observes:

> Many social services departments around the country have to deal on a regular basis with children who have arrived in this country from abroad. Even in those cases in which the country of origin of the child concerned is without a developed welfare system, the child may well have passed through such a country on his or her way to the UK. The social services departments of those countries are a potentially valuable source of information. Social workers should be provided with clear guidance and procedures explaining how best to access such information.
>
> (para. 6.619)

One of the recommendation of his report was, therefore, that 'Directors of social services must ensure that social work staff are made aware of how to access effectively information concerning vulnerable children which may be held in other countries' (para. 6.619). However, it could be argued that the Inquiry failed, perhaps reasonably given the limitations of its brief, to interrogate this spatial and economic dimension. Nonetheless, it is apparent, even in the early stages of social work involvement with Victoria and her aunt in Ealing, that the pair were seen to be 'out of place', with intervention entirely focused on trying to get them restored to what was perceived as their rightful place, France.

Victoria travelled, of course, across a number of local authority boundaries within London, but the focus, in what follows, is on the transnational movements.

## Responding to the 'out of place'

Victoria was born, on 2 November 1991 in the Republic of Côte d'Ivoire (or Ivory Coast), which from the 1840s until 1960 was a colony of France. The country is the world's leading cocoa-growing nation and since the late 1990s it has been periodically wracked by civil war and related strife. However, such turbulence can also be rooted in the 'artificial depression engineered by the International Monetary Fund (IMF) and the White House' throughout many parts of urban Africa during the previous decade (Davis 2006: 155). Abidjan, the country's sprawling capital was formerly one of the few tropical African cities with a significant manufacturing sector and modern urban services. However, an IMF 'structural adjustment programme' led to 'deindustrialization, the collapse of construction, and a rapid deterioration in public transit and sanitation'; as a consequence of such neoliberal inspired 'adjustments', urban poverty in the Ivory Coast – the 'tiger economy' of West Africa – doubled in the late 1980s (Davis 2006: 156; see also Klein 2007).

Victoria's parents, Berthe and Francis lived in Abidjan and chose to send their daughter to Europe with Marie Therese for a 'better life' (Israel and McVeigh 2001).[3] In acting in this way they were following a tradition whereby extended families help poorer relatives by taking responsibility for a child. Indeed, many West African children enter England each year under similar arrangements. Perhaps also relevant here, is the ancient custom, practised throughout West Africa of nieces being sent to work, as *petite bonnes* (or 'little maids'), in the home of family members. Often these 'little maids' are perceived within the Ivorian family as a category of foster child (see Jacquemin 2004 and 2006 for a fuller discussions of some of the complexities and, indeed, exploitative elements often integral to such arrangements).

Victoria spent approximately five months in France and it is possible that she lived in Rue George Meliés, Villepinte, which was the address given by her aunt to Ealing Social Services shortly after they arrived in the UK. Alternatively, it could have been at a different address, in Tremblay-en-France (para. 3.7). Initially, Marie Therese seemed willing to honour her promise to make sure Victoria received a proper education and the child was enrolled at the Jean Moulin primary school in Villepinte. However, by December 1998, Marie Therese began to receive formal warnings from the school about Victoria's absenteeism. The situation became serious enough by February 1999 for the school to issue a Child at Risk Emergency Notification (para. 3.8). A French social worker had also become involved and noted a 'difficult mother daughter relationship' between Victoria and her aunt (para. 6.618).

Some time in the spring of 1999, Marie Therese gave the school notice that she was removing Victoria so she could receive 'treatment' in London. The address of a distant relative was given as a forwarding address (para. 3.10). The Laming Report observes, 'why Kouao decided to leave France for the UK is unclear. For a long while before leaving, she had been claiming benefits that she was not entitled to. The French benefits agency was trying to recover money for these benefits, and this could have influenced her decision' (para. 3.11). Marie Therese did, however, provide Ealing social services with her French social security number which erodes the idea that she was fleeing from the French benefits agency and was keen to 'cover her tracks' (see para. 4.185). It is also clear that, Marie Therese, together with Victoria, made three trips back to France in late 1999 (para. 6.498).

As observed earlier, a key feature of social work intervention with Victoria and her aunt was the aim to get them *put back in place* and that place was France. Laming observes that one of the Ealing social workers concluded after interviewing Marie Therese, that she was not

> habitually resident in the UK. Her ties at that stage were with France . . . Kouao had provided documentation to confirm her identification and proof of the date of her arrival into the UK. Although [a social worker] was shown both Kouao's travel documents and her passport, which included Victoria's 'details' and her 'photograph', she paid no further attention to them, believing Kouao's application to be ineligible on the grounds of habitual residence.[4]
>
> (para. 4.55)

The Ealing file on Marie Therese and Victoria noted that social services should consider paying for their return fare to France (para. 4.151). Indeed, one of the social workers involved confirmed to the Laming Inquiry that 'from quite early on that Mrs Kouao should go back to France or the child should be accommodated' (para. 4.156). The case plan to restore Victoria and her aunt to their *proper* place was made on the basis that:

1. Client has no connection with this country, has no significant family/friends
2. There has been no appropriate/adequate planning prior to coming to this country
3. Reasons for coming are weak – to learn English
4. She has family/friends in France, has access to housing and state benefits in France
5. She has children who she left back in France whom she intends to return to France to collect and bring back to this country, who will subsequently become dependent on social services funding
6. Based on the above the department has decided that we can no longer fund Ms Kouao as it is apparent that she will need intermittent funding for a long period of time. Ms Kouao has left a stable

lifestyle to come to this country where she has no recourse to public funds or accommodation and has therefore placed herself in a
vulnerable situation. We are in a position to provide Ms. Kouao
with return tickets for herself and child to France.

(para. 4.157)

Perhaps not surprisingly, this response from Ealing Social Services pivoting on
a plan to 'repatriate' Marie Therese and her 'daughter' prompted the former's
solicitor to ask for a review of the 'case plan'; if this was not done it was
suggested that judicial review proceedings would be sought (para. 4.167).
However, it appears that the only response from social services was the suggestion that 'as an alternative to the family returning to France . . . social services
could offer to accommodate Victoria in their care until Kouao had found full-
time work' (para. 4.167).

Sensibly, but possessing the wisdom of hindsight, the Laming Inquiry
concludes, therefore, that all

the emphasis was on Kouao's lack of significant ties in this country,
the fact that she had left family and friends in France and that her stay
in the country was intended to be short term. There is not a single mention of Victoria. Indeed, there can be no doubt that the 'client' referred
to was Kouao. Nothing more had been learnt about Kouao, let alone
Victoria, in the two months since the case had been referred to Ealing
Social Services.

(para. 4.158)

The crucial, early social work intervention with Victoria, founded upon an
operational desire to prevent potentially long-term expenditure on the family,
was, therefore, fixated with 'place' and the fact that she and her aunt needed to
be returned 'home' to France.

## Suspicion and deterrence: the 'absent presence' in Laming's Report

Within political, economic and sociological debates, 'globalization' is frequently the contentious framing narrative for analysing social and economic
change (for a critique, see Bourdieu and Wacquant 2001). In very broad terms,
debates on globalization can be broken down into 'two camps', with one camp
maintaining that we are 'witnessing a qualitative shift in the structures of
international capital', and the other countering that this new era of so-called
'globalization' is 'nothing new at all, that it is the same old story of capitalist
exploitation, intensified and extended, but in essence the same' (Bhattacharya
et al. 2001: 28). Indeed, Marx's comments on the increasing 'entanglement of
all peoples in the net of the world market, and, with this, the growth of the
international character of the capitalist regime' perhaps, bolster the latter perspective and have fresh resonance in the early twenty-first century (Marx
1990: 929; see also Renton 2001). In terms of some of the social consequences
of contemporary turbulence and destabilization, it has been claimed that
globalization should not be interpreted as the dissolution of the nation-state,
but the 'unsettling presence of the "world" within the nation state' (Clarke

2004: 82). Certainly, the latter half of the twentieth century saw a 'rapid increase in the volume of people moving across internationally recognized borders. For example, in 1965 the number of international migrants was put at 75 million, by 1990 this had increased to 120 million while in 2000 168 million people were living outside the country of their birth' (Home Office, in Lewis and Neal 2005: 425).

Importantly, for the reading to be developed in this chapter, it is clear that the movement of people across national borders may have had an impact on how Victoria was responded to during her time in England. That is, people from outside the national territory, more specifically asylum seekers, were increasingly forming a part of social workers 'caseloads' (see also Humphries 2004). Related to this, there were no protocols, Laming was told, laying down how these 'referrals' were to be dealt with. All of this was placing immense pressure on services in the capital and undermining social workers' ability to provide a decent service. In Ealing, for example, the social worker eventually allocated to Victoria thought that perhaps 60 to 70 per cent of referrals came from abroad. According to a senior practitioner, within the same authority, 'there were not very clear protocols and guidance for dealing with people that were presenting from abroad and presenting as homeless, and quite often I felt that people were left to rely on . . . professional judgement' (para. 4.21). Similarly, in Brent, an increase in the number of asylum seekers appeared to have had an impact on the social work services available during the period when Victoria and her aunt were in contact with this authority. More speculatively, a political and generalized antipathy towards refugees and asylum seekers *could* have had an impact on how the pair was responded to by social services (see also Fekete 2001; Bauman 2004; Schuster and Solomos 2004; Goodman and Speer 2007). In this context, therefore, although it cannot convey important aspects of the orchestrated public mood, particularly the tenor of the press coverage of the asylum question, Table 4.1 provides a brief overview of the evolving New Labour policy making agenda during the period.

Perhaps a little more emphatically, issues related to immigration and asylum can be interpreted as the *absent presence* within the pages of the report which Lord Laming and his team produced. From the period stretching immediately prior to Victoria's arrival in March 1999, until her death in February the following year and continuing after the publication of the Laming Report in 2003, the agenda of the New Labour administrations was dominated by the meshed issues of 'race', asylum and immigration. Indeed, McGhee (2005: 67–71) has maintained that the White Paper *Fairer, Faster, Firmer* (Home Office 1998) and the eventual Immigration and Asylum Act 1999 indicated that 'suspicion' and deterrence were the 'organizing principles' of New Labour's immigration and asylum policy.[5]

Moreover, Michael Rustin (2004: 11) has referred to the 'evident ambivalence', of some of the services concerned, to migrants (even legal migrants such as Marie Therese and Victoria who came to England from another member state of the European Union). He suggests, that some of the 'stigma and hostility congealing around asylum seekers and refugees at this time was a factor contributing to the misrecognition of, and official indifference' to,

**Table 4.1**  Victoria in England: the immigration policy context

| Victoria in England and evolving policy on social work with children and families | Evolving policy on 'race', immigration and asylum |
|---|---|
|  | October 1998 – Publication of *Fairer, Faster, Firmer* White Paper. |
| March 1999 – Victoria arrives in Britain. Until her death, she remains for 308 days. | November 1999 – Immigration and Asylum Act: introduces vouchers, no choice 'dispersal system'. |
| February 2000 – Victoria dies | April 2000 – Race Relations Amendment Act |
| January 2001 – Inquiry into Victoria's death announced | December 2001 – Anti-Terrorism, Crime and Security Act 2001. Also in 2001, publication of the Cantle Report, *Community Cohesion* |
|  | February 2002 – Publication of *Secure Borders, Safe Havens* consultation paper |
|  | November 2002 – Nationality, Immigration and Asylum Act 2002 |
| January 2003 – Publication of the Laming Report |  |
| September 2003 – Publication of *Every Child Matters* White Paper |  |
| November 2004 – Children Act 2004 | July 2004 – Asylum and Immigration (Treatment of Claimants, etc.) Act 2004 |

Victoria and her aunt (see also Runnymede Trust 2000: 212–17). Rustin (2004: 11) concludes that the Laming Report simply does not explore the possibility that 'animosity towards refugees in this period may have been a contributory factor to the neglect of Victoria's needs, or indeed that other children who are in this situation might now for the same reasons be at risk'. More fundamentally, the fixation with getting Victoria and her aunt back to *where they belonged* can be interpreted as reflecting not simply isolated administrative and bureaucratic decision-making, but more embedded and political and cultural currents derived from neoliberalism.

### 'Flexibility' in action: the temporary, transient, transnational workforce

Migrants also featured in another significant way in the Victoria's life in that a number of the social work staff who had contact with her were from places other than England. The Inquiry was informed by a former Director of Ealing Social Services that many 'of the staff coming into post were relatively inexperienced in that they had not many years post qualification experience and/or were from [overseas]' (para. 4.20). In the referral and assessment teams, 'managers knew that "a lot of work had to be done with individual members of staff around core basic skills" ' (para. 4.20). Similarly, at the time Victoria's case was handled by Brent, 'all the duty social workers had received their training abroad and were on temporary contracts' (para. 5.14). The Inquiry was informed that when two referrals relating to Victoria passed through the Duty Team it was staffed entirely by agency workers who had not qualified in England. There 'were occasions where a person will get off a plane in the morning, arrive in the office just after lunch, be interviewed and start work in the duty team or the child protection team. It was happening very, very often' (para. 5.60). Furthermore, at no point in the Inquiry was this extraordinary account challenged.

In 2000 a number of social services departments began to recruit staff from Australia, Canada and South Africa. This resulted in, largely ignored, protests from the South African government.[6] Indeed, this 'drive to import child protection workers (along with teachers and nurses)' could result in 'ideal recruits for New Labour's public service regime' because they are 'mostly young, single and willing to tolerate Spartan accommodation' (Jordan 2001: 529). Clearly, there should be concerns about the impact on countries such as South Africa of social work staff being enticed to England, no longer available as a national resource to the aid in the process of post-apartheid reconstruction (see also Mackintosh et al. 2006; Yuval-Davis et al. 2005). Jordan's point is also correct in that it is easy to see how recruiting overseas fits in with the government's 'flexible', neoliberal approach to public welfare provision which is a recurring theme in this book. Moreover, 'the mobility of staff and numerous locum arrangements in frontline services render staff much less likely to be able to cope with the troubles of families who are themselves dislocated' (Rustin 2005: 18).

This is not, of course, to suggest that health and social care services should be entirely staffed by 'home grown' workers. Indeed, in 2001–02 over 40 per cent of new entrants to the UK's nursing profession came from outside the UK, compared with 15 per cent in 1989–90 (Clarke 2004: 79): in March 2008, the *Guardian* reported that the UK now has 22,000 social workers from other countries (19 per cent of social workers) (Rawles 2008). This does not mean that the calibre of service available is undermined for the key issue is clearly the degree of professional experience of the individual staff member and their level of knowledge of relevant local factors, as opposed to their geographic point of origin. Indeed, in some respects, an international and culturally diverse social work and social care workforce is, perhaps *better* equipped to provide understanding and expertise which is relevant to populations of service users which are themselves diasporic and diverse (Braziel and Mannur 2003).

The importance of specific professional *and* 'local' knowledge, deployed 'out of place', is also apparent in the Climbié case. This is reflected in the pivotal – but devalued – assessment of Victoria undertaken by Ekundayo Ajayi-Obe, the on-call paediatric registrar at the Central Middlesex Hospital (CMH), on 14 July 1999 (see paras 9.18–9.28). The Laming Inquiry observed that her examination had been 'a thorough one' and in 'marked contrast to any of the other doctors who saw Victoria' her 'notes were detailed and comprehensive'. She obtained a great deal of information about Victoria's social situation which, together with her examination findings occupied some 'seven pages of hospital notes' (para. 9.18, 9.24). What was particularly important about Dr Ajayi-Obe's intervention was her professional opinion on some of the marks on Victoria's body. Significantly, she was able to make use of professional knowledge, but also her 'local' knowledge derived from her work in West Africa: 'As to the question of whether Victoria's injuries might have been attributable to scabies, Dr Ajayi-Obe said such a diagnosis did not cross her mind. This was despite the fact that she had seen a number of scabies cases while practising in Lagos' (para. 9.23).

Indeed, one of the tragedies of the Victoria Climbié case was that the Ajayi-Obe assessment and her reluctance to accept that the 'scabies explanation' for some of the marks on the child was, in effect, disregarded by the 'highly respected' consultant paediatrician, who subsequently examined her (para. 5.137). A diagnosis by the more senior medical officer was, in part, grounded in misconceptions about life in West Africa (paras 9.54–5).[7]

## Conclusion

Part of the argument developed in this chapter, therefore, is that the Laming approach to Children's Services, 'race' and ethnicity was undermined because it was far too brief and interwoven with a sterile and misplaced attack on so-called 'political correctness'. What is more, it has been suggested that the concept of 'safety first' is unconvincing and hints at a wish to return to the days when a 'colour blind' approach was dominant and damaging in theory and practice. Indeed, it could also be suggested that ECM failed to emphasize adequately how issues related to 'race' and ethnicity influence 'outcomes' for children (Chand 2008). More fundamentally, both ECM and the Laming perspective can now be situated alongside the 'partial shift away from affirmations of British multiculture towards a (re)embracing of older notions of assimilationism with a newer de-racialized, language of social cohesion' (Lewis and Neal 2005: 437; see also Back et al. 2002; Sivanandan 2006). Indeed, following initial concerns about 'institutional racism' after the publication of the Macpherson Report (1999) into the death of Stephen Lawrence, a revised approach is now detectable across a range of government interventions. This altered policy perspective is reflected in, for example, the idea that 'new arrivals' in Britain need to become fluent in English and the abolition of the Commission for Racial Equality (see also Lewis and Neal 2005; see also Home Office Border and Immigration Agency 2008). Furthermore, the New Labour government's Asylum and Immigration (Treatment of Claimants, etc.) Act 2004, particularly section 9 of this Act which gave the Home Office powers to terminate all welfare support to 'failed' asylum-seeking families, runs entirely counter to the idea that 'every child matters' (Cunningham and Tomlinson 2005). This led to the BASW, along with other organizations, condemning the fact that this legislation may lead to demands on social workers to take children into public care simply because their parents have no recourse to financial assistance (BASW, 2003; 2004).

More generally, there has been a sustained attempt – rhetorically related to a number of factors including concerns about separatism, Islamism and terrorism – to bind people to a renewed sense of 'Britishness' (see also Gilroy 2005). This hegemonic project has, of course, been reflected in the speeches of Gordon Brown, whose first prime ministerial speech to the Labour Party conference startled many because of its heavily nationalistic emphasis. Wedded to 'our closest ally America', Brown asserted that he aspired to forge a 'patriotic Britain' with 'British jobs in British businesses' (Brown 2007). The 'vision' was, moreover, of Britain, 'up against the talent of two billion people in China and India . . . leading the global economy' (Brown 2007). Indeed, this nationalistic tone was, possibly, the key ingredient in the speech which provided some evidence of a shift, a recalibration, within the New Labour project in a post-Blair period. The rest of the Bournemouth speech was, however, mostly in keeping with the former Prime Minister's political vision. Subsequently, a discourse pivoting on 'the common bond of citizenship', ideas such as developing a new 'national day' and enhancing people's 'sense of shared belonging along all stages of a citizen's journey through life', have also entered into mainstream political debate (Ministry for Justice 2008).

The Conservative Party has also called for a reinvigorated 'narrative of Britishness – a confidence in the history and the institutions of our country, a basic belief that we're lucky to live here' (Cameron 2008). This has been coupled to attacks on what has been dubbed 'state multiculturalism' which according to its leader was one of the factors which contributed to the failure to respond adequately to Victoria (see also Gilroy 2005; Modood 2005). Indeed, this has been attached to the erroneous idea, partly encouraged by the Laming Report's treatment of the issue, that the 'cloak of cultural sensitivity is also one of the reasons why no one intervened in the case of eight year old Victoria Climbié' (Cameron 2008).

Laming's influence has also been detectable in the controversy surrounding the plan to set up the national database on children, the CPd. Indeed, during the House of Lords' Committee Stage debate of the Children Bill, in May 2004, Baroness Ashton was to maintain, on behalf of the government that the 'reason' the databases plan 'came up was that it was very much part of the recommendations that emerged from the Climbié inquiry'. Certainly Laming called for improvements in the exchange of information; he asserted that information systems that 'depend on the random passing of slips of paper have no place in modern social services' (para. 1.43). A close reading of his report suggests, though, that most of the problems relating to the exchange of relevant documentation was a reflection of defective intra-agency processes (within, for example, social services), not inter-agency ones. However, Laming did go on to argue that a 'national children's database', for all those under 16, would aid information exchange processes. He was, though, alert to some of the potential problems with a 'national children's database' notion and, interestingly related his idea to plans for national identity cards; something that the government has worked hard to avoid because of its political implications. Moreover, he noted that the 'indiscriminate sharing of unchecked information can have the counterproductive effect of presenting a misleading picture to the receiving agency, as well as swamping it with more information than it can process effectively' (para. 17.45).

The government has, of course, argued that the databases are 'not primarily a child protection measure. They aim to enable information sharing so that a preventive approach can be taken, through early identification of the needs of children, in order to promote their wellbeing' (Baroness Ashton, House of Lords' Hansard, col. 1094). Nonetheless, it is still the death of Victoria Climbié which has been pivotal, for Children's Services in terms of how New Labour has promoted the case for having done with data-protection related obstacles, to greater sharing of electronic data. More emphatically, the government has subsequently used the Climbié case to argue that the need for the envisaged electronic databases is simply beyond contestation. This aspect of the 'transformation' of Children's Services, therefore, forms part of the focus for the next chapter.

**Reflection and talk box 4**

Is the notion of 'safety first' promoted in the Laming Report a helpful maxim for child protection work or does it fail to address complex intertwined issues associated with 'race', ethnicity and culture?

Why have questions of 'race' and ethnicity frequently been controversial in social work with children and their families?

How did tensions between (and within) the various professions engaging with Victoria and her aunt, impact on the service provided?

Heron (2004) has commented on how 'race' (and anti-racism) appears, certainly in 'official' publications and protocols for social work and social work education in England, to be at risk of fading from view. Moreover, this is significant because rendering such issues 'invisible', marginal (or the fixation of the 'politically correct') will undermine Children's Services available to minority ethnic families. What is your view?

Heron (2004: 292) also maintains that the 'demise' of 'race' and anti-racism, as an subjects for professional inquiry and action may 'signal' that there is also to be an attempt to eliminate other forms of progressive practice because the ideas that 'undermine the anti-racist agenda may be the same ones that attack egalitarianism in all forms'. Is this credible?

Identify some of the tensions, even contradictions, which may exist in promoting the notion that 'every child matters' alongside current policies seeking to enforce tighter immigration controls.

Does the 'transformational reform agenda', promoted by the government adequately address the fact that many children are part of families that stretch *beyond* the borders of nation states?

Is the 'social cohesion' concept likely to provide an adequate conceptual framework for responding to cultural differences?

How might a multinational and multicultural workforce impact on the evolution of Children's Services?

Does the Laming Inquiry furnish the case for the establishment of ContactPoint?

# 5 'Transformation', technology and surveillance

In spring 2004, a council in the English East Midlands advertised for social workers in the *Guardian*. The advert (featured in Appendix A of this book) was headed 'Investing in You' and potential new recruits were advised that the council's Children's Services had 'achieved excellent standards of performance against national indicators'. Somewhat predictably given the hegemony of the (not so) new managerialism, the staff group were, moreover, reported to be 'vibrant and motivated'. However, what is of interest for this chapter is the pictorial imagery featured in the advert. The largest image was of a computer positioned on a desk. Three smaller, accompanying images, included: a female worker, smiling to the camera while nibbling her laptop's keyboard; another female worker using a telephone; and an office complex. Elsewhere, a magazine reported that this particular office complex was highly innovative in that it 'accommodates 114 employees where a traditional office would house only 88 employees'. The council had achieved this feat by 'introducing hot desking, where staff can work from home or out in the field or in the office. When they do need to come into the office, they collect their personal storage unit and roll it over to a free workstation where they can log on using a desktop PC or their own laptop' (Winchester 2004: 30).[1]

It has been argued that in the area of criminal justice, the 'habitus of many trained professionals – their ingrained dispositions and working ideologies, the standard orientations that "go without saying"' has been transformed over the past few years' (Garland, 2001: 5). Promotional iconography should not, of course, be read as illuminating the *real* or actual world of Children's Services and there is a need to be alert to how conspicuous displays of technology 'buttresses an image of efficiency' (Grint and Woolgar 1997: 130). Nonetheless, perhaps this pictorial representation and the magazine report hints that, albeit unevenly across local authorities, something similar is now taking place within Children's Services.

This chapter, therefore, particularly focuses on how information and communications technologies are central to the 'transformation' of Children's Services in England. Initially, it will comment on the 'e-government' agenda which forms a key part of the government's 'reform' of services for children and, more generally, the public sector. This is followed by discussion on what has been termed the 'surveillance society' or – what is preferred here – the 'surveillance state'. Related to these conceptualizations, in England – and, perhaps, elsewhere in Europe – two dominant and intertwined policy themes increasingly influence intervention into the lives of children and families. The first theme stresses the need to ensure that young people are adequately prepared for what is often referred to (rather euphemistically) as the 'world of work' and become compliant, well-presented employees able to function 'flexibly' in global markets. The second theme emphasizes the need to ensure that the criminal proclivities of the children of the unemployed and working poor are detected, regulated and contained. Given these dynamics, it is also argued that children (perhaps more specifically *particular* children) are increasingly apt to be the 'targets' of surveillance strategies and practices.

The latter part of the chapter examines – what is now referred to as ContactPoint, the database which, as mentioned in Chapter 3, is to contain basic details on all children in England. This 'innovation' has resulted in a good deal of controversy with some particularly viewing the introduction of CPd as eroding the privacy of children and their parents. Finally, the chapter comments on how the mass deployment of computer technology is potentially (as the image mentioned earlier suggests) remaking the *work* in social work with children and families. This, moreover, is also a theme which has been referred to in some of the debates generated on contemporary social work practices following the death of 'Baby P'.

## The e-government agenda: technologizing and marketizing the public sector

The notions 'joined up thinking' and 'joined up working' underpin the Children Act 2004 and some of the 'transformations' taking place in terms of the use of ICT in Children's Services (see also Gilling 2007: 49–53). More broadly, 'joined up' approaches characterize New Labour's orientation to government and approaches to public policy throughout a number of 'developed' of countries: for example, Sweden, the Netherlands, Australia, Canada and the USA (Ling 2002; Allen 2003). Significantly also, the 'integration of services clearly requires a freer sharing of data between agencies' and it is here that ICT is fulfilling a crucial role (Hudson 2002: 525). Furthermore, it is apparent this development is partly driven by transformations within the private sector, where 'excellent' companies – often themselves the designers, promoters and sellers of IT 'solutions' – are perceived to be providing a template for 'joined up' and 'flexible' public services (see PIU 2002: 2, 22).

Perhaps somewhat surprising, given the pace of recent developments, it was not until 1996 that the government 'produced an overarching vision for the use of ICTs in the public sector' (Hudson 2002: 517–18). However, since the late 1990s, a plethora of policy documents have been produced. Moreover, the government has created an e-minister, an e-envoy and a cadre of departmental 'information age government champions' (in Hudson 2000: 271; see also Central Information Technology Unit 1996; Cabinet Office 1998; 1999; 2000). Indeed, policy switches such as these have led to the assertion that we are now seeing the 'technologising of the public sector' (Selwyn 2002: 2).

More expansively – and, indeed, contentiously – prior to the General Election in 1997 New Labour confidently asserted that the nation stood 'on the threshold of a revolution as profound as that brought about by the invention of the printing press' (in Golding 2000: 169). Similar proclamations can be found emerging from administrations located elsewhere given that the 'often evangelical zeal of futurologists and technologists has now been taken up with equal determination by governments around the world' (Selwyn 2002: 2). Indeed, in some respects, this has merely served to bring into the 'political sphere ideas that have been gestating in the sociological literature for more than a quarter of a century' (Hudson 2002: 516). This literature includes some of the ideas on technology promoted by Daniel Bell with his 'post-industrial society' in the late 1960s and Alvin Toffler with the so-called 'third wave' in the 1970s and the 1980s (see Dyer-Witheford 1999). Perhaps, more recently, the influential ideas of Manuel Castells (2000) on the 'network society' can be interpreted as having had an impact.

Unmistakably, though, much of the rhetoric associated with the 'e-government' agenda fits rather cosily alongside the marketing rhetoric of the corporate communications industry. Indeed, the discourse on 'e-government' is saturated in the drizzle of 'the market', with 'children in need', for example, even being referred to as a 'key customer group' (PIU 2002: 114; see also Needham 2004). The fact that the e-economy is also driven by the desire of multinational corporations to reduce wages by, for example, relocating jobs to telephone call centres in the 'third world' is rarely alluded to in the relentlessly upbeat 'e-government' presentation (Khan 2003). More fundamentally, the government is now locked into relationships with multinational communications corporations which foster 'dependency on the technological expertise of the private sector' (Hudson 2002: 524; see also PA Consulting Group 2004).

Specifically, in relation to Children's Services and other fields within the public sector, forms of practice and engagement with the users of services are also being steered, directed, ordered and shaped not only by elected governments and various regulatory bodies, but by corporate designers and suppliers of ICT: this is so, even though this dimension is often insufficiently stressed in most – even critical – accounts of the use of ICT with Children's Services. Indeed, as well as selling ICT to the government, corporations are, because of the evolution of public–private 'partnerships', enmeshed in a complex (and profitable) web of contractual undertakings which enable them to gain better access to new 'customers'. Moreover, there are a number of other points that can be briefly mentioned in respect of how the 'e-agenda' can be seen as connected to the marketization of the public sector. First, the accelerated introduction of ICT in Children's Services and across this sector is frequently associated with the aim of 'saving' money and better 'targeting' not simply those 'in need', but those in *real* need (PIU 2002: 110, emphasis added). Second, despite some of the hyperbole attached to the e-government agenda, many people remain unable to access ICT (May 2002: 88–92). Indeed, in a global context, as Stallybrass (1995: 11) observed in the mid-1990s, only a fifth of the world's population even had access to telephones. Within England, this issue has come to be framed by the notion of 'digital exclusion' or the 'digital divide' (DCLG 2008a; 2008b; 2008c; see also Hudson 2000; Selwyn 2002).

Third, a good deal of the mainstream literature on ICT and the 'e-society' can be interpreted as rooted in the notion that, in the past, the needs and requirements of service providers have dominated those of 'consumers'. For example, the Performance and Innovation Unit (PIU), located within the Cabinet Office, has argued that by making better use of ICT, service providers 'will be able to deliver key consumer benefits, such as more "24×7" services, built around consumer needs rather than the convenience of service providers – accessible and flexible services that meet demand quickly, efficiently and accurately' (PIU 2000: 53–4). This claim that ICT can help to combat 'producer capture' gels, of course, with the sociology of Giddens and, as noted in Chapter 2, 'Third Way' policy-making (Giddens 2003). More practically, ICT now impacts on the providers of services by enabling the introduction of, for instance, electronic timesheets for home helps. Such a system was introduced in 1997 by Derbyshire County Council and required these care providers to continually telephone a call centre throughout the day to enable the employer to better track their movements (Owen 2000). Related to this, local authority employers in London, aided by a private sector ICT company, have been reported to be using a form of 'e-procurement' to create an 'electronic market-place to buy temporary social workers' more cheaply (Hunt 2004: 17). Some of these issues will be returned to later in the chapter. However, more encompassing and diffuse concern is focused on how the use of ICT – viewed here as related to the neoliberal aspiration to reshape working practices – is also contributing to the evolution of new and more pervasive strategies of governance and what has been termed the creation of a 'surveillance state' or 'surveillance society'.

## The 'surveillance state'

Surveillance is not, of course, intrinsically repressive and dominant. Economic and social forces in society determine how surveillant practices evolve. In the 1970s Foucault (1980) famously related the significance of surveillance to the evolution of the 'disciplinary society'. David Lyon (2001a: 2) defines 'surveillance' as 'any collection and processing of personal data, whether identifiable or not, for the purposes of influencing or managing those whose data has been garnered'. He goes on to maintain that it is now 'hard to find a place, or an activity, that is shielded or secure from some purposeful tracking, tagging, listening, watching, recording or verification device' (Lyon 2001a: 1). For Nik Rose (2000: 325) surveillance is now 'designed in' to the flows of everyday existence'. In short, we now live in, what the sociologist Gary T. Marx has referred to as, a 'surveillance society' (in Lyon 2001b: 32):

> The concept of a surveillance society denotes a situation in which dis-embodied surveillance has become socially pervasive. The totalitarian fears of Orwellian control all relate to *state* surveillance, whereas the notion of surveillance society indicates that surveillance activities have long spilled over the edges of government bureaucracies to flood every conceivable conduit.
>
> (Lyon 2001a: 33, original emphasis; see also Lyon, 2006)

Rose (2000: 325) is also of the opinion that 'control is not centralised but dispersed' flowing from 'a network of open circuits that are rhizomatic and not hierarchical'. Part of this analysis suggests that vertical or state surveillance 'still exists but it tends to be less centralised as personal data circulates more and more between public and private (commercial) realms' (Lyon 2001a: 33).

Within sociology and criminology, complex debates are, therefore, now taking place which examine whether surveillance is centralized, in the Orwellian sense, or whether the growth of surveillance systems is more dispersed, decentralized and 'rhizomic', more 'like a creeping plant than a centrally controlled trunk with spreading branches' (Lyon 2001a: 4). Perhaps expressed somewhat differently, rather like God in the old Roman Catholic catechism for schoolchildren, surveillance is, for the latter perspective, *everywhere.*

However, the idea that surveillance is now diffusing into society at large and is no longer so dominated by the state apparatus is somewhat contentious. Indeed, the perspective developed in this chapter is that the concept of 'Surveillance *State*' is, perhaps, more convincing (Jameson 2002). This is because, on account of the commencement of an endless 'war on terror', surveillance can be interpreted as actually becoming *more* 'vertical' (see also Lyon 2003; Elmer and Opel 2006): also, of course, most of the surveillance systems targeted at children, referred to in what follows, are *state*-generated endeavours. Nonetheless, it may be that the main utility of the 'surveillance society' motif is that it perhaps captures better the sheer omnipresence of surveillant practices in neoliberal societies. The 'mood music' – the political, social and cultural ambience, or temper, of the age in which we live – is, perhaps, also important. Here, a panoply of factors, including technological transformations, genetic determinism and, as suggested, the 'war on terror' may provide, to differing and complex degrees, part of the foundation for developments which are taking place within Children's Services and related fields. Indeed, promoting 'security' and averting or managing 'risk', albeit in a somewhat different sense, can be interpreted as indirectly influencing and steering policy in relation to interventions with children and their families and in the shaping of ideas fixated with 'tracking' socially wayward young people. Moreover, the 'focus of the risk gaze', as Rose (2000: 332) argues, is increasingly organized and 'packaged by structured risk assessments, risk schedules, forms and proformas [and] database fields' (see also Webb 2006).

## Surveillance today

The New Labour government has, of course, announced that it will press on with its plans to introduce identity cards, so-called 'entitlement cards', which will include biometric eye and fingerprint scans (Home Office 2002; Home Office Border and Immigration Agency 2008). It now also seems likely that the Brown administration may endeavour, in future, to put in place a centralised database of all telephone, email and online usage (see 'Bigger databases increase risks, says watchdog', *Guardian*, 29 October 2008: 4; 'Private firm may track all email and calls', *Guardian*, 31 December 2008: 1). Moreover, this information, once gathered and stored, could be made accessible to the security and law enforcement agencies, local councils and other public bodies.

Indeed, radical developments such as this have led to concerns about surveillance spilling from the discourse of sociology and criminology and into wider civil and public discourses. Moreover, such concerns are now even 'officially' recognized and pondered over, with the Information Commissioner's Office (ICO) publishing a report, in 2006, which unambiguously maintained that we now 'live in a surveillance society. It is pointless to talk about surveillance society in the future sense' (ICO 2006a: 1).[2]

The ICO has, however, been keen to stress that the evolution of this 'surveillance society' is not the product of a conspiracy: 'Conventionally, to speak of surveillance society is to invoke something sinister, smacking of dictators and totalitarianism [but it] is better thought of as the outcome of modern organizational practices, businesses, government and the military than as covert conspiracy' (ICO 2006a: 1). Furthermore, some forms of surveillance had 'always existed' (ICO 2006a: 1). The ICO report did not directly address the notion that the 'surveillance state' designation may be a more appropriate term and it predictably fails to furnish a political interpretation of some of the key factors leading to the new prominence of surveillance. However, substantial parts of the report remain important for those in Children's Services, and elsewhere in the public sector, because of the methodical way it goes about identifying some of the main processes and issues.

For example, in a section of the report analysing the context for the 'surveillance society', it focuses on three elements. First, a preoccupation, in England – and elsewhere – with *risk and security* has given rise to a '*pre-emptive* as opposed to a *preventative* approach to risk' (ICO 2006a: 11, original emphasis). As a result, it is maintained, current and 'emerging practices feature technologies and data-mining to this end'. Significantly also, 'pre-emptive risk profiling shifts surveillance practices toward the screening of the actions and transactions of the general population' (ICO 2006a: 11). Also influential, for the authors of the report, is the rise of epidemiology and the modelling associated with medical surveillance; for instance, the monitoring and tracking of individual disease cases, recording occurrences of disease for statistical analysis, and screening whole populations to identify individuals or groups at higher than average risk for a disease. Indeed, this notion is important because, it might also be argued that this orientation may be impacting on some of the prevention strategies, discussed in Chapter 3, and practices which are intent on 'targeting' those children 'at risk' of becoming criminal or 'anti-social'.

A second factor having an impact on the way the 'surveillance society' is evolving is what the authors refer to as the *militarization of surveillance* and the 'complex interaction between military and economic logics' (ICO 2006a: 14). The report, also notes the way in which many 'surveillance technology companies are intimately bound up with the military yet sell increasingly to civilian users' (ICO 2006a: 14). Related to this contextual dynamic, is the 'increasingly military way of talking about everyday safety' (ICO 2006a: 14); for example, the 'war on drugs', 'war on crime' and so on (see also Beckett 2003). Finally, the growth of elective 'personal information economies' may also be a significant; for example, some people's willingness to use, for example, 'MySpace', 'Bebo' and 'Facebook' may be serving to domesticate surveillance technologies.[3]

The ICO also usefully differentiates some of the main surveillance technologies. These include telecommunications, video surveillance, the database, biometrics and locating, tracking and tagging technologies. Indeed, all of these technologies are increasingly being deployed within Children's Services and other areas of social work and social care provision. Technologies concerned with electronic monitoring (EM), particularly tagging, for example, are increasingly prevalent. The Criminal Justice Act 1991 legislated for EM for those in curfew orders and, in 1999, EM curfews became a national scheme. The Criminal Justice and Court Services Act 2000 introduced EM for young offenders (as a component in bail, community sentences and post-custody supervision). Significantly, and gelling with the politics of neoliberalism, England and Wales are the only European countries 'to use the private sector to deliver EM' (Nellis 2005: 170).

Increasingly, satellite tracking is also beginning to play a significant a role in EM; global positioning system (GPS) technology was used, on a pilot basis, in September 2004. This 'targeted' sex offenders, domestic violence offenders and persistent offenders. Providing a good example of technological 'function creep', the following month it was extended to cover 'failed' asylum seekers – those awaiting deportation. This was the 'first use of EM in England outside a criminal justice setting' (Nellis 2005: 172). Private employers, however, are now deploying a variety of wearable devices for staff in the wholesale distribution industry; some

> consist of computers worn on the arm and finger computers to local area radio networks and to GPS systems . . . These devices calculate how long it takes to go from one part of the warehouse to the other and what breaks the workers need and how long they need to go to the toilet. Any deviation from these times is not tolerated.
>
> (GMB 2005)

Moreover, attention is now being given to the potential of using micro-chip technology to monitor an array of 'problem populations'. Early in 2008, for example, it was reported that government ministers, in England, were planning to implant 'machine readable' microchips under the skin of thousands of offenders, in the community, and that this could create more prison space. Radio frequency identification (RFID) microchips would be surgically inserted under the skin and this would carry scanable personal information, including offending record. Such a move would be in line with a proposal from the Association of Chief Police Officers (ACPO) that electronic chips should be surgically implanted into convicted paedophiles and sex offenders to alert authorities if they are in the environs of 'forbidden zones' such as schools, playgrounds and former victim's homes. These devices (already used to keep a track of dogs, cats and cattle) would be injected into the arm of an offender (see also 'Prisoners "to be chipped like dogs" ', *Independent on Sunday* 13 January, 2008: 1–4). In terms of social 'care', the Alzheimer's Society is of the view that satellite tracking systems could help families care for patients longer at home: a move opposed, in fact, by the National Pensioners' Convention ('Electronic tags to track dementia patients', *The Times*, 27 December 2007). In the USA, the market leader in RFID technology is VeriChip and its RFID devices are now being inserted into the bodies of people suffering from Alzheimer's disease and related conditions (see VeriChip 2007).

Given the creation of CPd, the evolution of database technologies is, perhaps, particularly important (see also Manovich 2001; Elmer 2004). Indeed, databases are now playing a key role throughout public services and are also more central in relation to policing and crime detection; for example, the National DNA Database.[4] Significantly also, multiple data can now be gathered, tabulated and cross-referenced far faster than with, what are now termed, 'old-fashioned 20th century paper documents' that were once a characteristic of bureaucracy (Home Office Border and Immigration Agency 2008: 4). These developments have, moreover, led some to stress the concept of 'dataveillance': 'a variation of surveillance [which] emphasises the importance of databases, rather than visual or auditory means of watching over people, in the practices of states and companies' (ICO 2006a: 20).

For the ICO, there are also a number of issues of concern about surveillance which remain highly relevant for the 'transformation' of Children's Services. First, there is the risk of *technical synergy and function creep* with information 'gathered for one purpose or in one domain' leaking through into others (ICO 2006a: 26). Second, there is a need to be wary about a drift towards *pervasive surveillance* with surveillance practices becoming 'ubiquitous, taken for granted, and largely invisible' (ICO 2006a: 27). Indeed, as Didier Bigo (2006: 49) has remarked, after 'a while, these technologies are considered so banal (such as ID checks in many countries . . . and biometric identifiers in documents) that nobody (including the judges) asks for proof of their legitimacy and their efficiency after a period of time'.

Third, there is an urgent need to be alert to *the limits of technology* given that the promise of technologies, often delivered by corporations intent on developing new markets or safeguarding and maintaining existing markets, 'is almost never quite delivered as anticipated' (ICO 2006a: 28). Finally, the ICO report reminds its readers of the dangers of *technological lock-in and regulatory lag*. Once again, moreover, important points are made in relation to the potential problems which could result for children's and related services:

> Surveillance as the first port of call in response to any kind of problem is a strongly managerialist solution, frequently proposed to governments by management consultants who operate on measurement-based world views . . . However, the more that states, organisations, communities and people become dependent on surveillance technologies, the more there is apparent 'lock-in' which prevents other options from being considered, and a comprehension gap which increases a dependence on expertise outside the democratic system.
>
> (ICO 2006a: 29–30)

Turning to examine surveillance processes, the ICO suggests that one of 'most significant developments is how surveillance, that was once reserved for the "suspect" or "deviant", has become extended to cover the majority of the population, which can then be sorted, categorised and targeted' (ICO 2006a: 30). Specific processes which are related to 'information sharing' and 'joined up' systems might also give rise to public concern – despite the centrality of such themes and practices to New Labour 'modernization' – because one:

> effect of this key development is that the boundaries that were once thought to have provided certain, albeit fragile, safeguards to privacy and limits to surveillance are called into question, often leaving both the public and the service-providers bewildered about how personal information is, and should be, managed. Personal data flow into new channels – some of them private – through organisations that never before had access to them, and whose traditions of confidentiality and privacy protection may differ substantially from each other, and from those agencies in the public sector.
>
> (ICO 2006a: 34)

In general, therefore, the Information Commissioner is explicitly and lucidly mindful of a series of complex issues and problems which are detectable within public services and which are impacting on Children's Services during a period of 'transformation' where ICT is fulfilling an increasingly central role. His report is also alert to some of the adverse social consequences of surveillance; discrimination, for example, 'in the form of differential speed, ease of access and various degrees of social exclusion is a major outcome of the social sorting processes produced by surveillance' (ICO 2006a: 43). Moreover, there are fundamental questions (concerning democracy, accountability and transparency) which are raised by the surveillance. In policy terms it is proposed, therefore, that 'surveillance impact assessments' should be produced before any proposed 'reform' is introduced (ICO 2006a: 93–5).

Indeed, it is vital to recognise that surveillance has a differential impact. Clearly, no one evades surveillance although some surveillant practices intrude into certain lives more emphatically than they do in others. In this context, children are 'arguably more hemmed in by surveillance and social regulation than ever before' (James and James 2001). Table 5.1, for example, attempts to identify some of the major databases concerned with children (see also Garrett 1999; 2003a: 145–8; 2005):

## Examining ContactPoint (CPd)

In what follows the aim is to provide a critical commentary charting the evolution of one particular database, the CPd, and to explore: the contested origins of the plan and ECM's initial references to it; the original idea to have the database feature 'flags of concern'; the opposition to, what has been variously termed by opponents, the 'electronic dossiers' (Williams 2004), a scheme to aid the 'virtual electronic tagging of families' (British Association for Adoption and Fostering 2004), even a 'search engine for paedophiles' (Carvel 2004); and the evolution of CPd, including the decision to not press ahead with the 'flags' notion.

**Table 5.1** Children and dataveillance: the major databases which collect (or will soon begin to collect) personal information on children in England[5]

| Scheme | Contents |
| --- | --- |
| ASSET | Used by Youth Offenders' Teams, Youth Inclusion and Support Panels and Youth Courts: features profiles of young offenders for the purpose of sentencing and rehabilitation |
| Centrally devised assessment schedules used by local authorities: materials associated with LAC; the AF; the CAF/eCAF | Children/young people receiving local authorities: which specific templates are used is determined by how the child/young person is classified |
| Connexion's Customer Information Service (CCIS) and Connexions Card | Information on all 13–19-year-olds. Smart Card for 16–19-year-olds operated by private company Capita which is enabled to carry out consumer profiles |
| ContactPoint (CPd) | To contain basic details on children (and some adults up to 25 years old) |
| DNA Database | Nearly 1.5 million 10–18-year-olds will have been entered by 2009. ACPO seeking even more extensive use |
| Fingerprinting for access to services and facilities | A number of local education authorities compile biometric information on children in the form of fingerprints e.g. to enable children to access libraries |
| Integrated Children's System (ICS) | An 'electronic social care record' for children: continues to be 'rolled out' nationally. Aims to store and analyse personal details on children in contact with Children's Services |
| 'Lost pupil' databases | Data on children not currently in state education in England |
| MERLIN | Used by the Metropolitan Police: records information on children 'coming to notice' (CTN) of the police. Some other constabularies use similar systems |
| National Pupil Database (NPD) | Extensive factual details on every child in state education in England |
| National Register of Unaccompanied Children (NRUC) | Promoted by the Association of London Government: used to exchange information between local authorities and the Immigration and Nationality Directorate (IND) on unaccompanied under-18 asylum seekers; used to manage funding and to respond to concerns about asylum seekers giving false ages |

| NOTIFY | Used by Greater London Authority and London boroughs: records information on the movement of homeless households |
| --- | --- |
| ONSET | Same as ASSET but for those not convicted: also used to try and identify those thought *likely* to offend |
| RAISEonline (Reporting and Analysis for Improvement through School self-Evaluation | System for analysing data in the NPD |
| RYOGENS | Produced by private company Esprit and deployed by a by a number of local authorities: logs 'concerns' about children and young people regarded as 'vulnerable' |

## *(Re)writing history: the CPd and Laming*

As mentioned earlier, the New Labour government has been keen to connect the development of CPd to the Laming Report (see, for example, Bawden 2006). However, evidence suggests that attaching the evolution of the database idea to Victoria's Climbié's death is misleading because plans to introduce new electronic systems for monitoring and tracking children were *already* under way *before* the publication of the Laming Report into her death; perhaps rather embarrassingly for the government, given the assertion that a system such as the CPd 'might have saved her life' (Baroness Ashton, in Foundation for Information Policy Research, 2006: 31), it has also been suggested that had the CPd had been in operation during Victoria's time in England, she would not have been featured on the system because draft guidance appears to rule out the inclusion of children who are only temporarily in the country.

In April 2002 the PIU report, *Privacy and Data-sharing: The Way Forward for Public Services*, was published (PIU 2002) and here the government conceded that the public was concerned about developments relating to electronic technologies and data-sharing. Public attitude research revealed, for example, worries about data-sharing being contaminated on account of 'infection with inaccurate data', and the 'use of soft data (such as professionals' opinions or assessments of individuals or clients)' (PIU 2002: 38). However, the authors of the PIU report were clear that the public sector did not want to 'lock information into a particular organisational form' (PIU 2002: 105). Moreover, the 'current legislative approach to data sharing' was 'restrictive' (PIU 2002: 106). In this context, it was argued, two key changes were needed: 'enabling data sharing where the individual consents to their personal data being disclosed to a third party'; and 'changes to the way in which data-sharing gateways are established in statute. This is particularly important in instances where consent is not viable'. The report went on to argue that public services could 'make progress' and referred to a number of 'service specific proposals'.

First on the list was 'identifying and supporting children at risk of social exclusion' (PIU 2002: 108–9). Here, it was maintained, that there was a need to try to promote better use of data with information-sharing 'across agencies to build up an holistic view of children's needs, and ensure children do not slip through the net' (PIU 2002: 108). These children needed to be kept 'on track' and common 'information-sharing practices' would aid this activity. The setting up of IRT projects, announced in August 2002, reflected this policy aspiration (Cleaver et al. 2004): subsequently renamed Information Sharing and Assessment projects these were then 'repackaged' as retrospective 'pilots' for the envisaged CPd.

### ECM and the 'local information hubs'

As discussed in Chapter 3, in autumn 2003, the government published ECM, its plan for reorganizing services for children. While New Labour's vision for change was broadly welcomed by child welfare professionals and others, the idea of introducing – what was referred to at the time as – 'local information hubs', an electronic system to facilitate the collating and sharing of information about children, was viewed much less favourably. *Every Child Matters* stated the aim was that, in localities, the 'hub' would consist of 'a list of all the children living' in the area and other 'basic details':

- name, address and date of birth
- school attended or if excluded or refused access
- GP
- a 'flag' stating whether the child is known to agencies such as education welfare, social services, police and YOTs, and if so, the contact details of the professional dealing with the case
- where a child is known to more than one specialist agency, the Lead Professional who takes overall responsibility for the case.

It was also stated that these envisaged 'information systems' would 'be based on national data standards to enable the exchange of information between local authorities and partner agencies, and be capable of interacting with other data sets' (Chief Secretary to the Treasury 2003: 53). A 'Lead Professional' would act as 'gatekeeper' for this information-sharing system and, in order to indicate that there were concerns about a child or family, readers of ECM were advised:

> [T]here is a strong case for giving practitioners the ability to flag on the system early warnings when they have concern about a child which in itself may not trigger or meet the usual thresholds for intervention. The decision to place such a flag of concern on a child's record, which may be picked up by another agency making a similar judgement, lies with the practitioners . . .
>
> [W]e are consulting on the circumstances (in addition to child protection and youth offending) under which information about a child could or must be shared, *for preventative purposes*, without the consent of the child or their carers. We would also welcome views on whether *warning*

*signs* should reflect factors within the family such as *imprisonment, domestic violence, mental health or substance misuse problems amongst parents and carers.*

(Chief Secretary to the Treasury 2003: 53–4, emphases added)

In addition, 'information would be updated by practitioners in response to changes in the child's life' (Chief Secretary to the Treasury 2003: 55). The New Labour administration was also convinced that the then existing arrangements for sharing information about children were 'too rigid' and it was intent on swiftly addressing any factors that might stand in the way of the introduction of the 'hub'. It was, therefore, committed to removing a whole series of legal, technical, professional and cultural barriers (Chief Secretary to the Treasury 2003: ch. 4).

As early as 2003, therefore, it was apparent that the envisaged system would result in more information being collated on children and potentially more 'tracking' taking place. Equally important, there were a number of key omissions. Would, for example, the police be able to access the databases and seek out data when investigating matters unrelated to children, but connected to other facets of criminal detection or intelligence? Would the Immigration Service be able to access the hubs when determining if an individual or family has the right to remain in the UK? Was there a danger of (external and internal) hacking or misuse? However, it was, perhaps, the notion of 'flags of concern' which appeared to be the most concerning and ill-conceived.

## The original plan for 'flags of concern'

Indeed, the very idea of a 'flag' could be read as problematic because a flag is a universal signifier of national belonging.[6] Moreover, this symbol could be read as particularly inappropriate and jarring given that social workers and others in Children's Services were increasingly becoming involved in 'scrutinising immigration status' (Sales 2002: 461). In more practical terms, it was also left unclear *when* a 'flag of concern' would be electronically placed on a child's personal database. Indeed, it appeared that the government's plan left far too much room for the discretion of individual practitioners about when 'thresholds' may have been crossed. Other aspects of the plans indicated that there were likely to be substantial civil liberties concerns. It was also unclear if a child, young person or parent would be informed that a 'professional' had electronically inserted a 'flag of concern' on a computer database. Neither was there any information provided about how these 'flags' would be treated when a young person reached 18 years of age. As is clear from the extract from ECM, referred to earlier, the government also seemed intent on expanding categories in order to insert 'warning signs' where there were instances of 'imprisonment, domestic violence, mental health or substance misuse problems amongst parents and carers'. In short, a mixture of hardships and woes, some of which may not always result in child protection concerns.

Furthermore, some felt that this plan, featured in ECM, could be dangerously counterproductive because it could deter a hard-pressed family from seeking help and support because they might be fearful of their private information being placed on the electronic 'hub'. Perhaps also social-class location can be connected to concerns that some children and parents might be deterred from seeking help because they are fearful that their 'details' will be entered onto a database. MORI, for example, undertook research on public awareness and perceptions of privacy and data-sharing for the Department of Constitutional Affairs in 2003. Extraordinarily, given the government's plans for accumulating and sharing information on over 11 million children, only the views of those aged 15 and over were sought. However, 60 per cent of those asked stated that they were 'very or fairly concerned' about public services sharing their personal information, with 22 per cent *very* concerned'. Only 12 per cent stated that they were 'not at all concerned' (Skinner et al. 2003: 4, original emphasis). These percentages reflect the public's wariness about privacy being undermined by electronic 'information sharing', but also of note is the fact that a 'fairly consistent trend' is for the middle social classes to be least concerned (Skinner et al. 2003: 5). Related to this, those in 'the middle social classes are more likely to trust public services to handle information responsibly than working class people/those on benefits' (Skinner et al. 2003: 21; see also 'ID cards may put poorer people at risk of fraud', *Guardian*, 16 May 2008: 11). It could be argued, therefore, that the setting up of databases might *particularly* deter working-class children and parents from seeking out help.

Additionally – and reflecting some of the thinking contained in the ICO report – it was felt, by some commentators, that the belief in an enhanced electronic monitoring system risked being perceived as something of a 'panacea' which would 'solve' a panoply of highly complex social problems relating to children and their families (Winchester 2003). More generally, in fact, it could be maintained that this simplistic orientation is detectable across the literature associated with 'e-government' agenda for Children Services (see, for example, PIU 2002: 77).

## The opposition to 'electronic dossiers'

Following the publication of ECM, criticisms of plans for databases were voiced not only from children's rights groups, but from organizations as diverse as the Women's Aid Federation and the British Medical Association (see also Cushman 2004; Dowty 2004). Upon publication of the Children Bill, the parliamentary Joint Committee on Human Rights went on to express serious concerns about the proposed databases (House of Lords and House of Commons Joint Committee on Human Rights (hereafter JCHR) 2004). More specifically, the JCHR felt that the information-sharing provisions in the bill involved 'serious interference' with Article 8 of the European Convention on Human Rights (ECHR), which seeks to ensure respect for private life. Related to this, it was maintained that the government was failing to provide evidence that this interference was proportionate and justified under Article 8 (2) of the ECHR (JCHR 2004: 29–35). The JCHR was, moreover, concerned about the 'breadth of the regulation-making powers being conferred on the Secretary of State' (JCHR 2004: 32). In this context, the government simply maintained that it needed to retain 'flexibility to develop the databases in light of the

experiences of the current pilot projects being carried out and technical advice
. . . commissioned but not yet delivered' (JCHR 2004: 32). Given this position,
the JCHR reasonably maintained that parliament was 'being asked to author-
ize in advance a major interference with Article 8 rights without evidence
demonstrating its necessity being available' (JCHR 2004: 32). Importantly also,
the measured report from the JCHR asserted:

> Maintaining a child protection register, or even a register of children 'in
> need' and therefore in receipt of Children Act assistance from the local
> authority, is a much more targeted measure aimed at protecting vulner-
> able children. But a universal database seems to us to be rather more
> difficult to justify in Article 8 terms. Adults are also the beneficiaries of
> universal services such as health care and other services, such as com-
> munity care, for which they may be eligible in certain circumstances. It
> appears to us that the strict logic of the Government's position is that it
> would be justifiable interference with adults' Article 8 rights to maintain
> a similar database of all adults in the UK in order to ensure that those
> amongst them who are or may be entitled to receive certain services from
> the state actually receive them.
>
> (JCHR 2004: 33)

Within Parliament it was a handful of unelected, albeit well-briefed, Conservative and Liberal Democratic peers who provided the substantial opposition.
This was most apparent in House of Lords' Committee Stage debate of the
Children Bill in May 2004. For the Lords, the plans for the databases were
vague on a number of key points. Indeed, it was asserted that 'the whole thing
is ill-formed' and 'wishy-washy' and the government had difficulties in trying
to rebut this charge (see the comments of Earl of Northesk, Lords' Hansard,
24 May 2004: col. 1159).[7] The lack of definition and skeletal nature of the legal
framework, which has provided for the databases, was targeted for particular
criticism. Critics maintained, for example, that the Children Bill delegated
exceedingly wide powers to the Secretary of State, permitting him or her to
'establish and operate databases' with regulations setting out the operational
details.

The government's chief spokesperson in the Lords argued, without referring to any evidence, that information needed to be electronically logged
because 'time and again, professionals cannot act on . . . early concerns
because they do not know who else is involved' (Baroness Ashton: col. 1095).
What was being proposed, therefore, was merely an electronic 'telephone directory', a 'yellow pages' to facilitate the work of busy child welfare professionals. Importantly, for the government, the envisaged databases would,
moreover, contain nothing that 'would constitute opinion about any child'
(Baroness Ashton: col. 1097). In short, according to the government's rather
bland presentation of the issue, all that was being proposed was a rational and
technical solution to a perceived social problem.

In some respects, the claim that the envisaged databases could be perceived as a sensible measure is convincing. In broad terms it seems sensible, of
course, for Children's Services to continue to exchange *relevant* information.
Moreover, as observed earlier, the policy aspiration to utilize ICT to facilitate

such exchanges fits neatly alongside the endeavour to 'transform' Children's Services (Harlow and Webb 2003; Geoghegan et al. 2004; Parton 2006b; Tregeagle and Darcy 2007). Moreover, the plan for the databases and the 'wiring up' of these services gels with the notion of 'joined up thinking' (Ling 2002). Furthermore, ideas about 'preventative' action to respond to children 'at risk' of 'abuse' or (somewhat more ambiguously) 'social exclusion' can have a 'common sense' appeal to child welfare professionals and to the wider public. However, as was observed in the House of Lords, when concerted attempts were made to clarify the purpose and scope of the government's plans, we:

> have here what is potentially a very large-scale system of data recording by the state on its citizens. The system is to be set up in the name of improving the welfare of all children. The names and key personal details of all 11 million children in England are to be recorded for access by professionals from a wide variety of disciplines. The vast majority of children so recorded will not be at risk of suffering significant harm or anything approaching it . . . [H]ow can we not regard this mammoth information gathering and information sharing exercise as anything other than grossly intrusive on the privacy of families?
>
> (Earl Howe: col. 1154)

Another contentious issue related to the ambiguity of the government's intentions. Were the databases instruments for research and social policy formulation or a 'tool' for child welfare professionals? This type of damaging ambiguity also characterised the evolution of the LAC materials in the 1990s (see Parker et al. 1991, Ward 1995; for criticism see Garrett 2003a). One of the Lords contended:

> I suspect that part of the problem is that the Government are attempting to cohere two related, but quite distinct, functions. There is something to be said for a database system that seeks to use anonymised data to guide and inform the development of child welfare policy. But that is quite distinct from using sensitive personal data as a mechanism for identifying individual children at risk. In effect, by melding those two disparate functions, the Government are inviting the possibility of entrenching the worst of all worlds – an unresponsive system that implodes under its own weight.
>
> (Earl of Northesk: col. 1156)

### 'Technologizing' the politically contested: implementing CPd

The New Labour administration has been keen to try, via regulations and protocol, to blunt criticism. Consequently, a number of changes have been made relating to the operation of the CPd. However, unfortunately for the government and senior local government officers wanting to press ahead with implementation, a whole series of mishaps, even scandals, connected to the 'loss' of government electronic data occurred in 2007 and 2008. These included the disappearance 'in the post' of HM Revenue and Customs discs containing the personal records of 25 million individuals, including their dates of birth, addresses, bank accounts and national insurance numbers; also 'lost' were the personal details relating to 7.25 million families in receipt of child benefit. Subsequently, it was reported that the personal details of approximately 3 million learner drivers had been 'lost' by a contractor in the US state of Iowa.[8] In the summer of 2008 it was then reported that PA Consulting, the consultancy firm involved in the development of national identity cards, had been responsible for losing a memory stick containing the details of all of the 84,000 prisoners in England and Wales.[9] Unsurprisingly these events, as well as illuminating one of the potential pitfalls associated with neoliberal inspired 'outsourcing' or 'contracting out' of core government tasks and functions, led to renewed criticism that storing the personal details of 11 million children on the envisaged CPd was an inherently 'risky' business. More emphatically, this was a reckless 'reform' of Children's Services which could still be avoided.[10]

The New Labour administration remains, however, intent on introducing the CPd. The present aim is that it will be a national system, but the data will be partitioned into 150 compartments, each relating to a different local authority. The government has, however, remained sensitive to the criticisms which have been deployed since the database plan was first mooted. For example, the 'flags of concern' idea has, therefore, been abandoned, but the envisaged scheme will alert practitioners if an eCAF has been completed on a child. Thus, it appears likely that a CAF/eCAF symbol or icon will replace a 'flag' when CPd begins to function on a national basis. Fundamentally, though, the government appears not to have given ground in terms of the core and problematic conceptual underpinning of the system. Hence, the defensive emphasis has latterly been on how the 'security' of the CPd will be safeguarded and how access to and use of the system will be established. Thus, the more recent presentation has switched from seeking to provide a rationale for the CPd to 'making the CPd work' (Ofsted 2007) and stressing that there will only be 'authorized users', within each locality, aided by 'specialist teams' with technical 'know-how'. In this way the New Labour administration can be seen as intent on 'technologizing' a 'politically contested issue, by translating the issue into technical and "common sense" understandings that serve to depoliticise' the CPd project (Penna 2005: 145). Nonetheless, some of the key criticisms referred to earlier have not been adequately addressed. Concerns remain not only about the security of the system, but about questions related to the core rationale for the CPD and to issues related to consent, confidentiality and the retention of information on certain children beyond their eighteenth birthday.

The final part of the chapter alters focus to briefly address how electronic forms of working, reflected in the development and deployment of systems such as the CPd and CAF/eCAF are potentially remaking the work in work with children and their families: even prompting the creation of a new 'techno-habitat' for social workers and other practitioners within Children's Services.

## The 'e-turn' and the remaking of practitioners' temporal frameworks

In *Capital*, Marx (1990: 560) referred to the 'constant advance of technology' in the *new* workplaces of the mid-nineteenth century (see also Garrett 2009):

he was, however, clear that 'machinery' was not to blame for the hardships and oppression of the industrial working class. As he lucidly remarked, it 'took both time and experience before the workers leant to distinguish between machinery and its employment by capital, and therefore to transfer their attacks from the material instruments of production to *the form of society which utilizes those instruments*' (Marx 1990: 555, emphasis added).

In this – a different time – it would seem that social work, and related forms of work with children and families is (on account of the ICS, the CPd and other databases and electronic templates) now becoming an activity that is characterized by a more frequent recourse to ICT. Moreover, if there is an 'e-turn' taking place in social work (Garrett 2005) this is likely to become accelerated over the next few years. In this context, it is also likely that the boundary between home and work will become more porous for those working within Children's Services, with practitioners finding their workplace at risk of being 'abolished altogether, or rather dissolved into life' (Bauman 2002: 149).

Perhaps sensitive to some of the changes impacting on direct work with children and families, BAAF (2004: 24) has called for the restoration of what it dubs 'people-focussed social work'. Related to this suggestion, in an early and important intervention on the use of computers in social services, Bob Sapey (1997: 806) observed:

> As a medium, the computer . . . also has an influence on the nature of the texts in much the same way that painters are influenced by their materials, or musicians their choice of instrument. The obvious example of this is the plethora of 'tick-box' assessments that have accompanied the community care changes. In this case, the nature of the assessment task is being changed to fit the parameters of the technology.

Certainly the technological basis for engagement with children and families is changing and with it the function of practitioners (UNISON 2008a). More fundamentally, there cannot, of course, be any return to the type of work practices elaborated on the basis of technological and social circumstances that no longer exist. Nevertheless, some of the neoliberal-inspired developments discussed in this chapter (as well as highlighting how notions related to the evolution of the 'surveillance state' relate to children and, more broadly, Children's Services) suggest that 'labour processes' are being assembled anew and (re)constructed in a potentially damaging way.

One area this is apparent relates to the 'temporal frameworks' for working with children and families (Waterworth 2003). Essentially, the assemblage of databases and e-assessment schedules is being constructed and deployed not only with a view to managing and governing the users of services, but to reorder and regulate practitioners and the time devoted to undertaking particular aspects of their work. The literature associated with the CPd is, in this respect, illustrative: for example, the ECM website[11] promoting the CPd emphasizes how the new system will contribute to 'faster' intervention and will contribute to a 'reduction in unproductive time spent by practitioners'; similarly 'efficiency gains' are likely to accrue 'expressed as time saved by practitioners'. At present, we are advised these practitioners 'can spend days trying to find out ... basic information: CPd, therefore, is a 'practical tool that frees up ... time.'

This emphasis on the temporal dimension to the 'transformation' of Children's Services is clearly complex. However, it could be argued that these new temporal standards initially emerged within the private and corporate sectors where the 'fast' and the 'efficient' are often discursively conjoined and valorized. It is also clear, of course, that it is not just in England where these developments are apparent. For example, Donna Baines has referred to similar 'reforms' in Canada where although

> social service provision is purportedly motivated by notions of social and/or individual caring ... the new public management compatible labour process within Canadian public and non-profit social services sector systematically strips out the work of caring content, replacing it with flexible, routinized models of work organization.
>
> (Baines 2004b: 268)

Given this orientation to engaging with children and families some 'non-profit agencies, such as child welfare, have introduced computer technologies that standardize work processes, dictate detailed time lines and order of tasks, provide electronic monitoring, and, in effect, remove most discretionary decision-making previously enjoyed by workers' (Baines 2004b: 272). Thus, 'standardization and workforce flexibility ... may prove to be a halfway station between the old welfare state and the neo-liberal, residual state' (Baines 2004b: 273).

Baines and others are also sensitive to how the 'standardization of social services delivery abstracts the lived in realities of individuals and communities, replacing multi-service, holistic approaches with narrowly calibrated ones to diverse problems and issues' (Baines 2004b: 277; see also White et al. 2008). This is a concern shared by Katja Franko Aas, the Norwegian criminologist, who has observed that the 'success' of the form and e-templates lie in their 'timelessness and disembeddedness' and the apparent 'insistence that people and their circumstances can be turned into *objects of information*, independent of the subjects that give them meaning. They insist that there is no "mystery" behind decision-making' (Franko Aas 2005: 157, emphasis added). She goes onto to argue that:

> Forms simplify choices, they create transparency and predictability, they ease the classification and processing of data, and ... they are the tools of control and surveillance. They are the tools that enable a shift of discretion and power from professionals to administrators ... Managerial control in contemporary ... systems is based on limiting the access of certain groups to introduce alternative types of knowledge and language that do not correspond with closed-ended formats and classifications.
>
> (Franko Aas 2005: 153)

This, for some, can be connected to more profound and far-reaching cultural shifts which suggest a 'crisis of narration' with narrative increasingly 'being replaced by the database as the privileged form of cultural expression' (Franko Aas 2005: 156). Importantly, a 'database organizes information through a markedly different ontology than narratives. A database is a medium for storing and organizing *information* rather than discursive knowledge . . . it is "byte-like" and compressed' (Franko Aas 2005: 156). That is, information is different from narrative because it is 'produced in a much shorter time span and, therefore, leaves little time for reflection . . . Every item of information is isolated in its self-sufficiency' (Franko Aas 2005: 156).

Clearly, this analysis can be contested and there will always continue to be some room, or space, for practitioner discretion (Robinson, G. 2003; Clarke et al. 2007; White et al. 2008): those working in Children's Services and elsewhere will not be entirely 'hemmed in' by ICTs, new techno-habitats and new time disciplines. However, it seems clear that 'transformation' projects launched across a number of jurisdictions and national settings are intent on *remaking* practices and 'speeding up' encounters with the users of services. Moreover, within emerging paradigms for practice there does appear to be a new, flattened emphasis on gathering 'information' at the expense of narrative and discursive knowledge. In this sense, the 'e-turn' may run counter to ideas, previously embedded in social work and related spheres, that exchanges with the users of services should be founded on notions of 'respect' and that there should be associated commitment to promote open dialogue (Garrett 2008b).

Equally important, of course, despite the beaming faces of the workers featured on the advert referred to at the beginning of the chapter, there is a need to remain mindful of the 'prevailing social order's systematic tendency to create unsatisfying work' (Bellamy Foster 1998: ix; see also Ferguson and Lavalette 2004). Within the emerging 'lean' work organizations the *work* in Children's Services is increasingly being ordered, devised and structured by academics, policy-makers and e-technicians far removed from the day-to-day encounters with users of the services. This is reflected in the emerging software architecture and, as already observed, in the greater use of centrally devised e-assessment templates which attempt to map the contours of engagements with the users of children's services and which construct new 'workflows' (see also White et al. 2008). In this way, the work is becoming more Taylorized:[12] broken down into bytes with social workers, for example, aided by less costly 'social care assistants', providing 'customers' with discrete packages, or micro-packages, of (often purchasable) support and intervention (Coleman and Harris 2008). Related to this, work with children and families, partly on account of ICT and the evolution of the 'techno-habitat', is becoming an even more 'flexible' activity. Here, the laptop – the portable office – will begin to play a more substantial role and electronically mediated forms of information exchange are likely to become more central, more contentious and, perhaps, more resisted.

## Conclusion

This chapter has not, therefore, tried to promote a dystopic and technophobic essentialism or a form of neo-Luddism. Indeed, it must be conceded that ICT has many potential beneficial uses for both practitioners and users within Children's Services. Databases, for example, are a useful 'tool' which can help in the collating and storage of information on the 'race' and ethnicity of users of services and can assist in identifying where particular groups are not receiving services (see, in this context, Garrett 2004). The Internet also provides many interesting possibilities for childcare social work and, more politically, for social movements seeking to combat neoliberalism and to champion a more 'democratic technics' (May 2002: 29–32).

However, there is also a need to be alert to the *ideological* atmosphere in which social workers and others in Children's Services perform their new technological role. Following Adorno's (2003: 118) lead, there is a need to try to ascertain *how* the technology is imbricated 'within the relations that embrace it'. Moreover, assessment 'tools' devised for intervention are underpinned, in part, by the functional aspiration to police the socially marginalized. Such 'tools' for practice, with their neoliberal, narrow, normative and prescriptive view of the world and economic relationships are increasingly being formulated to enable (maybe even to compel) practitioners to complete them electronically. Perhaps, in this context, a dual strategy (taking account of the threat to the civil liberties of users of services and to the working conditions of practitioners) needs to evolve which will respond constructively to the *negative* consequences ICT deployment in Children's Services.

This next chapter contends that there is a need to interrogate factors which are influencing and driving the ASBO agenda during the period of New Labour. It begins by, once again emphasizing the significance of keywords and phrases in the 'transformation' of services and orientations to working with children and their families. This is followed by a critical overview of the White Paper, *Respect and Responsibility: Taking a Stand Against Anti-Social Behaviour* (Home Office 2003a). It is then argued that Tony Blair and David Blunkett played distinctive roles in creating England's 'ASBO politics'. This, moreover, is a politics which potentially narrows the focus of practitioners' involvement with children and families.

**Reflection and talk box 5**

Why is social class connected to the degree of trust people have in the state safeguarding the integrity of personal data?

Why do children – or more specifically, *particular* children – seem more subject to surveillant practices?

Which concept is more enlightening for those working in Children's Services: 'surveillance society' or 'surveillance state'?

Should changes to practices within Children's Services, be subject to, what have been termed, 'surveillance impact statements'?

How does the use of technology relate to ideas pivoting on the 'flexibility' of workers referred to in, for example, Chapter 2?

How might the increasing use of ICT and related surveillant practices be viewed alongside professional codes of ethics, such as that of BASW?

Can you identify any instances of 'function creep' in terms of how technology has been deployed in your particular workplace? Are there any instances of what has been termed 'technological lock-in'?

How is ICT impacting on the work you do? Are you more likely to 'take work home'? Do you feel that your work, within Children's Services, is more subject to electronic surveillance?

Is the idea that Children Services are undergoing an 'electronic turn', or 'e-turn', convincing?

'Today there is a good deal of criticism – in the context of promoting "joined up" approaches – of "silos". However, so-called "silos" can be also be welcomed because members of the public are clear what particular service will or will not be provided. In contrast, with more "joined up", electronically mediated, approaches to Children' Services, matters tend to become blurred and there is also greater likelihood that personal information might "wash around the system".' Discuss.

# 6 Making 'anti-social behaviour': ASBO politics

In early 2005, BASW signed the statement of aims of the campaign group, ASBO Concern (Foot 2005). This broad-based coalition has fulfilled an important role in drawing attention to some of the problems resulting from the introduction of ASBOs and highlighted a range of seemingly outlandish instances where individuals have been subjected to these orders. These included the serving of ASBOs on an '87 year old for being repeatedly sarcastic' and on a '17 year old deaf girl for spitting' (Office of the EU Commissioner for Human Rights (OEUCHR) 2005: 37). Elsewhere, a 63-year-old peace campaigner was the subject of an ASBO application by police after regular protests at Menwith Hill US military 'listening post' in Yorkshire. Specific concerns have also been raised about how ASBOs and associated measures are regulating and constraining children's temporal and spatial worlds, infringing their human rights and increasingly subjecting them to criminalization (OEUCR 2005: 39; see also James and James 2001; Muncie et al. 2002; Walsh 2002). Indeed, 'something like three-quarters of ASBOs are imposed upon young people' (Squires and Stephen 2005: 519): for some of these, according to research conducted for the government's own Youth Justice Board, ASBOs are seen as a 'badge of honour' ('Teenagers see Asbos as badge of honour', *Guardian*, 2 November 2006: 2); 42 per cent of ASBOs, imposed between June 2000 and December 2003 were breached and of these 55 per cent resulted in custodial sentences (in Squires and Stephen 2005: 520; see also Matthews et al. 2007).

Although entirely welcoming the work of BASW and others undertaking the vital work of illuminating the injustices associated with ASBOs and what the EU Commissioner on Human Rights (OEUCHR 2005: 38) has referred to as 'ASBO-mania' promoted by the government, this chapter is not chiefly concerned with rehearsing the well-aired criticisms of these measures and again highlighting that troubling cocktail of authoritarianism and absurdity which characterizes ASBO deployment (see, for example, Walsh 2002; Payne 2003; Brown 2004; Burney 2005; Rodger 2006; Squires 2006; Gilling 2007). In what follows, the main focus is on the initial evolution, during the period of the Blair administrations, of what will be referred to as 'ASBO politics'. In this context, as Bourdieu has maintained, each 'society, at each moment, elaborates a body of *social problems* taken to be legitimate, worthy of being debated, of being made public and sometimes officialized and, in a sense *guaranteed by the state* (in Bourdieu and Wacquant 2004: 236, original emphases). We might also be guided by the suggestion that we

> must retrace the history of the emergence of these problems, of their progressive constitution, i.e. of the collective work, oftentimes accomplished through competition and struggle, that proved necessary to make such and such issues known and recognized . . . as *legitimate problems*, problems that are avowable, punishable, public, official.
>
> (Bourdieu and Wacquant 2004: 238, original emphasis)

In this sense, the words used to construct social problems and to hegemonize particular dominant perspectives is, of course, of immense significance.[1]

## 'Anti-social behaviour': putting it into words

Beckett (2003) and Gregory and Holloway (2005) have pointed to the significance of the words deployed in social work and related fields of activity. Building on their contributions, 'anti-social behaviour' can be interpreted as keywords within the New Labour political lexicon (Williams 1983; Fairclough 2000; Bennett et al. 2005). Perhaps the work of Bourdieu also helps us to illuminate how 'anti-social behaviour' has been constructed. More specifically, his understanding of how – what he terms – capital operates inside particular fields assists in interpreting the role of 'primary definers'. For Bourdieu, the 'position of a given agent in the social space can . . . be defined by the position he [*sic*] occupies in the different fields, that is, the distribution of powers that are active in each of them. These are principally, economic capital (in its different kinds), cultural capital and social capital, as well as symbolic capital' (Bourdieu 1991: 230). Moreover, the 'kinds of capital, like trumps in a game of cards, are powers which define the chances of profit in a given field (Bourdieu 1991: 230; see also Bourdieu and Wacquant 2004: 118–19; Garrett 2007a; 2007b).

From the perspective developed throughout this book, symbolic capital is particularly important because not 'all judgments carry the same weight, the holders of large amounts of symbolic capital . . . are in a position to impose the scale of values most favourable to their end products' (Bourdieu 2002: 240). In this sense, symbolic capital is a form of 'credit' which can be drawn on and deployed in order to advance one's likelihood of success in a particular struggle (Bourdieu 2002). Thus, in the 'symbolic struggle for the production of common sense or, more precisely, for the monopoly of legitimate *naming* as the official – i.e. explicit and public – imposition of the legitimate vision of the social world, agents bring into play the symbolic capital that they have acquired' (Bourdieu 1991: 239, original emphasis). This discursive deployment of symbolic capital is also, of course, especially significant in the struggle to establish political and social hegemony for particular policies and here 'leading' politicians and 'esteemed' academics play significant roles.

In this context, David Blunkett (Home Secretary 2001–04) and Tony Blair were each equipped with political power, yet each also had sizeable reserves of *distinctive* forms of symbolic capital. They can, therefore, be interpreted as fulfilling quite different roles in terms of how they endeavoured to frame the ASBO issue. Inevitably, each of them was apt to amble into the other's discursive space and the political work which each of them *did with words* was not tidily separable. Nonetheless, these two primary political definers of 'anti-social behaviour' endeavoured to draw on different types of 'symbolic capital' to construct the ASBO agenda somewhat differently. What reserves of symbolic capital did each of them seek to draw on and deploy? What meanings and associations have they mobilized in terms of their specific public comments on the issue? Some answers to these questions are, perhaps, apparent if we briefly look at some of their own comments and media reports. However, a concern about 'anti-social behaviour' pre-dated the first Blair administration of 1997 and so first it is useful to chart the evolution of this concern (see also Burney 2005).

## Tracking 'anti-social behaviour'

Perhaps surprisingly, even in the late-1960s the Seebohm Report on the future of social services contained a passing reference to 'anti-social behaviour' (Committee on Local Authority and Allied Personal Social Services 1968: 56). In the mid-1990s, though, it was the Conservative government of John Major which endeavoured to focus attention on the behaviour of those who were, it was maintained, unsettling, even harassing members of the public. For him, beggars – an 'eyesore' in many cities – were a prime target (see, for example, 'Keep beggars off the street says Major', *The Times*, 28 May 1994: 1; 'Major chases votes in new attacks on beggars', *Observer*, 29 May 1994: 1). Tony Blair, then shadow Home Secretary and poised to become Labour leader after the death of John Smith, responded to these attacks on beggars by claming that the Tory leader was merely seeking to divert attention from far more substantial problems. Moreover, Major was guilty of 'vindictiveness' against a group of people 'some of who will be genuinely destitute'. In addition, maintained Blair, 'the pettiness and small-mindedness ... will affront people and bewilder them' ('Bishops attack Major over beggars', *Daily Telegraph*, 30 May 1994: 1).

It was, however, the council estate (or, drawing on prevalent US vocabulary, the so-called 'sink estate') which was to become the theatre in which the performance and regulation of 'anti-social behaviour' was to be enacted.[2] Council tenants were advised by the Major government that local authorities would not 'tolerate anti social behaviour by tenants and will take action against them' (see, for example, Papps 1998; Flint 2003; 2004a; 2004b). In the most serious cases, this could result in tenants losing their homes (Department of the Environment 1995). Related to this warning, 'probationary tenancies', one 'more weapon in the armoury of local authorities tackling anti-social behaviour', and other assorted measures were introduced, under the Housing Act 1996, which made it explicit that maintaining a tenancy was to become conditional on behaviour (Department of the Environment 1995: 3; see also Haworth and Manzi 1999). Attempting to shadow the Conservatives and pre-empt them using the 'anti-social behaviour' issue to their political advantage in the General Election of 1997, Labour was also swift to deploy its own policy documents which laid out how it would deal with the problem (see Labour Party 1996; Straw and Anderson 1996). Importantly, though, Labour was not simply acting in a strategic and pragmatic fashion. Changes — reflected in the ascendancy of Blair and the *New* Labour ideological rebranding – were also taking place, in terms of the political orientation of the party. Furthermore, a foundational facet of these changes was a new preoccupation with remodelling the behaviour, and more fundamentally, the culture of socially and economically marginalized communities. Central to this programme of remoralization was to be the evolution of a new type of welfare state in which, as noted earlier, 'welfare' was to be 'a hand-up not a hand-out' (Blair 1999: 13, 17) and its provision was to become more and more conditional on behaviour and a willingness to become 'economically active' (Blair 1999; see also Levitas 1996). The 'anti-social behaviour' construct was, moreover, to fulfil an emblematic role within this emerging and coercive paradigm of governance.

New Labour introduced ASBOs under the Crime and Disorder Act 1998 and these became 'live' in April 1999. However, there was concern, on the part of the government, that an insufficient number of these orders was being sought (see also Burney 2002). In 2003, therefore, a concerted effort began to reinvigorate the ASBO agenda. This was reflected in the setting up of the Anti-Social Behaviour Unit at the beginning of the year and then, in March, by the publication of the White Paper, *Respect and Responsibility: Taking a Stand Against Anti-Social Behaviour* (Home Office 2003a). *Respect and Responsibility*, which was to culminate in the Anti-Social Behaviour Act 2004, is a focal document in terms of the defining of 'anti-social behaviour'. It remains important, therefore, to interrogate its key elements because it continues to illuminate the tone and texture of New Labour rhetoric and policy-making.

## Creating 'respect' and 'responsibility'

*Respect and Responsibility* stated that there are 'many forms of anti-social behaviour, a definition given in the Crime and Disorder Act 1998, is that a "person has acted in a manner that has caused or was likely to cause harassment, alarm or distress to one or more persons not of the same household as himself" ' (Home Office 2003a: 14). 'Anti-social behaviour', we were advised, was a 'problem manifested in hundreds of ways and locations, but the effects of each incident were immediate, real and personal. They could be long-lasting, causing distress to individuals and sometimes scarring communities for years afterwards' (Home Office 2003a: 14).

The ministerial foreword to the White Paper, by the then Home Secretary David Blunkett, illustrates a number of key dimensions related to the discursive construction of 'anti-social behaviour'. We were told that the White Paper was 'all about . . . responsibility: an acceptance that anti-social behaviour, *in whatever guise*, is not acceptable and that together we will take the responsibility to *stamp it out*, whenever we come across it' (Home Office 2003a: 3, emphases added). These remarks hinted at the potential elasticity of the 'anti-social behaviour' construct and also served to emphasize the *toughness* which rhetorically underpins the New Labour approach to crime and related forms of social disorder (see also the critiques of the vagueness of the construct in Millie et al. 2005; OEUCHR, 2005). Importantly also, Blunkett maintained:

> We have seen the way communities spiral downwards *once the windows get broken* and are not fixed, graffiti spreads and stays there, cars are left abandoned, streets get grimier and dirtier, youths hanging around street corners intimidating the elderly. The result: crime increases, fear goes up and people feel trapped.
>
> (Home Office 2003a: 3, emphasis added)

These comments refer to key facets of the government's 'case': the notion that 'communities' are apt to 'spiral downwards' if relatively minor infractions and incivilities are not dealt with when they occur. Moreover, the reference to 'broken windows' has particular resonance in the context of the discourse on crime and 'zero tolerance' in the USA (Kelling and Coles 1996; see also Newburn 2002).

The main body of the White Paper began by conceding that 'anti-social behaviour' 'means many things to different people' (Home Office 2003a: 6). Here, notions popularly associated with so-called 'neighbours from hell' (see also Home Office 2007) were alluded to, but also an odd and disparate list of troublesome behaviours was provided which can be located within a range of referential frames:

> Anti-social behaviour means many things to different people – noisy neighbours who ruin the lives of those around them, 'crack houses' run by drug dealers, drunken 'yobs' taking over town centres, people begging by cash-points, abandoned cars, litter and graffiti, young people using airguns to threaten and intimidate or people using fireworks as weapons.
>
> (Home Office 2003a: 6)

Furthermore, 'anti-social behaviour' was presented as fluid and omnipresent and an impression was conveyed that communities were under siege given that it 'can occur anywhere – in people's homes and gardens, on estates in town centres or shopping parades and in urban and rural areas. It blights people's lives, undermines the fabric of society and holds back regeneration' (Home Office 2003a: 6). 'Fundamentally', though, 'anti-social behaviour' was caused by a lack of respect for other people' (Home Office 2003a: 7). Similarly, respect was viewed as 'all important, and this is missing in families that behave dysfunctionally' (Home Office 2003a: 8). This notion, that in some communities there is a respect deficit, was subsequently to emerge as a key New Labour trope following the third Blair victory in 2005 (Blair 2006b; Respect Task Force 2006).[3]

## 'Radical' and 'modern' approaches to 'chaotic families'

As Prime Minister, Blair (2006b) maintained that 'chaotic families lack the basic infrastructure of order' and, more broadly, the identification of this type of family was and remains a pivotal aspect of the New Labour framing of 'anti-social behaviour':

There are a small number of families that can be described as 'dysfunctional'. Two or three families and their wider network of contacts can create havoc on a housing estate or inner city neighbourhood. It is always in areas of greatest disadvantage that this corrosive effect is seen and felt most clearly. Sometimes it occurs where there has been considerable family breakdown; multiple partners can pass through the house; children do not have a positive role model; there is little in the way of a predictable orderly routine; and the lifestyle is such that it makes the lives of neighbours a complete misery. Some professionals have refrained from demanding changes in standards and behaviour from such families, in an effort to remain 'non-judgmental'. This stance alienates those living alongside chaotic families and who legitimately complain that professionals can go home to areas not beset by this kind of misery. It also fails children in dysfunctional families by not asserting their need for care and discipline by their parents.

(Home Office 2003a: 23)

For parents who were unable or unwilling to improve their parenting there was, moreover, a need to consider a more radical strategy: a form of 'preemptive or preventive detention' (Rose 2000). Thus, a 'residential option' would be considered for some parents and their children and a 'residential requirement' could, it was pointed out, be 'attached to Parenting Orders' (Home Office 2003a: 9). However, the government confided: 'We hope that families who are at the stage where only drastic action will work will accept such support voluntarily' (Home Office 2003a: 28–9, emphases added). Given this enthusiasm for the extraordinary 'residential option', the White Paper referred favourably to the influential Dundee Families Project established by the National Children's Home (NCH) Action for Children which will be examined in the next chapter (Home Office 2003a: 28: see also Hill 2007; 'Sinbins scheme for 1,500 antisocial families a year', Guardian, 12 April 2007: 13).

The government also signalled its intention to 'consult on whether to give local authorities an enabling power to withhold payments of housing benefit to tenants where local authorities believe this is the most effective way of tackling anti-social behaviour' (Home Office 2003a: 11). In this context, it would be looking 'at introducing an automatic trigger for Housing Benefit sanctions either in designated geographical areas where this is a problem or once individual anti-social behaviour has reached a particular level and requires enforcement action' (Home Office 2003a: 62).

The White Paper also laid great emphasis on intervening in families and on – a recurring focal theme in the 'transformation' of Children's Services – the early 'identification of children at risk of committing crime or anti-social behaviour' (Home Office 2003a: 8). Hence, work was to continue on developing IRT which, as discussed previously, was targeted at young people viewed as potentially criminal, and on enhancing the commitment and ability of local authority agencies to share information (Home Office 2003a: 22). Reflecting some of the focal preoccupations referred to in the previous chapter, the importance of 'sharing information' was viewed as important in seeking to tackle 'anti-social behaviour' 'effectively' and 'local agencies should disclose relevant information, including personal information, to other relevant authorities in a way that is consistent with legal requirements' (Home Office 2003a: 52). However, and perhaps alluding to the existing legislation on data protection, action against 'unacceptable behaviour' must be 'unfettered by unnecessary bureaucracy' (Home Office 2003a: 74). Technology might also aid 'communities' since local authorities could consider 'lending or buying hand held cameras or diaries so people can collect information on problems' (Home Office 2003a: 66). Indeed, there were 'many examples of good work around the country – small groups are given portable hand held cameras as well as diaries to capture evidence of the perpetrators' (Home Office 2003a: 68).

Significantly, traditional forms of intervention in families (and the professional vocabulary used to describe that intervention) were to be relocated within a discourse fixated with the struggle against 'anti-social behaviour'. Hence, it was envisaged that fostering was to be used as an 'alterative to custody' and as a 'remand' option for the courts.[4] In relation to 'persistent young offenders', the Intensive Supervision and Surveillance Programme (ISSP) would be extended from 6 to 12 months (see Home Office 2003a: 34–5). Readers of the document were also referred to practices in Portsmouth where 'case conferences' were taking place to discuss 'anti-social behaviour', as opposed to child protection concerns which would be the professional norm (Home Office 2003a: 61). The White Paper also asserted that 'positive work with families must always be allied to a clear understanding – by professional agencies and the perpetrators – that the protection of communities must come first' (Home Office 2003a: 29): a notion which appeared to substantially erode, even contradict, the position, contained in the Children Act 1989, that the welfare of the child (or children in the family) must be the 'paramount' consideration.

More generally, unruly young people appeared as the main concern and a picture was painted that 'communities' were under threat from what one senior police officer termed 'feral youths' who had 'no parental control or respect for anybody' ('The trials of living with the feral youths of Salford', *Guardian*, 21 May 2005: 8; see also Garrett 2002a). As the White Paper asserted: 'It is important that communities are not afraid to use parks, playgrounds, streets and shopping centres. Young people gathering together in groups can be very intimidating to the public and trouble does sometimes occur when gangs gather together in the street' (Home Office 2003a: 53). Moreover, it seemed from comments such as this that 'young people' were being constructed as somehow separate, apart and partitioned off from that larger, ambiguous constituency, 'the public'. This approach was, therefore, to result in specific measures which would enable the police to regulate and control young people both spatially (in terms of envisaged new police powers of 'dispersal') and temporally (in terms of 'fast-track child curfew powers') (Home Office 2003a: 53).

As mentioned earlier, in the 1990s, Blair had been critical of Major's targeting of 'beggars'. However, less than ten years later, beggars were another group singled out for criticism, censure and sanctions in New Labour's 'modernization' plans:

> No one in this country should beg – it is degrading for them, embarrass-
> ing for those they approach and often a detriment to the very areas
> where environmental and social improvements are crucial to the broader
> regeneration of the community itself . . . The public feel intimidated by
> people begging at cash points, outside of shops or asking them for
> money in the street of on trains. Using children and pets to make money
> from begging is completely unacceptable.
>
> (Home Office 2003a: 47)

Oddly, given the centrality of 'evidenced based' policies and practices for New
Labour, no convincing evidence was furnished to support these comments.
Where evidence was provided, it remained inconclusive and ambiguous:
members of the public 'often' found 'begging *intimidating*. Results from a
recent survey indicate that 65% of respondents *resented* being approached'
(Home Office 2003b: 16, emphases added). However, beggars, seemingly acting as a brake on the process of 'regeneration' were, in future, to be dealt with
more vigorously by the government. Thus, the Blair government signalled its
intention to make begging recordable under the National Police Records
(Recordable Offences) Regulations 2000. This would 'make begging convictions a part of an individual's criminal record and *enable police forces to fingerprint offenders*. This will not only lead to more appropriate sentencing but also
*will enable the police to keep a track of persistent offenders*' (Home Office 2003a:
47, emphases added).

The government followed up the publication of *Respect and Responsibility*
with *Together – Tackling Anti-Social Behaviour* (Home Office 2003b). This 'action
plan' included the announcement that a 'together academy' was to be set up in
early 2004. This would be a 'centre of excellence on all aspects of tackling the
problem, running training, conferences and specialist master classes for all
relevant practitioners' (Home Office 2003b). The initiative reflected the fact
that tackling 'anti-social behaviour' was 'in many ways . . . a "new discipline"
(Home Office 2003b: 11). Moreover, this rather contentious and fragile idea
has, for some, been built on with the recent setting up postgraduate courses
entirely concerned with the management of 'anti-social behaviour'.[5]

Thus, it seemed, from these and related developments impacting on
children and their families' that a range of urban and social problems, many
rooted in questions related to poverty and other material hardships, was to
be refracted through the 'anti-social behaviour' lens. Here, the chief actors
responsible for promoting ideas associated with 'anti-social behaviour' have
been in political, academic and media fields. In what follows, however,
particular attention will be accorded the first of these locations.

## 'Been there': the ASBO politics of Blunkett

David Blunkett brought to his engagement with the issue very specific types of
symbolic capital. The fact that he is a 'blind man' was associated with his
personal experiential understanding of being 'disadvantaged'. Indeed, this
disability was apt to be used as a form of capital which could be used against
opponents of New Labour's wider 'welfare reform' programme. Thus, in his

subsequent role as Work and Pensions Secretary, it was reported that Blunkett who '*is blind himself*, [insisted his neoliberal plans to remove sick and disabled people off incapacity benefit] should not be seen as a threat to the disabled but as "liberating" their ambitions' ('Blunkett plans clamp on benefits for disabled', *Observer*, 15 May 2005: 11, emphasis added). How, it was implied, could a man for whom 'guide dogs and Braille machines [were] essential tools' (Dudley Edwards 2005: 25) possibly seek to rob the disabled of benefit entitlement?

However, in terms of the political discourse on ASBOs it was Blunkett's former 'tough', 'working class' background – the fact that he had to 'rise from the bottom' (Dudley Edwards 2005: 25) – which acted as a political resource and source of symbolic capital.[6] These experiences (irrespective of their authenticity) were, therefore, crudely deployed by the then Home Secretary and amplified by the media. Blair might have gone to the 'posh' public school, Fettes, but Blunkett 'went to a boarding school for the blind when he was four and had to live off bread and dripping with his widowed mother' (Thomson 2005: 25). On the day that *Respect and Responsibility* was published it was reported, for example, that the White Paper would 'draw on the home secretary's roots' in a working-class community ('Blunkett goes back to his roots to fight disorder', *Guardian*, 12 March 2003: 11).

Responding to critics who argued that intervention and help was more appropriate to deal with the issue of disruptive behaviour, Blunkett – in a manner reminiscent of the style of Norman Tebbit (Conservative Party chairman, 1985–87) – attacked those who still 'argued this garbage from the 1960s and 1970s that you should not be judgemental about anti-social behaviour: You can't be non-judgemental when you live next door to the neighbours from hell' ('Tackle lawless streets or face sack, councils and police told', *Guardian*, 15 October 2003: 4). Similarly, Louise Casey, director of the Anti-Social Behaviour Unit felt able to assert that 'youth workers, social workers and the liberal intelligentsia' who criticized ASBOs were 'not living in the real world' ('Asbo chief rounds on liberal critics', *Guardian*, 10 June 2005: 9). Yet it was Blunkett whose presentation of the case for ASBOs almost entirely pivoted on his rather crude (but perhaps still effective) depiction of his having *been there* (having lived on the troublesome estates where 'anti-social behaviour' was, apparently, rife).

The approach adopted by Blunkett – founded on his own professed working-class *experience* rooted in the *real world* – is one that can also be associated with others seeking to install a more authoritarian and disciplinary politics.[7] Thus, Mary Curran, Scotland's Minister for Communities, the lead minister responsible for carrying through the politics of 'anti-social behaviour', was born, it was claimed, to 'working class parents' (in Holman 2003; see also Tisdall 2006). More theoretically, as Hall et al. (1978: 152) observe, experience 'here, means something specific – primary experience, unmediated by theory, reflection, speculation, argument, etc. It is thought superior to other kinds of argumentation because it is rooted in reality: experience is "real" – speculation and theory are "airy-fairy" '.

Hazel Blears, presently Secretary of State for Communities and Local Government, played a subsidiary role, concentrating on how ASBO politics can reach inside the private sphere, the family. Thus, she was reported as suggesting that parents should enforce sensible bedtimes for children and that they should restore 'structure' to family life by eating meals together ('US-style uniforms for yobs in new disorder crackdown', *Observer*, 15 May 2005: 1–2). Blears also endeavoured to give ASBO politics some degree of intellectual respectability and to locate this preoccupation within the historical current of Labourism. These efforts have focused on her attempt to map out a 'politics of decency' (Blears 2004). In seeking to do this, she also tried to draw on George Orwell and suggested that her *experience* of representing the largely working-class constituency of Salford had informed her perspective.

### Excavating the 'problem family' in an age of 'terrorism' and 'insecurity': the ASBO politics of Blair

Blunkett, therefore, was the prime voice of 'experience' from the 'real world' intent on cleansing the discourse on 'anti-social behaviour' of 'airy-fairy' non-sense. In contrast, Blair can be interpreted as having performed three main functions. The first aspect of his presentation of the ASBO issue was founded upon a combative, *up for it*, masculinity. This is the Blair who has '*battered* the criminal justice system to get it to change' (Blair 2005, emphasis added). He was also the leader of a government which was prepared to be 'firm' and 'tough' and, as Johnson (2004) has rightly maintained, this was an element in the Blairs' relationship with the US administration of Bush. Second, he worked hard to excavate the anachronistic and pernicious 'problem family' construct and to relocate it within twenty-first-century ASBO politics (see also Hall 1960: ch. 10).

In the 1950s many families of the urban poor were characterized as 'problem families' who were, it was maintained, indolent, feckless, dirty and a drain on the resources of the post-war welfare state (see Spinley 1953; Philp and Timms 1957; Welshman 1999a; Starkey 2000). Yet the excavation of the 'problem family' appears to be a project which Blair personally (or perhaps his main speech writers and chief cohort of advisers) had been intent on for many years. In this context, he played a key role in reactivating the construct and repositioning it within New Labour's 'modernization' drive. Indeed, Blair was, for example, apt to use the term even when the party was in still in opposition (see *Guardian*, 26 July 1993) and he was to use it again at the launch of the 'Respect Action Plan' in 2006. This 'plan', the launch of which involved 16 ministers, contained half a dozen references to so-called 'problem families' in just three pages of the document (Respect Task Force 2006: 21–4; see also 'Sinbins for problem families as Blair attacks yob culture', *Guardian*, 11 January 2006: 1). In this context, the earlier *Respect and Responsibility* also drew attention to the Kent Constabulary which has developed a 'problem family manual' (Home Office 2003a: 55). Furthermore, this retrogressive ideological category is continuing to seep into professional exchanges, and media reports on interventions in the lives of children and families (see, for example, 'How problem families learn self-respect', *Observer*, 30 September 2007: 24–6).

The third aspect of Blair's role relates to his ability to deploy the symbolic capital he has accrued on account of his (controversial) role as a 'world states-man'. More specifically, he repeatedly worked to inflate the significance of 'anti-social behaviour' by conflating it with terrorism (see also Guru 2008). This was particularly apparent in Blair's keynote address to the Labour Party conference in 2005 (Blair 2005). Following a section of the speech devoted to 'anti-social behaviour' he moved seamlessly to address 'a new challenge: global terrorism' (Blair 2005).[8] Blunkett also, to some extent, made statements which functioned to blur or conflate the ASBO agenda with that of the 'fight against terrorism'. Thus, he asserted in an interview on the planned introduction of ASBOs, that 'Britain has never been at a more insecure moment . . . I think it is my job to provide some stability and order. Anti-social behaviour is actually at the foundation and root of insecurity' ('Blunkett goes back to his roots to fight disorder', *Guardian*, 12 March 2003: 11).[9] However, it was chiefly Blair who has endeavoured to conflate these two ostensibly distinct domains.

Indeed, this discursive move provides a good example of the type of 'signification spiral' identified by Stuart Hall and his colleagues, in the context of the analysis of 'mugging' (Hall et al. 1978: 223). As they observed the 'signification spiral is a way of signifying events which also intrinsically escalates the threat' (Hall et al. 1978: 223). A key part of this spiral is 'convergence' or 'the linking, by labelling, of . . . [a] specific issue [of concern] to other problems' (Hall et al. 1978: 223). Thus, 'convergence' occurs when 'two or more activities are linked in the process of signification so as to implicitly or explicitly draw parallels between them' (Hall et al. 1978: 223). In the late 1980s, for example, one of Blair's predecessor's, Margaret Thatcher, notoriously converged terrorists, terrorist states, and the left within the trade union movement:

> At one end of the spectrum are the terrorist gangs within our borders and the terrorist states which arm them. At the other are the hard left, operating inside our system, conspiring to use union power and the apparatus of local government to break, defy and subvert the laws. Now the mantle has fallen to us to conserve the very principle of parliamentary democracy and the rule of law itself.
>
> (in Scraton 1987: 161)

Similarly, Blair (and Blunkett), in linking 'anti-social behaviour' and the threat posed by terrorism, endeavoured to equate 'two distinct activities on the basis of their imputed common core' (Hall et al. 1978: 223). There can, of course, 'be real convergences . . . as well as ideological or imaginary ones. However, signification spirals do not depend on a necessary correspondence with real historical developments' (Hall et al. 1978: 224). Moreover, such convergences serve to simplify complex issues which 'would otherwise have to be substantiated by hard argument' (Hall et al. 1978: 224). In this sense the

> use of convergences . . . in the ideological signification of societal conflict has an intrinsic function of escalation. One kind of threat or challenge to society seems larger, more menacing, if it can be mapped together with other, apparently similar, phenomena – especially if, by connecting one relatively harmless activity with a more threatening one, the scale of the danger implicit is made to appear more widespread and diffused.
>
> (Hall et al. 1978: 226)

## Conclusion

All welfare states 'have something to do with the management or regulation of "problem" populations' (Clarke 2004: 1) and this chapter has suggested that the politics of 'anti-social behaviour' illuminate transformations taking place in terms of how such populations and their perceived wrongdoings, incivilities and infractions of the law are interpreted, dealt with and managed (Hillyard et al. 2004). Viewing this in a historical context, it can be maintained that the

> criminologies of the welfare state era tended to assume the perfectibility of man [sic], to see crime as a sign of an under-achieving socialization process, and to look to the state to assist those who had been deprived of the economic, social, and psychological provision necessary for proper social adjustment and law-abiding conduct.
>
> (Garland 2001: 15)

In contrast, the control theories, which encase 'anti-social behaviour' begin

> with a much darker vision of the human condition. They assume that individuals will be strongly attracted to self-serving, anti-social, and criminal conduct unless inhibited from doing so by robust and effective controls, and they look to the authority of the family, the community, and the state to uphold restrictions and inculcate restraint. Where the older criminology demanded more in the way of welfare and assistance, the new one insists upon tightening controls and enforcing discipline.
>
> (Garland 2001: 15)

Perhaps, on a more fundamental and material level, the shift which Garland identifies can be related to how the state seeks to manage and contain those groups whom Rose (2000: 333) dubs the 'usual suspects' – the poor, benefit recipients, petty criminals, discharged psychiatric patients, beggars and so on: those troubling (and troublesome) groups whose prime and defining characteristic is that they are surplus to the requirements of global capital. Indeed, as Millie and his colleagues have observed, in one of the more thoughtful contributions to a usually rather narrow ASBO debate, levels of what has come to be regarded as 'anti-social behaviour' tend to be highest in inner cities, poor council estates and other 'low-income areas – the kinds of neighbourhoods worst affected initially by the decline in the industrial and manufacturing base over the 1970s and 1980s' (Millie et al. 2005: 3). More fundamentally, 'anti-social behaviour' can be interpreted, in part, as a 'screen discourse' (Bourdieu and Wacquant 2001) which is serving to mask the impact of neoliberalism on impoverished communities.

During the period of the Brown administration, confusing signals have been sent on ASBOs: for example, in late 2007 it was decided to terminate the Respect Task Force set up by the previous Prime Minister (see 'Minister's scrap Blair's Respect taskforce', *Guardian*, 12 December 2007: 4; see also 'Every Asbo a failure, says Balls, in break with Blair era on crime', *Guardian*, 28 July 2007: 13). A Youth Taskforce – established in October 2007 – would, it was claimed, seek to 'take the work of the Respect programme to the next stage and put an even greater focus on the twin track approach to promote earlier intervention and more positive activities for young people' (DCSF 2008c). However, the publication of the Youth Crime Action Plan 2008 again highlighted how ASBOs were to remain central within New Labour polity. Indeed, readers of the plan were advised that a 'new national Action Squad of ASB experts will troubleshoot across the country . . . targeting areas that are not using the anti-social behaviour measures available to them' (Home Office 2008: 20).

Approaches to 'anti-social behaviour' are far from uniform across the country: indeed, there are interesting differences between places such as Nottingham and Milton Keynes which highlight how local forces and local practitioners can deflect the intent of centrally devised measures (Burney 2005: ch. 6). However, ASBO politics, now embedded in a 'whole new infra-structure for governance' (Gilling 2007: 129), remain a politics committed to reframing Children's Services and associated fields of activity. So, for example, in one of the 'intensive family support projects' (or 'sinbins'), to be com-mented on in the next chapter, a manager told researchers that his 'project is not anything revolutionary, but simply *welfare support provided through the lens of ASB*' (DCLG 2006: 85, emphasis added). Similarly, a social worker reported that the 'underlying rational' of the project she had contact with, was 'shifting from one of child welfare to one of ASB' (DCLG 2006: 86). If this is occurring (and it seems likely to be so, given that 'anti-social behaviour' is a greedy, consuming discourse) it runs entirely counter to the Children Act 1989 which maintains that the child's welfare is the *paramount* consideration for those working with children and families.[10] Not surprisingly, this has prompted ten-sions between childcare social workers, often seen as a 'barrier to dealing' with' 'anti-social behaviour', and a more punitively inclined housing management (Foord and Young 2006: 170, 177).

More generally, 'ASBO politics' – populist and authoritarian – can be interpreted as part of a wider ideological matrix which is expansionist and seeks to reorientate a range of occupational and professional perspectives. When *Respect and Responsibility* was published, for example, it was argued by the then Home Office minister that the White Paper provided social workers with an 'exciting agenda for working positively with families' (in 'Social work-ers are told they must understand the effects of clients' conduct', *Community Care*, 20–26 March 2003: 14). However, as BASW opposition indicates, this agenda is retrogressive and gives rise to particular forms of intervention, tar-geted at 'failed citizens, anti-citizens, comprised of those who are unable or unwilling to enterprise their lives or manage their own risk, incapable of exer-cising responsible self-government' (Rose 2000: 331). In short, it is a role which is narrow, constrained (and constraining) and entirely at odds with the more progressive aspects of the profession's ethical base. This is a theme which is examined further in the next chapter.

**Reflection and talk box 6**

Why did 'anti-social behaviour' become such a key theme for New Labour?

Can you identify ways in which concern about 'anti-social behaviour' and 'security' or even 'terrorism' have been conflated or blurred?

Do you feel that 'ASBO politics' is having an impact on the 'transformation' of Children's Services? If so, how and in what ways?

Is there a leading group of policy-makers and/or practitioner group more intent on 'pushing the ASBO agenda' than others? If so, why should this be the case?

The Children Act 1989 states that the welfare of the child in the 'paramount consideration'. However does a fixation with 'anti-social behaviour' dilute this orientation to child welfare practice? Can you identify any instances where this might have occurred? Can you think of any instances – perhaps in your work with children and families – where 'paramouncy' won out over an approach more concerned with combating 'anti-social behaviour'? To what do you attribute this?

Is the question of gender significant either in terms of those defining 'anti social behaviour' or in terms of those identified as being responsible for such behaviour?

Are there connections between 'anti-social behaviour' and neoliberalism: more specifically, what was referred to, in Chapter 2, as 'accumulation by dispossession'?

Why did the Brown administration opt to disband the Respect Task Force?

What other words and phrases, central to the 'transformation' of Children's Services', can be analysed in the way we have examined the construction of 'anti-social behaviour'?

How does the use of keywords and phrases contribute to ruling blocs constructing hegemony and 'winning hearts and minds' (see also Chapter 2) for 'transforming' practices?

# 7 'Problem families' and 'sinbin' solutions

As observed in the previous chapter, the 'problem family' – the discursive antithesis of the vaunted 'hardworking family' – has been re-excavated by New Labour and located at the centre of the drive against 'anti-social behaviour' (Home Office 2007). In some senses, within New Labour's referential frameworks, 'problem families' are, perhaps, positioned and perceived as being from another age: living anachronisms, 'anti-modern', seemingly 'out of time' families that are unable or unwilling to exhibit a commitment to be self-activating and responsibilized neoliberal citizens. Furthermore, 'problem families' remain an important component within the complex constellation of discourses, policies and programmes which are focused on the 'transformation' of services for children and families.

Associated with re-emergence of the 'problem family' is also a drive, contained in the Respect Action Plan, published in early 2006, to put in place a network of 'intensive family support' projects, the so-called 'sinbins'.[1] The then Prime Minister reaffirmed that his administration was to 'bear down uncompromisingly on anti-social behaviour' (Respect Task Force 2006: 1). Furthermore, as mentioned early, the 'problem family' appeared to be the central focus of concern.[2] Moreover, it was to become 'mandatory' for local authorities to establish IFSPs modelled on those in Dundee and similar projects located in the north of England (Respect Task Force 2006: 22). It was maintained, therefore, that the government would 'roll out schemes which "*grip*" problem households and the array of services involved with them and change their behaviour' (Respect Task Force 2006: 21, emphasis added).

ADSS responded that many councils were facing 'radical cuts' in family support services ('Sinbins for problem families as Blair attacks yob culture', *Guardian*, 11 January 2006: 1). Thus, it was implied, the IFSPs might be something of a distraction and drain on resources (see also Foord and Young 2006: 181). Indeed, it was reported elsewhere that there was a £600 million funding shortfall in Children's Services ('Children's groups warn punishment not a panacea', *Guardian*, 11 January 2006: 7). However, mainstream comment and opinion on the Respect Action Plan was largely favourable. The *Guardian*, in an editorial, criticized the launch speech of Blair, but felt that the 40-page plan was 'well-written, succinctly argued and packed with sensible approaches to a complex social problem' ('Beyond the boundary', *Guardian*, 11 January 2006: 28).

This chapter – likewise – implicitly acknowledges the potential usefulness of 'outreach' provision for families encountering difficulties; indeed, this used to be called 'local authority social work' and was not situated within a damaging and delimiting 'anti-social behaviour' discourse. However, in what follows, it is maintained that the 'sinbins' plan is a retrogressive development and needs to be viewed in the context of debates which took place on the 'problem family', in England and elsewhere in Europe, in the past. That is, in order to better understand the contemporary construction of the 'problem family', and some of the organizing principles related to the inception and proliferation of the IFSPs, there is a need to 'look backwards' and to have regard to when the 'problem family' first emerged as a focus for intervention. In the 1930s, for example, projects in England and elsewhere also set out to create what were viewed, at the time, as 'pioneer' residential units. More theoretically, this willingness to look backwards is important because it can prompt a 'rupture' from dominant, taken-for-granted ways of understanding. Indeed, one 'of the most powerful instruments of rupture lies in the social history of problems, objects, and instruments of thought' (Bourdieu and Wacquant 2004: 238). Thus, it vital to try and retrace 'the history of the *emergence* of these problems, of their progressive constitution' (Bourdieu and Wacquant 2004: 238, original emphasis).

Next, the chapter examines the first two research reports which have been undertaken to evaluate the IFSPs, particularly the residential components of such schemes (Dillane et al. 2001; Nixon et al. 2006). Here it is suggested that the reports are, perhaps, lacking in reflexive hesitancy and insufficiently critical. More fundamentally, the intention is to try to bring the 'undiscussed' into discussion and to focus on what can be interpreted as ambiguous, unconvincing, unfinished, omitted and insufficiently stressed facets within these research publications. It is, moreover, important to dwell on the *hidden* aspects of this research – the missing words – because a message is now being conveyed, by at least one of these studies, that 'overwhelmingly those families interviewed were positive about the effects of the projects on their lives' (Nixon et al. 2006: 59). Furthermore, it is also argued that academic researchers, frequently funded by government grants when investigating 'social problems', need perhaps to retain a certain wariness and scepticism before providing research 'products' which seem largely to endorse, the policy and practice 'solutions' which the state, never independent of class relations and committed to the maintenance existing economic relationships and associated patterns of social regulation, has formulated. Indeed, if there is a failure to interrogate IFSPs, these establishments – which seem to erode any sense of authentic citizenship on the part of residents located in the residential units – could quickly become mundane, predictable and commonplace mechanisms for dealing with 'problem families'.

## The state, 'social problems' and the backward glance

As mentioned in the previous chapter, every society, at different moments in history, constructs a series of social problems 'taken to be legitimate, worthy of being debated' (in Bourdieu and Wacquant, 2004: 236, original emphasis). In this context the state also fulfils a key role because through 'the structuring it imposes on practices, the State institutes and inculcates common symbolic forms of thought, social frames of perception or memory, State forms of classification or, more precisely, practical schemes of perception, appreciation and action' (Bourdieu 2000: 175). Furthermore, 'problems that are taken for granted in a given social universe are those that have the greatest chances of being awarded grants' (in Bourdieu and Wacquant 2004: 240).

These comments may, therefore, illuminate what may be taking place in terms of the construction of the 'problem family' and the strategies – specifically IFSPs – which are being initiated, researched and highlighted as the response to it. For example, in seeking to generate support for what might appear to be a more punitive approach to such families, research findings (frequently emanating from projects funded by the state and embedded in the discursive frames of reference promoted by the state) are being deployed to support the direction of policy. Indeed, 'evidence-based' research and practice seemed to be an important element in the plan to establish the national network of 50 IFSPs (Respect Task Force 2006: 22). Thus it was maintained that the influential project in Dundee was successful in 84 per cent of cases (Respect Task Force 2006: 22).[3] A study, undertaken by a research team mostly based at Sheffield Hallam University (Nixon et al. 2006), which examined 'six similar projects' in the north of England also revealed that in '82% of cases studied, there was a reduction in the level of complaints, and that 95% of families, *where data is available*, achieved *housing stability*' (Respect Task Force 2006: 22, emphases added).

Neither of these two reports resorts to the term 'problem family'. Moreover, both of the publications are complex and cannot be crudely interpreted as *entirely* amplifying a New Labour 'message' on 'anti-social behaviour' and the 'sinbins'. That is, these reports should not be crudely interpreted as simple and uncomplicated narratives of successful policy implementation and practice. Nonetheless, the two reports need to be critically scrutinized. At this stage, one significant omission in the researchers' presentation of the issue can be identified: the failure to locate the various and proliferating residential schemes in a historical context. On account of this lacuna, it can, therefore, be argued that these research reports reveal a certain 'forgetfulness', perhaps a lack of patience with the past. However, a brief backward glance refutes the notion that, in truth, these New Labour schemes and the classifications in which they are embedded are, in fact, truly 'pioneer'. John Macnicol (1987), for example, has traced the various formulations, or ideological categories, constructed to identify and classify an 'undeserving' segment of the population in the late nineteenth century and twentieth centuries Hence, 'industrial residuum', 'social problem groups', 'problem families', 'underclass', even the 'new rabble' have all been deployed (Stedman Jones 1984). Each shifting conceptualization refers to essentially the same alleged behaviour traits (fecklessness, lack of foresight) of the group identified. Importantly also, each of these classifications were suffused with biological metaphors of breeding and generation and it was the family which was identified as the prime location which served to produce and reproduce social characteristics which polluted the wider public domain.

In this context, therefore, the 'problem family' invites particular attention because of its reactivation and reification by New Labour. For example, the Wood Committee, set up in 1926 and reporting in 1929 referred to the 'social problem group'. However, it was the publication of *Our Towns* by the Women's Group on Public Welfare (1943) which led to the 'problem family' becoming a commonplace term in academic, political and other public discourses (Hall 1960; see also Blacker 1952; Spinley 1953; Philp and Timms 1957). The study, which sold well, was undertaken as a result of a resolution from the National Federation of Women's Institutions deploring the conditions of English town life revealed by evacuation (Welshman 1999a; 1999b). Significant, for the authors was the notion that there was a 'submerged tenth' and, among these were 'problem families'; that is, families 'always on the edge of pauperism, crime, riddled with mental and physical defects, and in and out of the courts for child neglect, a menace to the community' (in Hall 1960: 157).[4] What is more, these families were perceived as a breeding ground for 'juvenile delinquency' (Welshman, 1999b: 795). Frequently, it was the 'feckless' mother of the 'problem family' who was identified as the chief obstacle and impediment on account of her failure to be appropriately domesticated (Starkey 2000).

Associated with the identification of the 'problem family' was also an interest in what New Labour now refers to as the 'residential option' (Respect Task Force 2006). In this context, commentators and policy analysts looked to Europe and Penelope Hall (1960), in her popular guide to social services in 'modern' England, referred to some of the experiments being conducted in the Netherlands. In Rotterdam, 'socially weak' families were, she noted, transferred to a group of dwellings called the Zuidplein Project which housed 570 families. Here, they were ' "re-educated" socially with a view to rehousing among normal families in another part of town' (Hall 1960: 166). Experiments along similar lines had also been conducted in Utrecht and Amsterdam with 'special camps established for the "anti-social" in Drenthe and Hilversum'.[5] Reflecting, in part, the eugenicist thinking underpinning these schemes, Hall (1960: 166) confided:

> Families so separated from the normal community are regarded as 'diseased biological units, social deterioration being the chief symptom of the disease' and it is considered proper that for the sake of society in general, such families should be removed to an environment where they are protected against their own inadequacies and there is a chance for the children to develop.

(See also Hauss and Ziegler 2008.)

Special legislation had, moreover, been formulated 'which would enable the authorities to place "anti-social" families under supervision, and, should that prove fruitless, in a re-education camp' (Hall 1960: 166). The Women's Group on Public Welfare did not feel that policy in England should replicate that of the Netherlands, but Hall was more favourably disposed towards these European initiatives because 'the Dutch experiments, however we may criticise them, at least show an awareness of the problem and determination to take active measures against it' (Hall 1960: 167). This was because 'problem families' were 'a continual drain on the man – and money – power of social services . . . and their presence in our midst lowers the whole tone of neighbourhood and community life' (Hall 1960: 167).

Although not referred to in Hall's discussion, what is striking about the initiatives in the Netherlands, is how closely they resemble some of the initiatives taken by the National Socialists in Germany in the 1930s. In this context, a number of social historians have examined responses to 'asocial families' and other 'social outcasts' after the party seized power (see, for example, Pine 1995; Evans 2001; Gellately and Stoltzfus 2001; Wachsmann 2001). 'Asocials' were portrayed as the 'dregs of society' who were marked by 'weakness of character', 'lack of restraint', 'loose morals', 'disinterest in contemporary events', 'idleness' and 'poverty of mind'. The term was applied in a flexible manner to include 'large families' that were 'inferior', 'criminals', 'idlers', 'good for nothings' and 'wastrels' (Pine 1995: 182). Essentially, ' "performance" and "success in social life" were the yardsticks by which the "value of individuals and families" were measured' (Pine 1995: 183). Many 'asocials', however, failed to achieve an adequate level of 'performance' and 'success' in social life, and were sterilized in accordance with the Law for the Prevention of Hereditarily Diseased Offspring of 14 July 1933.

Lisa Pine has performed vital scholarly work in excavating the history of Hasude, an experimental 'asocial colony' set up by the welfare authorities to establish whether or not 'asocial families' could 'be socially engineered into "valuable members of the national community" ' (Pine 1995: 183–4). Families had no choice in deciding whether or not they were sent to the facility which consisted of 84 family houses, an administration building, a bathing area and children's home. They could find themselves sent there if they had, for example, been responsible for 'begging' or 'disturbing community life' (Pine 1995: 188). Once sent to Hasude, the leader of the colony played a vital role: they had 'to have a "strong character", which corresponded with the National Socialist *Fuhrer-Prinzip* or "leadership principle" ' (Pine 1995: 191). A key task of the leader was, therefore, to get a grip on individual families, to ensure that they obeyed the rules of the colony and to facilitate, if this was warranted, their integration back into the community. At 'worst, serious and repeated flouting of house rules could lead to being placed in concentration camps by the police' (Pine 1995: 193). Within these camps the 'asocials' were identifiable because of the 'black triangle' they were compelled to wear (Wachsmann 2001: 180).

Prior to examining some of the reported operational modalities of the emerging network of residential units for 'problem families' in contemporary England – and Scotland – it needs to be emphasized that what is *not* being suggested here is that the new 'residential options' seek to replicate those set up by the National Socialists. In plainly avoiding such a highly misguided and foolish interpretation, it nonetheless appears important to remind ourselves what was encompassed within the discourse on the 'problem family' in England, and elsewhere in Europe, in the not too distant past. Furthermore, Theodor Adorno's comment that 'the survival of National Socialism *within* democracy' is 'more menacing than the survival of fascist tendencies *against* democracy' appears pertinent (Adorno 2003: 4, original emphasis). Writing in a West German context, he stated: 'National Socialism lives on, and even today we still do not know whether it is merely the ghost of what was so monstrous that it lingers on after its own death, or whether it has not yet died at all' (Adorno 2003: 3; see also Bauman 1991). Perhaps these remarks encourage us, therefore, to try to remain watchful for the ghost within contemporary neoliberalism and its chosen modes of governance. Indeed, Adorno might encourage us to remain alert and attentive to some of the ways that *thinking* about, *describing* and *acting* upon the 'problem family', during a period stretching from the 1930s into the 1960s, may be informing the 'new', 'transformed' and 'modern' ways of working with troublesome families (see also Kunstreich 2003).

## Promoting the 'empowerment' of families: the Dundee Families Project

The Dundee Families Project (DFP) was established, in 1996, with Urban Programme funding to 'assist families' who are homeless or at severe risk of homelessness as a result of 'anti-social behaviour' (Dillane et al. 2001: 1). The Project is run by NCH Action for Children Scotland in partnership with Dundee Council Housing and Social Work Departments. It operates from premises on the St Mary's housing estate in Dundee and provides 'a range of individual, couple, family and group work interventions' (Dillane et al. 2001: 1). The service is offered in three main ways: admission to the core block, which comprises accommodation for up to four families; support to a small number of dispersed flats run by the Project, mainly for families to move into from the 'core block'; an outreach service provided to selected families in their existing accommodation, where they are at risk of eviction by the City Council due to 'anti-social behaviour' (Dillane et al. 2001: 1).

Dillane et al. (2001), based at Centre for Child & Society and the Department of Urban Studies at the University of Glasgow, undertook an evaluation of the DFP for the period stretching from May 1999 to 2001. The research team accessed the records of 69 families (11 who had resided in the 'core block') and interviewed 20 families (only four of which either were or had been in the 'core block') (Dillane et al. 2001: 38, 55). With this latter group of families, there were, moreover, only seven individuals interviewed (Dillane et al. 2001: 55). Elements of the evaluation which appear to invite comment include at least three themes: the characteristics of the families in contact with the DFP; the problematic 'anti-social behaviour' label attached to the families; the constraints and restrictions, nonetheless, placed on those families living in the 'core block'. These themes, in fact, provide the foundation for the chapter's discussion on both this and the more recent research report by Nixon et al. (2006).

The DFP faced a good deal of opposition from local residents who organized themselves into the St Mary's Action Group, and a local councillor stated that the launch of the project, initially located inside perimeter fencing, was a 'public relations disaster' (in Mitchell 1996: 18; see also Dillane et al. 2001: 11) However, by the time the research was undertaken it was maintained that the relationships with the local community had been transformed and the DFP enjoyed a much better profile. Indeed, by

> 2001 the coverage was unanimously positive. . . . This led to the project being cited in the Westminster Government's Social Exclusion Unit report on Anti-Social Behaviour as an innovative and ground-breaking idea that others were urged to follow . . . The Chartered Institute of Housing also conferred a 'Good Practice' award . . . Interestingly, while the public profile of the project had changed positively, some of the stakeholder interviewees felt that the image of the project to potential users had become more negative.
>
> (Dillane et al. 2001: 14)

The most striking family characteristics relate to poverty and ill-health. 'Virtually all the families were poor. Where information was available on family income, this almost always indicated reliance on state benefits' (Dillane et al. 2001: 41). In terms of the 20 families interviewed, eight comprised 'individuals with physical health problems or impairments'. In

> one family, 2 sons had heart problems. One was born with 17 holes in his heart and the other with a heart murmur. Whilst the boys were able to have a normal life their condition had to be closely monitored. The daughter was born with a cleft palate and had had several operations to correct this, but it left quite a pronounced speech impediment, coupled with feelings of low self-esteem.
>
> (Dillane et al. 2001: 57)

In a different family,

> one of the girls had been born with cerebral palsy. She required someone constantly present to help out with her daily routine and to monitor progress. Another girl developed kidney problems at an early age. She had had several operations to help overcome the problem, but these proved unsuccessful. The youngest daughter was born 7 weeks premature and suffered from nocturnal enuresis. In another family, the youngest son was diagnosed with leukaemia when he was 3 years old. As a result of the high level of care required, the son was looked after by the local authority for a period of several years. He was later returned to the family home when the cancer was in remission. The youngest daughter suffered from an eating problem, where she was unable to eat any solids.
>
> (Dillane et al. 2001: 57)

In another family,

> the mother and her 2 daughters had epilepsy. This required regular medication and close monitoring. The youngest daughter was also acutely deaf and had to wear hearing aids. Finally, there were 2 other

families identified whose children were believed to have epilepsy due to the blank spells they had experienced.

(Dillane et al. 2001: 57)

Half the mothers (10 out of 20) were prescribed anti-depressants; four fathers said that they suffered from depression and three of them had been prescribed anti-depressants (Dillane et al. 2001: 58). Fourteen young people interviewed (70 per cent) stated that they had been bullied at school (Dillane et al. 2001: 58). A high percentage of the children in contact with the DFP had, moreover, been the victims of child abuse (Dillane et al. 2001: 58).

Millie et al. (2005: 2), in an exploration of 'anti-social behaviour strategies', have pointed to the lack of 'conceptual clarity' when the issue of 'anti-social behaviour' is deployed in political and policy discourses. The staff working in the DFP, in part colluding with the reification of 'anti-social behaviour', also expressed concern about the utility of the label being attached to the families they attempted to engage with:

> There was a consensus among the staff that the term anti-social behaviour (ASB), as used by the referring agencies, was too broad and problematic . . . Staff believed that often the ASB reported by the referring person was a manifestation of other problems in the family or their circumstances, which only became apparent when further information was gained after the referral . . . Staff also expressed concern about the impact of applying the label anti-social behaviour, which families understandably experienced as stigmatising. It was expressed that ASB is like a form of 'racism' with the consequences being very hard to live down. Whether the term is applied explicitly or not, families feel they have to prove that they are not anti-social, rebuild trust and improve their reputation. Removing the stigma is very difficult and even when improvements occur they may be hard to demonstrate. One staff member remarked that 'with an alcoholic you can readily see the change but with someone that is ASB you cannot readily see change'. Another comment was that the term could apply to anyone at some point, even herself as she occasionally shouts at her children. Most staff said that it was not helpful or appropriate to use the term outside the staff group, but recognised there was a need to name what they were dealing with. One suggestion was to place a time limit on the application of the term to a particular family.
>
> (Dillane et al. 2001: 28)

The 'beauty of empowerment is that is that it appears to reject the logics of patronizing dependency that infused earlier modes of expertise. Subjects are to do the work themselves, not in the name of conformity, but to make them free' (Rose 2000: 334). Perhaps predictably, according to NCH literature, one of the foundational aims of the DFP is, therefore, to promote the 'empowerment' of families (NCH Action for Children Scotland 1995: 1). However, families who find themselves in the 'core block' at the DFP have restrictions placed on their liberty. Thus, although these restrictions are not legally enforceable, they are manifested in temporal and spatial frameworks being imposed which seek to address 'anti-social' tendencies.

Families who worked with the DFP did so 'due to a combination of "*persuasion and coercion*" ' (Dillane et al. 2001: 21, original emphasis). Once admitted to the 'core block', for example, many of the 'interviewees commented that the regime was fairly strict . . . Residents were expected to comply with the project's detailed rules and guidelines' (Dillane et al. 2001: 25). Thus the researchers were advised by a staff member:

> We have a set of boundaries – we call them – and they are in the information pack that goes to everyone. We have basic rules and that's about *visitors being out by 11 o'clock at night. You know, we're not chapping on the door at 11 o'clock at night, but that's something people sign up to when they come.* And that's around the needs of the children and them not being disrupted and them being in their bed and all that kind of stuff. Some families have additional *guidelines imposed* such as, if we think you are using alcohol inappropriately when your children are there, then an additional condition is that we will come at all times, or at variable times and check. But that's all up front and families know that.
>
> (Dillane et al. 2001: 25, emphases added)

Some of the families clearly resented the amount of 'supervision' and intrusion to which they were subjected in the 'core block'. However, compliance may, perhaps, have been forthcoming because there was a lack of housing alternatives available. One family, for example:

> [L]eft a few months afterwards and F [a worker in contact with the family] felt that their stay there 'did not turn out terribly well'. The family did not like being there and found the staff 'overly intrusive'. For instance, they were having what they regarded as a 'normal row' which any family might have and a staff member came banging on the door. The family expected the work to be focused on their housing situation not their personal relationships.
>
> (Dillane et al. 2001: 26)

The role of the police was also apparent in terms of the day-to-day running of the DFP and this can be perceived as, perhaps, adding to the 'control' dimension of the project's activities. The

> police had both a formal and an informal role. On a formal basis, the Project had an information-sharing protocol with the police . . . However, informally, the community police officer would offer advice and carry out training sessions with the staff. The community police officer saw himself as being 'integrated' with the Project and visited on a weekly basis. . . .
>
> (Dillane et al. 2001: 85–6)

The statement that the DFP is proving to be 'successful' should, perhaps, also be examined. For example, not all the 'cases' referred to the project were accepted. From late 1996 to a third of the way through 2000 there were 126 referrals, yet only 69 (55 per cent) of these were accepted (Dillane et al. 2001: 36). This appears to be potentially important because it suggests that those referrals not 'accepted' could still, within the DFP's frame of reference, be causing difficulties for others within their communities. Moreover, it could be that the DFP and similar projects might simply be working with those families who could be regarded as the most compliant or least able to resist coercion. In addition, there appears, according to the research team, to be a high proportion of re-referrals. Thus, included 'in the 126 referrals, were 25 re-referrals, accounting for 20 per cent of the overall referrals. These resulted from 12 families being referred twice and one family on 3 separate occasions' (Dillane et al. 2001: 39). Thus, and without dwelling on the ambiguity of 'success', it could be maintained that this sizeable number of re-referrals undermines the idea that such projects are as successful as the government maintains.

A number of the professionals' comments on the DFP are also, at best, ambiguous. The Social Work Department, for example, was one of the 'prime instigators of the project', but social workers were reported to hold 'mixed views' on the DFP. There 'were some positive comments about the work of the project and the improvements that it had made to families. However, other social workers . . . expressed views that, in some cases, child-care and parenting skills had not improved as a result of the projects' intervention' (Dillane et al. 2001: 84). Despite the less than emphatic success of DFP, it has been the foundation for a range of similar projects (see also Table 7.1).

**Table 7.1** 'Pioneers' the initial Intensive Family Support Projects (IFSPs)[6]

| Name of project | Type of intervention |
| --- | --- |
| Dundee Families Project | A core residential block for up to 4 families<br>Outreach support for an unspecified number of families |
| Sheffield High Support Service | Core residential unit for up to 3 families<br>Support for 14 other tenancies |
| Manchester Foundations Project | Includes a core residential unit for up to 4 families<br>Outreach service for 23 families |
| Bolton Families Project | Includes a residential unit for 2 families<br>Outreach support for 16 families |
| Salford ASSFAM Families Project | Planned to include a core residential unit in 2005<br>Outreach service for 10–20 families |
| Oldham Families Project | No residential element<br>Outreach service only for 12 families |
| Blackburn with Darwen Families Project | No residential element<br>Outreach service only for between 12 and 19 families |

## Getting a 'grip' on the 'anti-social family': examining the 'pioneers'

The report of Nixon et al. (2006) was published by the Office of the Deputy Prime Minister and it examined a number of 'pioneering' project set up in northern towns and cities to respond to what the researchers term the 'anti-social family' (Nixon et al. 2006: 43). These projects were initiated largely as a result of the government funding IFSPs in the context of the drive against 'anti-social behaviour', and the six projects which are the focus of the study appear to have been heavily influenced by the DFP. The authors state that, at the time they completed their interim report, there were eight projects in England and Wales. However, only six were selected because one was already in the process of being evaluated, another was only in the very initial stages of development (Nixon et al. 2006: 13; see also National Children's Homes 2006).

Five of the six projects have been developed by NCH (North West) in partnership with local authorities in Blackburn with Darwen, Bolton, Manchester, Oldham and Salford. These projects are located in 'peripheral social housing locations' with 'inadequate public transport links' (Nixon et al. 2006: 17): the sixth project, set up in the research team's own city by Sheffield City Council, is found in a 'leafy suburban location of mixed tenure' (Nixon et al. 2006: 67). The services provided, within each of the projects, tend to comprise both 'outreach' support and 'intensive support' which is available within 'core' residential units (see also Table 7.1). However, when the research was being undertaken we are informed that only the projects in Bolton, Manchester and Sheffield included the latter component, although there were plans for a 'core' residential unit to be included within the scheme, still in the process of development when the research was undertaken, in Salford. When the evaluation was taking place it would seem, therefore, that there was room for a maximum of only nine families across the six projects.

The evaluative exercise drew 'on "closed files" to provide a statistical profile of 99 families consisting of 131 adults and 259 children under the age of 18, who had worked with the six projects up to July 2004' (Nixon et al. 2006: 18). In-depth interviews took place with one or more of five families supported by projects operating in Bolton, Oldham, Manchester, Salford and Sheffield: in Blackburn 'only four families were interviewed due to problems encountered in securing an interview with a fifth family' (Nixon et al. 2006: 13). In 'total, therefore, 29 families agreed to take part in the study of which 23 were being provided with outreach support and [only] six were living in core residential accommodation at the time of the interview' (Nixon et al. 2006: 13): a research strategy which would seem to be significant because it means that representatives from only ten families who were living or had lived in the 'core' accommodation cumulatively featured in this and the DFP study. However, despite only a small group of families in this type of accommodation having been the focus of research, this approach to the 'problem family' is, under the Respect Action Plan (Respect Task Force 2006) now to proliferate.

Pat Starkey (2000), in her historical work on the 'problem family', has observed that, despite the term being used, what was really meant was 'problem mother'. Significantly, in terms of the characteristics of the twenty-first century families that the 'pioneer' projects had contact with, one of the main findings (which is not satisfactorily explored by the research team) is that they also are 'intensively' intervening into the lives of mothers. Seventy-eight per cent of the adults receiving services from the schemes were women and 'eight out of ten families were headed by a lone parent woman' (Nixon et al. 2006: 18). Where the ethnicity of the users of services could be identified from records, over 94 per cent of users of the projects' services were classified as 'white British'. Reflecting some of the findings from the Dundee study, these families were often ill. In '39% of families one or more member of the household were identified as having mental health problems most commonly depression related illnesses': members of 'more than one in five families were affected by chronic physical ill health such as asthma' (Nixon et al. 2006: 22, 6). The families also tended to be relatively large since on 'average there were at least two children per family, with one in five (22%) consisting of four or more children including two families with eight children' (Nixon et al. 2006: 18). Thus, by far the main target group for the projects would seem to be lone female parents, heading relatively large families, who are 'white', poorly or having to respond to the ill-health of others. Furthermore, Nixon et al. (2006: 26) concede, despite the 'high support needs' of these families, 'many of which had not been adequately addressed at the point of referral . . . there was found to be little consistency or pattern to the ways in which families came to be labelled "anti-social" '.

As with the DFP, classifications such as 'problem family' and 'anti-social family' failed to encompass the complexity of the families' predicament. For example, in 'just over a quarter of families (27%) it was specifically the behaviour of the children rather than the adult family members which caused concern' (Nixon et al. 2006: 29). Indeed, the researchers refer to 'the complex multi-layered reality of anti-social behaviour' and note that many families and agencies were reluctant to use the term 'anti-social' because it was counterproductive (Nixon et al. 2006: 32). However, the Sheffield based academics seem somewhat insensitive to their respondents' insights because they then go on to refer to 'anti-social families' (Nixon et al. 2006: 43) or, in a more recent report, simply 'ASB families' (DCLG 2006: 10). Furthermore, a key theme which emerges from the evaluation of the six projects in the north of England is that many of these families seem themselves, to have been the *victims* of harassment.

> In just under one in five cases (19%) it was reported that family members had been the victim of anti-social behaviour by others. It should be noted that families were not systematically asked whether they had been victims of anti-social behaviour and it is therefore likely that project case file records underestimate the scale of the problem. The finding, however, does indicate that one of the ways in which anti-social behaviour differs from usual models of criminal behaviour is that an individual can be simultaneously both a victim and a perpetrator of nuisance behaviour.
>
> (Nixon et al. 2006: 23)

Nixon et al. (2006: 24) add:

For a small number of interviewees, the alleged anti-social behaviour they had endured was serious in nature and included racial harassment and threats of violence, and had resulted in families being rehoused. The severity of the behaviour had contributed to health problems among family members. One woman, a single mother with three sons, all subject to ASBOs and all of whom had been the subject of local publicity campaigns, described how the local community had undertaken a course of harassment against her family in order to force them to leave their home. The police believed that the family were indeed at considerable risk of harm and recommended that the family be rehoused.[7]

However, such families felt that 'because they had been labelled "anti-social" their views were not taken seriously' (Nixon et al. 2006: 24). It is, therefore, hardly surprising that one of the respondents felt that the residential unit they were acquainted with felt like 'a place of safety' and that it 'instils a sense of security' (Nixon et al. 2006: 51). However, it is also maintained that 'a number of families' 'enjoyed' living in the 'core accommodation':

> What was perhaps an unexpected finding is that a number of families interviewed said they *enjoyed* the core accommodation . . . Although living in core accommodation brings with it restrictions on freedom, paradoxically, this enabled some families more freedom than they experienced previously. In some cases families had previously lived within environments characterised by risk, vulnerability and volatility and as a consequence, living in core accommodation enabled service users to feel safe.
>
> (Nixon et al. 2006: 51, emphasis added)

As mentioned earlier, some members from only six families who had spent time in the 'core accommodation' were interviewed and no responses are provided to substantiate the notion that 'a number' of families 'enjoyed' the period when they lived in the projects.

Turning to the constraints placed on those families it is, however, apparent that many respondents felt highly pressurized because of the 'restrictions' which the projects put in place. This is evidenced in the way in which referrals and admissions occurred. Families could have declined 'support', but referrers and project staff conceded that the actual 'choice' families had was very constrained and a 'fully informed decision to accept a referral . . . seemed rare' (Nixon et al. 2006: 40); particularly given that many families felt that if they did not accept a referral then an ASBO could be applied for, or a family might already have someone subject to an ASBO and they could be facing eviction. In this context, however, housing referrers were clear that in some instances, 'they were *unable* to collect the evidence they needed to start legal proceedings and so their only option, as they saw it, was the project' (Nixon et al. 2006: 37, emphasis added). That is, the existence of these projects provided a new disciplinary mechanism *beyond* due process of law which made some tenants 'wake up and smell the coffee' (Nixon et al. 2006: 37).

Indeed, the evaluation of these 'pioneer' projects suggests that many families likely to be headed by lone female parents were coerced and hood-winked at the point of referral. This is reflected in the comments of one parent, in Oldham, who was left uncertain who was speaking to them and what their powers amounted to:

> At first because she was at the Police Station, I didn't know what to expect. I didn't know whether she was a social worker, I didn't know whether she worked for the police, I didn't know whether she worked for social services. I didn't know who she worked for, I didn't know where she'd come from and I was a bit taken aback at first, cos I thought, why, why, why is it that I need help, are they trying to tell me that I need help cos I can't control him?[8]

(Nixon et al. 2006: 40)

All the projects examined were committed to promoting a 'positive lifestyle', 'social inclusion' and 'well-being' (Nixon et al. 2006: 16–18). However, the dominant approach, within the 'core accommodation' seems to be one of infantilizing the adults. The five NCH projects profess to have a practice methodology, based on 'narrative therapy', yet there was little evidence of this from service user interviews (Nixon et al. 2006: ch. 6). Instead, much of the emphasis, as in the DFP, would seem to be placed on the containment and surveillance of families:

> Families in core accommodation are required to adhere to a set of rules and regulations which vary between projects but which usually comprise of a *requirement* for children and adults to be in the accommodation at a set time in the evening; restricted access in and out of the project building where the flats are located; visitors by *permission* only; together with specific rules deemed *appropriate* for particular families.

(Nixon et al. 2006: 51, emphases added)

One respondent confided:

> I mean at first it was a bit of a shock having to stay in at ten o' clock. They changed the time, it was eleven o' clock they told me, then they said it was ten o' clock. But I mean that the first month I got that many warnings, cos you can't get in on time. And it's hard to . . . you've got to change into a routine. If they gave you a bit more time to get the routine going yourself. I mean from day one it was like . . . god, it was like a prison, you know what I mean? But I'm used to it now, sort of thing. I don't go anywhere.

(Nixon et al. 2006: 51)

Thus, the focus of project staff in the 'core accommodation' is placed on schooling families to accept new temporal frameworks and staff monitoring: 'For example, most families are visited each morning to ensure that they are out of bed and that the children are ready for school, and the NCH projects provide several observation visits during the day' (Nixon et al. 2006: 51). It is concluded, in a contorted and perhaps self-censoring, paragraph:

> Many families described how they found the rules strict and difficult to live by at first but had *gradually* become accustomed to them over time.

What's more the rules *seemed* flexible and service users were *allowed* to come home late for *special occasions*. No family *seemed* to *vehemently* resent the rules and regulations that they were expected to comply with.

(Nixon et al. 2006: 51, emphases added)

Perhaps also this extract draws attention to the role which research plays in aiding and facilitating New Labour's 'transformation' project. This is an issue which is briefly commented in the context of the IFSP research.

## Reporting the 'transformation' of Children's Services: researchers and the 'lives of others'

Part of the argument developed in this chapter is that Nixon et al. (2006: 53) appear far too buoyant and emphatic when, despite an apparent lack of sufficient and convincing supporting data, they maintain that the projects which they examined offer a 'lifeline' to families; certainly few interviews appear to have been conducted with those at the 'sharp end' in these projects, in the residential units. More generally, both the findings related in Dillane et al. (2001) and Nixon et al. (2006) are, perhaps, somewhat constrained on account of the role of the Scottish Executive and Office of the Deputy Prime Minister, but the research teams could, perhaps, have been a little bolder in critically interpreting their, often complex, findings which reveal a good deal about the trajectory of the fragmenting, and increasingly authoritarian, outer edges of the neoliberal 'welfare' state.

This lack of curiosity in respect of a number of seemingly pertinent themes directs us, to ponder the notion that Nixon and her colleagues are 'independent' (Nixon 2007). This is not to crassly imply that these researchers are merely seeking to operate as organic intellectuals of New Labour, but it is to suggest that they could be asked: 'independent' from what, from whom? 'Independent' from which structures, which processes, which orderings, which particular ways of seeing and describing? This is not a personalized critique, but there is, perhaps, a need to interrogate this proclaimed 'independence' and to question how structural determinants might impinge on it and dilute it (see also Allen 2005).

Neoliberalism has fostered and promoted a nexus of relationships of a particular character within the university sector in England (Cohen 2004; Scott 2004; Callinicos 2006). Central here is the need to 'win' research funding and to generate income, within a market of competing bidders, which then also functions as 'symbolic capital' which can be drawn on 'win' promotion and build careers. In this context, confronting funding bodies about the interpretation of data becomes particularly problematic on account of fear of jeopardizing the awarding of research monies from the same, or associated, sources in future (see also Garrett 2002b).[9] It is, however, asserted that the Sheffield based researchers 'continually resisted pressure [from the New Labour administration] to change our methods of production and interpretation of data' (Nixon 2007: 550). Thus, it is implied that they were engaged in a rather clever Gramscian 'war of position' with officials in the Office of the Deputy Prime Minister and the DCLG. However, where is the evidence of this resistance, this questioning of received ideas? Which particular issues, relating to the framing of this 'social problem' or the interpretation of data, caused friction? There does, however, appear to be evidence which hints at the incorporation of the researchers into the New Labour 'project'. Thus, there is, on occasions, something of slippage from research and analysis into a form of 'product promotion' and political 'spin'. Hence the IFSPs ('pioneer projects') are lauded as providing 'excellent value for money' (DCLG 2006: 15) and extracts from the research ('proven to turn families around') is embedded in a government press release featuring 'neighbours from hell' in the banner headline (Home Office 2007). Here there is, of course, no suggestion that the researchers are unthinkingly complicit in this process of incorporation (or that they may have been easily able to prevent what they may even regard as the misappropriation of their research). It is, however, to maintain that it is important to focus on how the 'dissemination' of research on the 'transformation' of services for children and their families can blur into the 'branding' and 'marketing' of state policy. Perhaps, more fundamentally, there should be a willingness to examine how 'research' or 'expert' interventions can, of course, also be understood as deeply *politicized* interventions.

Drawing attention to projects and programmes considered and implemented in the past, not only in England, but also in the Netherlands and Germany is also important. First, because it manifestly undermines, the essentially promotional language of the researchers with their repeated claims that the IFSPs are 'pioneering a new way of working', and that 'pioneer local authorities' are committed to innovation (DCLG 2006: 9). This proclaimed 'pioneering' status is contestable because of the evidence of antecedents. Second, there needs to be some analysis of an odd coincidence of language with similar keywords and phrases recurring and being put to work in different times and different places: for example, the need to 'grip' recalcitrant families and to embark on programmes of 're-education' with families (DCLG 2006: 34; Respect Task Force 2006: 21) appears to unify residential establishments such as the Hasude, in pre-war Germany, and New Labour discourse on the IFSPs.

## Conclusion

The New Labour administration has argued, more recently, that there are a 'minority of families', about 140,000 of them, representing around '2% of the population' which should be targeted (Social Exclusion Task Force 2007: 4). These families are now the focus of the government's 'Think Family' initiative which is committed to put 'them back onto the road to success and enabling them to enjoy the improved outcomes that the rest of society is experiencing' (Social Exclusion Task Force 2007: 57). In line with the neoliberal world view underpinning this form of intervention, it is also maintained that in 'a rich society like ours . . . the prime responsibility for a family's success or failure *always* lies with the parents' (Social Exclusion Task Force, 2008: 1, emphasis added).

In this context, the IFSPs are likely to fulfil a key role and the *distinctive* and potentially *disturbing* element of these projects – the 'core' residential components – can be perceived as a form of 'pre-emptive or preventive detention'

(Rose 2000: 330) which is intent on partially sequestrating specimens of the 'problem family'. In this sense the 'core' elements within the IFSPs may also provide evidence of how the 'neoliberal penality', mentioned in Chapter 2, is 'spreading and mutating' (Wacquant 2001). Furthermore, what might be termed an 'internment' dynamic, frequently promoted as a form of residential 'supervision' or 'support', is detectable in other spheres; for example, in the context of provision made available for asylum seekers and in relation to 'teenage parents' (Guillari and Shaw 2005). On account of this punitive, disciplinary dimension it is, therefore, particularly important that such strategies are examined in detail (see also Hillyard et al. 2004; Pratt et al. 2005).

Critically focusing on the IFSPs is also warranted because of the direction which 'intervention' could take with children and families in future. As one of the project workers explained to the researchers: 'You know, they [the families] get here [are admitted to the core units] and they're under so much surveillance and scrutiny that we find out loads' (DCLG 2006: 114). Given the intensity of the gaze at least aspired to by policy formulators and some IFSP staff, it is not difficult to foresee how the 'core units' might evolve into a type of 'research laboratory' committed to (even earlier) intervention in the lives of many families (see also Wintour 2008). To be fearful about such a development, one does not have to be a dystopian, drunk on the most outlandish science fiction. Rather, there perhaps needs to be a little sociological imagination and heed taken of the former Prime Minister's fascination in the 'prebirth' screening of 'families that are severely dysfunctional, that have multiple problems' (Blair 2006c).

There would also seem to be largely unexplored issues connected to class, ethnicity and gender given that the projects appear to be targeting poor, 'white' women and their children. Moreover, it is apparent that these women, as well as being poor, are frequently poorly. Indeed, they seem to reflect some of the corporeal characteristics referred to by Simon Charlesworth (2000: 9), in his ethnography of life in parts of post-industrial Rotherham. Here his respondents, and those he observed around him, were surplus to capital's requirements; casualties, 'people so vulnerable and atomized that they carry the marks of their impoverishment in their bodies as oddity and illness'. Certainly, it remains important to try to analyse the situation of the families targeted for the IFSPs within analytical frameworks which foreground economic factors. More specifically, researchers might investigate why these families tend to inhabit locations which capital has rendered 'obsolete' because they no 'longer provide a secure basis for sustained accumulation' (Brenner and Theodore 2002: 7). Perhaps also, the IFSP families are carrying, like those interviewed by Bourdieu and his colleagues, some of the 'weight' of the neoliberal world in their 'social suffering' (Bourdieu et al. 2002).

Furthermore, the setting up of the IFSPs, or 'sinbins', could be providing further evidence of the penetration of the neoliberal project into the social domain: targeted at recalcitrant, troubled and troublesome children and families these 'pioneer' endeavours indicate how the *social regulation* aspect of neoliberalism is being implemented' (Munck 2005: 63, emphasis added). Maybe there are also indications of an implicit privatisation agenda, given the role of NCH, is integral to the promotion of such schemes. That is, these units are now becoming more prevalent and numerous in a context where – as will be highlighted in the next chapter – services for children are increasingly likely to be provided outside the public sector and for profit.

---

**Reflection and talk box 7**

Why is the so-called 'problem family' so central again in terms of how certain families are being described?

Why do the IFSPs appear to be targeted at poor women?

How does a 'backwards glance' assist us in trying to better comprehend the contemporary 'transformation' of Children's Services?

In analysing the IFSPs, how useful is it to have regard to 'residential solutions' created, in Europe, in the 1930s?

Can you identify ways in which the views of those families engaging with the IFSPs may be being silenced, muted, or reframed in the emerging research discourse?

How reasonable is it to subject families to 'curfews' and other restrictions within the so-called 'core' units?

If you are a student writing a dissertation, how do some of the issues and themes highlighted in this chapter relate to your own particular research project?

Why does ill-health appear to be such a significant issue for families referred to the IFSPs?

How might the proliferation of IFSPs be connected to the privatization of public services?

How, more generally, can some of evolution of IFSPs be connected to some of the characteristics of neoliberalism outlined in Chapter Two?

---

# 8 Making 'happier' children and more 'fulfilled' social workers? Privatizing social work services for 'looked after' children

Young people in care 'have a unique place in society and a special relationship with the state' (DfES 2007a: 6). Furthermore, New Labour has appeared keen to address the situation of this group, and this was apparent in the strategies and plans put in place during the period of the first Blair administration. The 'Quality Protects' programme, for example, was an early attempt to improve the 'outcomes' of those in care (DoH 1998; Secretary of State for Health 1998). The Blair governments also introduced the Care Standards Act 2000 and the Children (Leaving Care) Act 2000. This 'modernizing' agenda was also, in part, embedded in a number of developments which had taken place during the Major period, which focused on introducing controversial changes to how assessments of children 'looked after' were undertaken by social workers and associated professionals (Parker et al. 1991; Ward 1995). More broadly, New Labour has also been apt to refer to the idea that local authorities are the 'corporate parents' of 'looked after' children. New Labour administrations have seemed, however, to bring a new energy and direction to this area of social policy. Moreover, since the late 1990s, initiatives have been characterized by particular thematic preoccupations. These included attempts to raise the educational performance of 'looked after' children and the former Prime Minister's endeavour to promote child adoption as a solution to some of the problems associated with the 'care' system (DoH 1999a; 1999b; 2000a; 2000b; PIU 2000).

Approximately 60,000 children and young people are 'looked after' at any one time; about two-thirds are the subject of 'care orders' and the remainder are accommodated or 'looked after' on a voluntary basis (Secretary of State for Education and Skills 2006: 15). In terms of placement location, 68 per cent are in foster care; 13 per cent in residential care; approximately 9 per cent are placed with their families and 'the rest are placed for adoption or in a variety of more specialist placements' (Secretary of State for Education and Skills 2006: 16). There is 'currently a mixed economy of provision' with 'around 65% of children's homes . . . run by the private sector, 32% by local authorities, and 6% by voluntary sector providers' (Secretary of State for Education and Skills 2006: 43). Furthermore, children's stay in the care system tends to vary; for example, very 'few children spend their whole childhood in' care'; some 40 per cent 'stay for under 6 months and 13% stay for 5 years of more' (Secretary of State for Education and Skills 2006: 16). Children in care are also 'ethnically diverse' with black and 'mixed race' children being 'over-represented' in the 'looked after' population. For example, over 'half of children in care in London are from black or minority ethnic backgrounds' (Secretary of State for Education and Skills 2006: 50). Around '3,000 unaccompanied asylum seeking children are cared for by local authorities at any one time' (Secretary of State for Education and Skills 2006: 16).

In October 2006, the government once again turned its attention to children 'looked after' with the publication of a Green Paper *Care Matters: Transforming the Lives of Children and Young People in Care* (Secretary of State for Education and Skills 2006) and *Care Matters: Time for Change* (DfES 2007a) a White Paper published, just over ten years after New Labour was elected to government, in June 2007. In what follows, attention will particularly focus on the plan to set up Social Work Practices.[1] The first half of the chapter, using extracts from these texts and from the crucial report of the SWP working group (Le Grand 2007a) aims to largely refrain from comment and is mostly descriptive. The latter part of the chapter argues that SWP heralds the privatization of a major area of social work with children and families and that particular attention should be given to how the drive to install these new organizational forms is being assembled and orchestrated. Here the discursive moves and tactics being deployed might also relate to what has been termed the contemporary 'spirit of capitalism' (Boltanski and Chiapello 2005). Moreover, in attempting to counter SWP, three dimensions could be focused on: the notion that the SWP working group is 'independent'; the casual assertion that local authorities are unambiguously 'failing' children; and the fact that parents and 'looked after' children are mostly excluded from the dominant SWP discourse.

## 'Transforming' the lives of children and young people in care?

In a forward to the Green Paper the Secretary of State conceded that the help provided for those in care has 'not been sufficient' and that this group of children and young people, still achieving relatively poor 'outcomes', were at 'greater risk of being *left behind* than was the case a few years ago' (Secretary of State for Education and Skills 2006: 3, emphasis added).[2] This was particularly troubling because children in 'care are a group who are especially deserving of our help precisely because they are in care. As their corporate parent the State cannot and must not accept any less for them than we would for our own children' (Secretary of State for Education and Skills 2006: 6). The government was, therefore, considering introducing a range of measures to respond to this situation. This was likely to include every local authority introducing: a 'pledge for children in care' which might feature a commitment that there would be '24/7 support from their social worker or an out of hours contact'; a 'Children in Care Council' which would be a mechanism to ensure that the voices of children in care would be heard and have influence on policy and practice (Secretary of State for Education and Skills 2006: 11); better strategies and forms of intervention, such as 'functional family therapy, which might aid 'children on the edge of care' and so prevent their entry into the care system (Secretary of State for Education and Skills 2006: 20). In addition to these and a plethora of other measures, local authorities, aided by central government under the auspices of the Options for Excellence programme, were to continue to address problems related to the recruitment and retention of social workers (Secretary of State for Education and Skills 2006: 34).

In general, it might be suggested that the Green Paper contained nothing particularly striking or radical. Indeed, most of the ideas mentioned appeared to indicate a 'bringing together' and (re)presenting ways of working which were largely in place – in some shape – already. In short, the Green Paper was, perhaps, characterized more by 'spin' that by a detailed presentation of new policies. However, in a document 120 pages in length, the major 'radical' proposal was referred to briefly, over a mere three pages, and this was the plan to set up (what was still termed at this time) 'social care practices' (Secretary of State for Education and Skills 2006: 34–6). In what follows, this short section will be referred to at length because it endeavoured to put in place the initial foundational rationale – and discursive framework – for the proposed new organizational forms.

Here it was maintained:

> Children's social workers are in no doubt that their job is to help children. They have told us that they are frustrated with a complex system that takes them away from direct work with children. They also have only limited freedom to act as a vocal and effective advocate for the child, ensuring they receive the support they need. In our most recent survey, over half of local authorities reported problems with both recruitment and retention because of the nature of the work.
>
> (Secretary of State for Education and Skills 2006: 34)

It was then asserted:

> There must be much greater scope for independence and innovation for social workers. Social workers want to be able to spend more time working with children and their families, but often find this difficult because of high caseloads and the need to respond to crisis situations. Clearly, child protection must be the first priority, but social workers also need the freedom to work with children on a sustained basis to improve their long term outcomes. *We need to shift the culture*, draw clear lines of accountability and improve working conditions *to free social workers* to do this.
>
> (Secretary of State for Education and Skills 2006: 34, emphases added)

It was argued that one of the major difficulties faced by social workers was attributable to the organizational setting in which they were located:

> We believe there can be an inherent tension for social workers operating within the local authority. On the one hand they must do what is best for children but on the other must defend the authority's existing policies and practices and work within its structures. And the many levels of management within authorities can mean that decisions about children

are taken by people who have no direct knowledge of that child and their needs.

(Secretary of State for Education and Skills 2006: 35)

To address this problem, the government proposed, therefore, to explore the model of 'social care practices': 'small groups of social workers undertaking work with children in care commissioned by *but independent* of local authorities' (Secretary of State for Education and Skills 2006: 35, emphasis added). A practice would:

be an autonomous organisation, whether a voluntary or community sector organisation, a social enterprise or a private business – similar to a GP practice – registered with the Commission for Social Care Inspection and responsible for employing social workers. This would be *a tremendous opportunity for social workers and for children* . . . Each practice would hold a budget, provided through the contract with the authority, and would use it for individual social workers to fund the placement, support and activities that they believe *'their'* children should have. *Social workers would be given the autonomy and the freedom from a complex management structure needed to be able to put the child above everything else.*

(Secretary of State for Education and Skills, 2006: 35, emphases added)

The social workers, employed by these 'independent' practices, would have 'a genuine financial and personal stake in a small organisation centred around them and the children in their care. *The opportunities are immense.* Practices would be able to develop multi- disciplinary teams including staff such as education welfare officers as well as social workers to develop a unique offer in response to particular needs' (Secretary of State for Education and Skills 2006: 35, emphasis added). Such practices would, it was confided, also proliferate:

Successful practices would be able to expand and grow and to invest in better support services through a model of performance contracting. Under this approach, agencies are offered a powerful incentive to achieve permanence for children through being paid a set amount per child. They would be free to retain unused funds – *either as profit or for reinvestment*, depending on the nature of the organisation – resulting from a successfully managed and supported return home, or to adoption.

(Secretary of State for Education and Skills 2006: 36, emphasis added)

Local authorities would 'continue to play a key role' by determining the budget for practices and by 'monitoring' the 'quality of care' being provided (Secretary of State for Education and Skills 2006: 35). It was, moreover, acknowledged that it was 'unlikely' that such a 'model' would become 'commonplace across the country quickly', but it was still 'important' to 'explore ways of *freeing* social workers to provide better services for children within a local authority. Having a budget can make a big difference to this' (Secretary of State for Education and Skills 2006: 36, emphasis added). Furthermore, both 'budget-holding and social care practices . . . will give social workers greater *flexibility* to obtain services from a wider range of providers' (Secretary of State for Education and Skills 2006: 38, emphasis added).

The government announced that it is intent on discovering responses to 'this vision' for change (Secretary of State for Education and Skills 2006: 100). Furthermore, 'in order to explore some of the big ideas . . . in more detail . . . four working groups of interested stakeholders' were to be formed. These would focus on: the future of the care population (chaired by Martin Narey); placement reform (chaired by, the ubiquitous, Lord Laming); best practices in schools (headed by Pat Collarbone) and – most importantly in the context of the focal concerns of this chapter – social care practices (headed by Julian Le Grand) (see also DCSF 2006).

## Examining the potential for SWP

The consultation period concluded in January 2007 and the government reported that many respondents believed that there 'should be a drive towards reducing caseloads, streamlining bureaucracy and increasing investment in more social work staff' (DfES 2007b: 12). A number of respondents were regarded as 'supportive' and agreed that social care practices could address the problem identified in the Green Paper 'that social workers often do not have the freedom to work with children on a sustained basis *due to the bureau- cratic systems* in which they work, high case loads and crisis managing' (DfES 2007b: 13, emphasis added). The CBI, for example, 'strongly welcomed the proposal' (DfES 2007b: 16; see also CBI 2006a; 2006b; Bentley 2007). Readers of the government's summary of the responses to the consultation exercise were also drawn to a response from Shaftsbury Homes & Arethusa which believed that the proposal for SWP was 'the single most important idea within the Green Paper' (DfES 2007b: 14).

However, it was conceded that there had been a 'very mixed reaction' to the proposal for SWP (DfES 2007b: 13). Many respondents, for example, 'feared a possible dilution of accountability and questioned the extent to which local authorities can, or should, delegate their "corporate parenting" responsibilities' (DfES 2007b: 14). BASW maintained that that there was a belief that 'it should not be possible for a corporate parent to devolve its responsibility to an external organisation for the exercising of its legal responsibility of care' (DfES 2007b: 14). ADSS worried that SWP could result in 'duplication of effort'; inhibit 'the recruitment and retention of local authority-based social work staff; reduce 'direct investment in frontline services for children in care as a result of the perverse impact of the "profit motive" '; and ossify 'patterns of expenditure, precluding strategic redirection of resources over time towards earlier, preventative interventions' (ADSS, LGA and Confed 2007: 5). These pointed remarks, culled from more detailed responses to the consultation exercise, featured alongside a bundle of other criticisms. One local authority 'queried why, when the ECM agenda advocates we join services together to create a Children's Services Authority, that we are seeking to create practices that will produce gaps and fragmentation in provi- sion' (DfES 2007b: 15). The Pan-London Group of Independent Reviewing Officers pondered how 'appropriate is it that a private business is permitted to take money and then not spend it on services for children and young people they exist to work with, but instead pass it on as a dividend to shareholders and partners?' (DfES 2007b: 15). Recognizing the direction in which policy was likely to move, some 'respondents pointed to the fact that the jury is still out on fund-holding GP practices', a model which SWP seemed likely to be based on' (DfES 2007b: 15).

## SWP: the Grand vision

The main document entirely focusing on the SWP idea remains, however, the working party report chaired by Julian Le Grand which became available in spring 2007. This maintained that the 'original idea was a relatively simple one. It was that there would be benefits for both looked after-children and for social workers if the latter were organised along the lines of professional partnerships, mirroring similar arrangements for legal and medical partnerships' (Le Grand 2007a: 3). However, it was acknowledged that the plan had 'attracted more critical attention that any other proposals in the Green Paper' (Le Grand 2007a: 3).

An important section of the report then set out to remind readers of the nature of the 'problem' (Le Grand 2007a: ch. 4). Here it was argued that what 'many looked after children do not seem to have under current arrangements is *a* champion, someone with a parental degree of concern and affection, *and* with the power to get things done' (Le Grand 2007a: 16, original emphasis). None of this

> implies that the social worker could or should fulfil all the roles of a parent, or even of a 'corporate parent', for the looked after child. In particular, it should be emphasised that, at any one time, looked after children should have the care and support of the foster family or the staff of the children's home where they live.
>
> (Le Grand 2007a: 16)

Next turning its attention to the perspective of the social worker, the Le Grand working group echoed some of the themes which were emphasized in the Green Paper:

> In general, social workers who deal with looked after children come to work with *a strong moral purpose, idealism, energy, enthusiasm and a commitment to rectifying injustice*. However, once into the job, social workers often feel de-motivated, overwhelmed by bureaucracy and paperwork and deprived of autonomy. Research, both national and international, suggests that job dissatisfaction and burn-out, are the most common contributors to social workers in the field of child care leaving their jobs. In turn, these seem to arise from high levels of depersonalisation, role ambiguity, role conflict, stress, work overload, lack of autonomy and influence over funding sources, lack of support and professional supervision, bureaucratic control.
>
> (Le Grand 2007a: 17, emphasis added)

Furthermore, and more 'controversially', it:

has been argued that social workers in Britain have become captured by an auditing regime involving accountability mechanisms that have increased managerial control at the expense of professional development. The accountability of social workers has become a rule-based managerialism, instead of knowledge-based professional accountability in which social workers were accountable to a professional body by delivering services based on evidence about best practice and to service users by providing good user outcomes. In short, it is claimed, in social work managerialism is increasingly dominating professionalism.

(Le Grand 2007a: 17)

In brief, it 'is not too much of an exaggeration to say that, *as a society*, we are training social work professionals and then offering them jobs, as one social worker put it to us, as social administrators' (Le Grand 2007a: 18–19). Moreover, it was implied, social workers were spending too much time 'in front of a computer screen' (Le Grand 2007a: 20). Problems were also apparent from an organizational perspective because, at present, the local authority is the 'monopolistic supplier of the social worker service to looked after children . . . [Yet it] is widely accepted that monopolies find it more difficult to sustain *the competitive edge* which is necessary for continually improving professional practice (Le Grand 2007a: 20).

The working group report, having framed what it perceived as 'the problem' next moved on to focus on what it viewed as some of the chief components structuring the 'debate' on SWP (Le Grand 2007a: ch. 5). By way of preamble it was maintained that the group had not found 'much disagreement' with – one of the motifs at the core of the discourse on SWP – the view that

> *in many ways*, managerial decision-making has replaced professional decision-making with respect to looked after children, that there is a dilution of responsibility away from the front line, and that the autonomy and responsibility of social workers is significantly restricted in various ways. Most would also seem to agree, *for one reason or another*, social workers are spending too much time on paperwork and on fulfilling other bureaucratic requirements associated with child protection, and too little on building relationships and engaging in direct interaction with children on their caseload.
>
> (Le Grand 2007a: 22, emphases added)

The working group's 'preferred model' would, therefore,

> be a group of perhaps six to ten partners of whom a majority (but not necessarily all) would be social workers. The partnership would contract with the local authority to provide field social work for looked after children, and to commission services that its own staff could not provide. It would own its assets and pay the partners and any staff that it might employ. The latter could include receptionists and other administrative staff, and a practice manager (although the last could also be a partner).
>
> (Le Grand 2007a: 22)

Local authorities would still have a 'major role to play' because they would 'still retain the formal responsibility of being the corporate parent; they will undertake care proceedings, they will commission; they will contract; they will monitor the contract' (Le Grand 2007a: 25).

This 'preferred model' could, it was argued, solve a plethora of problems which currently lie at the core of social work with the 'looked after' children. In terms, for example, of the criticism that social workers fail (perhaps because of high turnover in staff) to provide such children with a sense of continuity in the care, this might be addressed by the SWP model because there 'is evidence that those who have a stake in an organisation are more loyal to it and less likely to leave it than those who are not' (Le Grand 2007a: 22). Similarly, SWP could respond to childcare social workers' lack of adequate relationships with children in care and 'deprofessionalisation' (Le Grand 2007a: 23). This is because the 'absence both of the need to report continuously to a managerial hierarchy and other demands of a large organisation, would increase the time available for SWP partners to build the relationship' with a 'looked after' child (Le Grand 2007a: 23). Within SWP there would be 'more hands-on time' (Le Grand 2007a). In short, they would be '*independent* professionals, making *professional* decisions' (Le Grand 2007a: 23, emphases added). The envisaged framework also gelled with the government's plans to introduce, as outlined in Chapter 3, a LP role into Children's Services (DfES 2005f; 2006c; 2006d).

The issue of 'incentives' was vitally important, in terms of this reconfiguration of services for children 'looked after', because '*many* believe that there is a lack of incentives for innovation and responsiveness within present structures' (Le Grand 2007a: 22, emphasis added). Perhaps, attentive to the fact that this unfolding scheme might prompt the charge that local authority services were to become privatized and that children in care were to become commodified, Le Grand and his nine working party colleagues attempted to directly address this question. Thus, services being outsourced 'for profit' prompted reflection on two related issues: first, morality; should 'social workers (or indeed anyone) be in the business of making profits out of looked after children?'; second, a more 'practical issue', would a social work practice 'be more concerned with cutting costs to increase its profit margin than improving the welfare of the looked after child?' (Le Grand 2007a: 26).

Related to the morality dimension, it was asserted:

> There are already profit-making institutions and individuals working with looked after children, including independent fostering agencies, independent social workers working under contract, and private children's homes. Voluntary organisations working in the area, although often incorrectly described as not-for-profit, can also make profits (often described as surpluses): the *only* difference between them and profit making institutions is that these profits or surpluses are not distributed to shareholders or to other owners, but to improve staff pay and conditions or invested in improving facilities. It is also important to note that profit-making institutions exist in cognate areas of public service provision such as health care and education, including the institution most closely related to the professional partnership . . . the GP practice.
>
> (Le Grand 2007a: 26, emphasis added)

In a section of the report which – arguably – left the working group open to the charge that they are being rather misleading about major planned departure relating to local authority services for children, it is stated that, 'more generally', there are:

> many groups of people who make a living out of looked after children, including the employees of local authority children's services, foster carers, workers in children's homes, and the suppliers of goods and services to foster carers or children's homes. It is hard to see all of these as morally reprehensible, or to argue that one particular form of making a living from working with looked after children is more immoral (or indeed more moral) than any other.
>
> (Le Grand 2007a: 27)

In respect of 'incentives', it was maintained that there are, in fact, reasons to 'suppose that a professional partnership practice will actually prioritise the interests of the child' (Le Grand 2007a: 27). Social workers 'would still be trained and registered as professionals, with an emphasis on their professional ethos and motivation' (Le Grand 2007a: 27). Moreover, the 'small, intimate nature of the social work practice would be one that encourages the formation and maintenance of personal relationships, especially between the social workers and the looked after child – which would make it hard for the social worker to put their concerns above that of the child' (Le Grand 2007a: 27).

Another reason for believing that SWP 'will not engage in ruthless cost cutting or quality reducing is the pressure that would arise from contracting and potential competition or contestability' (Le Grand 2007a: 27). In this context, the 'local authority will be monitoring the contract, and will have the potential to transfer the contract to some other practice, or to take the service back in-house' (Le Grand 2007a: 27). More broadly, a profit sharing SWP 'will encourage a new dynamic – one that rewards responsiveness, industry and effectiveness, while penalising indifference and inefficiency' (Le Grand 2007a: 27).

Le Grand and his colleagues next examined the potential 'models' for social work practices. Here it was conceded that a 'fully developed' SWP could actually take over 'complete responsibility' for social services for children, including child protection and all services for children in need. However, their preferred model was one where SWP would 'take responsibility for children on care orders (section 31 cases) and those who are voluntarily accommodated (section 20 cases)' (Le Grand 2007a: 30). In attempting to map out how this might occur, it was suggested that for

> children on care orders *the formal transfer of responsibility* to the practice would occur *somewhere* between where the interim order is made and when the care orders are completed. For voluntarily accommodated children *the local authority would make a judgement* on where it would be best to transfer responsibility to the social work practice.[3]
>
> (Le Grand 2007a: 30, emphases added)

Social work practices could include 'forms of social enterprise, such as a professional partnership or voluntary organisation. It could also include private sector firms of various types from share-holder owned corporations to small owner-operated businesses' (Le Grand 2007a: 35).[4] In a more overtly ideological move, it is argued:

> *The idea that it is useful to distinguish between organisations on the basis of whether they aim to obtain a surplus of revenue over costs – that is, a profit – is a [sic] nonsense.* All organizations that wish to survive as independent entities will aim generate such a surplus, whether they are professional partnerships, private businesses or voluntary sector charities. The difference concerns the way in which they organisations dispose of those profits: private enterprises distribute some or all of their profits to their private owners, or, in the case of a listed company, to their shareholders; whereas voluntary sector or professional partnerships do not distribute the profits to any individuals outside the organisation. *So here we shall avoid the terms for-or not-for-profit, instead referring to professional partnerships, private businesses, or voluntary sector organisations.*
>
> (Le Grand 2007a: 35, emphases added)

The working group appeared especially keen on social work practices learning from 'employee-owned companies' (EOCs) such as the John Lewis Partnership (which employs 68,000), but also smaller enterprises. The

> hallmarks of EOCs are high levels of success in *business performance, staff that are more entrepreneurial and committed to the company*, a strong commitment to corporate social responsibility and involvement with the community, attractiveness to high quality staff who stay for longer periods, and notable levels of innovation.
>
> (Le Grand 2007a: 36, emphasis added; see also Reeves, 2007)

Acknowledging that the SWP plan has led 'many' to feel 'considerable anxiety over the possibility of distorting and diluting lines of accountability' (Le Grand 2007a: 39), the report attempted to address such concerns. In this context, it was stated that local authorities will make arrangements with a SWP for that practice to discharge their statutory functions in relation to looked after children through a contract (Le Grand 2007a: 39). Furthermore, local authorities would 'still retain their corporate responsibility even though key decisions will be made by the social work practice' (Le Grand 2007a: 40). The working group also suggested that if there practices appeared to be 'making *excessive* profits at the expense of children's needs . . . a cap on the amount of profit or surplus that could be made . . . [with the] practice having to share any profit/surplus with the local authority' (Le Grand 2007a: 40, emphasis added).

The 'considerable anxiety' felt by some readers of the Green Paper might, it was implied, be alleviated by the 'lean and sound structure' of regulation which would oversee SWP (Le Grand 2007a: 44). Here, the main regulatory bodies would be Office for Standards in Education (Ofsted) and the General Social Care Council (GSCC) and there would need to be a 'new set of Minimum National Standards for social work practices' (Le Grand 2007a: 45). Moreover, it would be important to pilot properly the SWP, and the piloting activity should 'last for at least two years from when the social work practice has taken over responsibility for its full allocation of children' (Le Grand 2007a: 46). Here, it was suggested that there should be '9 pilots in total (3 professional partnerships, 3 voluntary sector and 3 private sector) across a diverse range of local authorities' (Le Grand 2007a: 46). A national steering/ implementation group might also aid this activity and every effort 'disruption for children involved in the pilots' should be '*minimised*' (Le Grand 2007a: 48, emphasis added).

Following the completion of the working group's report, the White Paper, *Care Matters: Time for Change* was published, in the final week of Blair's premiership, on 21 June 2007 (DfES 2007a). However, despite SWP being, as noted earlier, the 'single most important idea' in the Green Paper (DfES 2007b: 14), it merited less than two pages and, in this sense, is almost *hidden* in the text of the White Paper (DfES 2007a: 129–30). Nonetheless, it was still clear that the government remained intent on progressing SWP. Here it was concluded that the proposal to institute these new organizational forms 'offers a new opportunity to enable professionals to work together with greater autonomy and flexibility in order to work more directly with children and young people and better meet their needs' (DfES 2007a: 129). While the 'commissioning local authority would remain the "corporate parent" . . . and the Director of Children's Services would continue to be accountable for ensuring that these children achieve and reach their potential' it was envisaged that each

> social worker in a practice would have the freedom to concentrate on the children in their care and would be accountable for their outcomes. The practice social worker would remain with them, as far as possible, throughout their time in care and beyond. Each practice would also hold a budget provided through the contract with the authority and would use it to enable social workers to fund the placement, support and activities that they believe 'their children' should have.
>
> (DfES 2007a: 130)

It was announced the piloting of SWP would commence, subject to parliamentary approval, in autumn 2008. However, in May 2008 – and even before the Children and Young Persons Bill had reached the statute book – the DCSF, together with the private consultants *iMPOWER*, launched a series of roadshows also involving Le Grand, to prepare the ground for the SWP pilots. In November the bill received Royal Assent and the following month it was announced that six councils had been selected to pilot the contracting out of social work services for 'looked after' children: Blackburn with Darwen, Hillingdon, Kent, Liverpool, Sandwell and Staffordshire.

How, therefore, can this plan to introduce SWP be assessed and interpreted? Just how is this project to create 'happier children' being orchestrated and developed?

## Tilting the balance: the 'war of position' against local authority social work

BASW (2007), in its response to the Green Paper, reported that the SWP proposal had been 'fiercely debated within our organization'. Indeed, it could be argued that a core element in the neoliberal plan for SWP is to divide and split the profession in that part of the strategy involves decoupling a key cadre, or section, of the profession from the public sector (CBI 2006a: 4). As some respondents to the Green Paper observed, those 'social workers . . . more likely to be experienced and confident, leaving the less experienced social workers to work within the local authority' (DfES 2007a: 14). Perhaps crudely, this could also be perceived as a form of (human) asset stripping which *removes* the most experienced professionally accomplished workers and leaves behind a residual pool of newly qualified, comparatively low-paid workers, whose work will be subject to Taylorist forms of ordering and regulation; work processes partly associated, in fact, with the assessment materials derived from the work of one of the members of the SWP working group (Ward 1995). More generally, the entire discourse focused on SWP provides evidence of a complex 'war of position' being waged against state social work and this is embedded in a more encompassing project to discredit public services provided by local authorities subject to democratic control.

The 'war of position' is derived from the work of Antonio Gramsci mentioned in Chapter 2 (see also Forgacs 1988). Writing during his period of confinement in prison, he argued that there was a need for Marxists to adopt tactical changes. This, for him, meant that there had to be a shift from a 'war of manoeuvre' to a 'war of position'. That is, it was no longer appropriate to embark on a frontal assault against capital: instead, there needed to be put in place a more subtle form of confrontation, more conducive to the conditions in the West, and which focused on a longer war of colonization and territorial conquest. In the context of the discussion in this chapter, therefore, it is suggested that the 'war of position' may also be helpful in terms of understanding how the forces of neoliberalism are forging a Gramscianism of the Right and are intent on the slow colonization and marketization of key areas of public services.

This 'war of position' does not, of course, seek to *entirely* shift social services provision into the private sector, but there is a constant attempt to *tilt the balance* in the direction of the private sector, increased commodification and marketization. This process is, in part, facilitated by a plethora of elite networks and complex professional and social ties. What is more, senior officers from local authorities are increasingly likely to be inside the same – formal and informal – networks as corporate management consultants. Moreover, many senior officers are now apt to move from public services into private consultancy work.

How the 'debate' (Le Grand 2007a: ch. 6) on SWP is discursively framed – formulated by means of libertarian rhetoric – is, as hinted throughout the earlier part of this chapter, immensely important and revealing. Table 8.1, for example, illustrates how keywords derived from the policy documents associated with SWP are incessantly deployed by primary definers in their attempt to achieve hegemony, organizational 're-modelling' (DfES 2007a: 125) and 'cultural shift in this field of public services' (Le Grand 2007a: 72). In this context, a seemingly new move in the evolving strategy to promote greater privatization (in, for example, the form of SWP) is to partly assimilate and *selectively* incorporate leftist critiques of social work, emerging over the past

**Table 8.1** 'Remodelling' social work: keywords in the SWP legitimating apparatus

---

**(Old/public service) local authority social work** =
(deprived of) autonomy
bureaucracy/bureaucratic control/bureaucratic requirements
burn-out
(high) caseloads
crisis situations
depersonalization
deprofessionalisation
job dissatisfaction
managerial control/rule-based managerialism/social work managerialism/
managerial decision-making
(dire) outcomes
paperwork
(lack of) professional supervision, support, time
(dilution of) responsibility
role ambiguity/conflict
stress
work overload

**(New/profit-making) social work practices** =
autonomy/autonomous organization
champion
committed
creative
decision-making
entrepreneurial
flexibility
freedom/freeing
independence/independent professionals
innovation
opportunity
professional
(good) outcomes
(adequate) time
trust

---

ten years, which have focused on job dissatisfaction (for example, Harris 1998; Jones 2001; Baines 2004a; 2004b; Ferguson and Lavallette 2004; Harlow 2004; Carey 2007; Coleman and Harris 2008). This involves recognizing social worker dismay, discontent and disappointment (illuminated in this research literature) about how work is becoming more dehumanizing and alienating, but then the attempt is made to *detach* such insights from the critique of neoliberal modernity in which they are mostly embedded. Thus, the project becomes one of 'reframing' or 'channelling' social workers' reported discontents, away from political and economic critique, so as to orchestrate and mobilize a particular tier or group to support *more* neoliberal 'innovations'; in this instance in the form of the outsourcing of a substantial element of local authority social work services for children 'looked after'. For example, in the documents referred to earlier, social workers are not criticised and, indeed, arrive in the profession with, as mentioned earlier, a 'strong moral purpose, idealism, energy, enthusiasm and a commitment to rectifying injustice' (Le Grand 2007a: 17).[5] They are, however, not furnished with an opportunity to blossom and realize high-minded and noble career ambitions because the current (democratic/public) structures stultify, fetter and constrain, while the potential for liberation and emancipation lies in the envisaged (private/profit-seeking) structures. Indeed, it would appear that with the 'new organizations, the bureaucratic prison explodes ... Discovery and enrichment can be constant' (Boltanski and Chiapello 2005: 90).

In this context, it could, for example, be argued that BASW was mistakenly won over by this strategy when a pro-SWP motion was narrowly adopted at the association's AGM in the spring of 2008. This welcomed the proposal to explore SWP and asserted, in line with the promotional rhetoric associated with the dominant official literature, that the envisaged model could be a viewed as a

> route towards the rediscovery of professional confidence for social workers in all areas of practice. We believe that the opportunity to have control over our working conditions will lead to the sort of ethically sound and imaginative practice that will benefit service users/clients/ customers as well as our own self esteem.
>
> (BASW 2008)

The strategy on the part of the promoters of 'modernization' chimes with trends in contemporary management literature in which workforce change is often 'presented as an attempt to inflect the world of work in a "more human" direction' (Boltanski and Chiapello 2005: 98). That is, the emphasis appears to be on responding to 'demands for authenticity and freedom' (Boltanski and Chiapello 2005: 97). More theoretically, the approach taken in promoting SWP gels, in many ways, with Luc Boltanski and Eve Chiapello's (2005) account of the contemporary 'spirit of capitalism'.[6] For Boltanski and Chiapello (2005: 10), the 'spirit of capitalism' is the ideology that justifies continuing engagement in capitalism and a belief in its emancipatory power: it is, therefore, a set of 'beliefs associated with the capitalist order that helps to justify this order and, by legitimating them, to sustain the forms of action and predispositions compatible with it'. In this sense, the 'spirit of capitalism ... presents two faces – one turned towards capital accumulation, the other towards legitimating principles' (Boltanski and Chiapello 2005: 58). The ability to assimilate critique into the legitimating apparatus is a vital aspect of this project. Moreover, the 'critiques to which capitalism is vulnerable constitute one of the determining elements in the formation of the spirit of capitalism peculiar to a period' (Boltanski and Chiapello 2005: 96). Thus, the 'price paid by critique for being listened to, at least in part, is to see some of the values it had mobilized to oppose the form taken by the accumulation process being placed at the service of accumulation' (Boltanski and Chiapello 2005: 29). They argue, therefore, that to:

> maintain its powers of attraction, capitalism ... has to draw upon resources external to it, beliefs which at a given moment in time, possess considerable powers of persuasion, striking ideologies, even when they are hostile to it, inscribed in the cultural context in which it is developing. The spirit sustaining the accumulation process at a given point in history is thus imbued with the cultural products that are contemporaneous with it and *which, for the most part, have been generated to quite different ends than justifying capitalism.*
>
> (Boltanski and Chiapello 2005: 20, emphasis added)

It might, therefore, be argued that SWP discourse furnishes something of a microcosm of how this process works. Perhaps, also the high moral tone of the working group report provides an illustration of how there is a need to 'restore meaning to the accumulation process, and combine it with the requirements of social justice' (Boltanski and Chiapello 2005: 19). More generally, Boltanski and Chiapello maintain that we are currently witnessing the 'formation in the developed countries of a spirit of capitalism that is more capable of attracting support (and hence also more directed towards justice and social well-being) with a view to seeking to galvanize workers and, at a minimum, the middle class' (Boltanski and Chiapello 2005: 19).

The 'spirit of capitalism', differently constituted in different epochs, needs to constantly shift and evolve so as to 'respond to the need for justification by people who are engaged in the capitalist accumulation process at a given moment, but whose values and representations, inherited cultural legacy, are still associated with earlier forms of accumulation'. In this dynamic context, what is 'at stake is making the new forms of accumulation attractive to them (the exciting dimension of any spirit), while taking into account of their need to justify themselves ... and erecting defences against those features of the new capitalist mechanisms that they perceive as threatening the survival of their social identity' (Boltanski and Chiapello 2005: 21). Importantly, contemporary management literature (which the SWP literature so resembles)

> cannot be exclusively orientated towards the pursuit of profit. It must also justify the way profit is obtained, give cadres arguments with which to resist criticisms that are bound to arise ... Management literature must therefore demonstrate how the prescribed way of making profit might be desirable, interesting, exciting, innovative or commendable. It cannot stop at economic motives and incentives.
>
> (Boltanski and Chiapello 2005: 58)

Once again, Table 8.1, derived from the emerging corpus of official literature on SWP, indicates how this process is being discursively amplified. As observed previously, this stress on the exciting possibilities inherent in SWP enterprises is coupled with an attempt to erase the significance of the core 'for profit' element. More emphatically, the SWP working group can, perhaps, be perceived as performing (fairly blatant and rather crude) *ideological* work and is intent on reinterpreting, even eliminating, mention of 'profit'. This is necessary (but should not be perceived as guaranteed to succeed) because using children in care to generate profits is likely to at best rest uneasily alongside the humanistic social work code of ethics (Hare 2004).

The concluding part of the chapter, however, tries to identify those areas where the official discourse on SWP may be vulnerable to a series of discursive counter-moves.[7] In this context, there are, for example, at least three zones of potential contestation which this leading discourse attempts to 'shutdown': the make-up of the SWP working group; the casual assertion that local authorities are unambiguously 'failing' children; and the fact that parents and 'looked after' children are mostly excluded from the dominant SWP discourse.

## Examining the SWP working group

The working group met formally on seven occasions over the period November 2006 to March 2007 to examine SWP (Le Grand 2007a: 14). Aside from Le Grand, the other members appointed by the government were: four senior officers from London boroughs; Paul Fallon, head of Children's Services and director of social services in Barnet; Alastair Pettigrew, a 'keen promoter' of SWP (Toynbee 2006: 37), co-author of Le Grand's and the director of children's social care in Lewisham (see also Le Grand and Pettigrew 2006); John Hill, service manager, Children's Services, Tower Hamlets; and Moira Gibb, chief executive of Camden Borough Council. The remaining members of the working group were: Lynne Berry, the chief executive of the GSCC; Polly Neate, executive director of public affairs and communications at NCH; and Modi Aboud, described as a 'care leaver and service involvement worker'. Le Grand was also joined by 'two *distinguished* academics that specialised in social work research and training' (Le Grand 2007a: 3, emphasis added): Peter Marsh, professor of child and family welfare, from the University of Sheffield and Harriet Ward, professor of child and family research at Loughborough University.[8] Given the composition of this group, it could reasonably be maintained, that the government construction of 'interested stakeholders' was rather narrow. That is to say, they seem to have been chosen from limited (and limiting) 'fields' of activity (Bourdieu and Wacquant 2004). For example, there was no representation from BASW, UNISON or ADSS. Furthermore, there was nobody representing parents with experience of having children located in the care system. In terms of the geographical dimension, it also seems rather odd that no local authorities from outside the capital – and its rather narrow pattern of associations and affiliations – were included on the working group.

In this context – and once again drawing on the work of Bourdieu – it is important to have regard to how key individuals (freighted in particular times and particular places with particular types of capital) come to be perceived as primary definers, authoritative articulators and champions for 'reform' programmes such as those pivoting on the introduction of SWP. Key senior academics, and other strategically located 'experts', are particularly important in this respect because their 'expertise' functions (or seeks to function) *outside* or *beyond* ideology.[9] However, even *prior* to the publication of the

Green Paper, Pettigrew (2006) was *advocating* for the introduction of the SWP model. Similarly, just days before its publication, Le Grand and Pettigrew (2006) argued in the *Guardian* that 'care' produced 'dire results' with 'shocking outcome statistics' for children and young people. This was related to 'local authority hierarchies' and 'an absence both of effective authority and of a sense of responsibility'. Their idea (to find echo in the Green Paper and then subsequently endorsed by them as members of the 'independent' working group) was for practices or partnerships that could be 'organised as a social enterprise, or, like GPs, as a small business'. These new structures they stated plainly would result in unambiguously 'happier children, growing up into more secure and more confident adults' (see also Le Grand 2007a: 155).

## The private sector rescuing a 'failing' care system?

Given the ascendancy of neoliberal ways of *seeing* and *doing*, the private sector has, over recent years, become increasingly important with regard to the 'delivery' of care for older people. This has, of course, been particularly the case with the residential and nursing sector where large corporate providers continue to increase their share of the market. This has led Peter Scourfield (2007: 162; 170) to conclude that residential care is now 'a commodity . . . there to be traded and exploited for its surplus value like any other commodity' and as a consequence 'the quest for profitability means that business values, reductions in costs and income generation have been prioritised over and above the quality of care'. The private sector's role in providing children's homes and related Children's Services is also, as mentioned earlier, increasing and there has been, for example, a 'stampede of private equity firms into the foster-care sector' (Mathiason 2007).[10]

The *Care Matters* agenda reflects this new emphasis on the role of the private sector, not only in terms of the promotion of the SWP model, but more generally.

In seeking to provide a 'first class education' for 'looked after' children, for example, it maintained that, for some children, private boarding schools 'provide an excellent means of stability and support' (Secretary of State for Education and Skills 2006: 59–60). Thus, the government stated that it was to set up a number of 'pilot' projects in 'order to test the effectiveness of boarding provision for vulnerable children': this was to include nine local authorities and around 50 independent and state maintained boarding schools (Secretary of State for Education and Skills 2006: 59; see also DfES 2006f). Related to this emphasis on the role of the private sector, the Green Paper referred to the role of the Hong Kong and Shanghai Banking Corporation (HSBC) in funding private tutoring for children in care (Secretary of State for Education and Skills 2006: 65; DfES 2007a: 76). More generally it was asserted that:

> the private sector has much to offer children in care. Major companies already do valuable work – increasing young people's access to structured leisure activities and the *world of work*. We will facilitate a long-term dialogue between private companies and the care system, exploring the

potential for building major sponsorship programmes which increase opportunities for children in care across the board.

(DfES 2007a: 13, emphasis added)

In a similar vein, it was claimed that 'major companies' do 'valuable work with vulnerable children and young people in the community as part of their corporate social responsibility programmes, increasing their access to structured leisure activities and the world of work' (DfES 2007a: 102).

It could, of course, be argued that the government is simply being pragmatic and is opportunistically making good use of available private sector resources and companies' desire to provide a veneer of 'corporate social responsibility' for their activities. However, this approach, which provides a more encompassing framework for SWP, perhaps neglects to address a range of interrelated issues. First, it could be maintained that the private sector and market mechanisms have often been complicit in prompting hardship, poverty and stress in families and so contributed to the need for a child to be 'looked after' in the first place. In short, children and young people in care may, in some instances, be viewed as *victims* or *casualties* of marketization (see, for example, Charlesworth 2000). Second, what is this 'world of work' which recurs in the *Care Matters* discourse? What are its characteristics and defining features? Who or what is seeking to provide children and young people 'looked after' with answers to such questions? This seems to be particularly important given that there are risks that 'major companies' chief concerns are likely to focus merely on 'employability'. Third, given this enhanced role for business, there may also be concerns about the leakage of confidential information relating to children and young people in care.

Finally, the centrality of the private sector serves to reinforce, implicitly and explicitly, the notion that public services (particularly local authorities) have failed 'looked after' children (see also ADSS, LGA and Confed 2007). However, this notion – part of the emerging 'common sense' associated with the SWP enterprise – can be contested. Mike Stein in a pithy, but devastating, critique of the government's plans has argued that the idea that the current 'care system' is an unambiguous failure can be challenged in a number of ways. For example,

> many of these 60,000 young people come into care for a few weeks or months and return to their parents; 40% return home within six months, a majority within 12 months, and the average length of stay for all young people in care is less than 2.5 years. Their time spent in care represents a very small part of their lives and therefore in no scientific sense could it be causally linked to future outcomes. The education, careers, health and wellbeing of these young people will be far more shaped by what happens to them at home and in their schools and communities.
>
> (Stein 2006: 6)

Moreover, there is, for Stein, a need for more robust research and analytical rigour when assessing 'outcomes' in the context of children's pre-care social and economic location. Indeed, the whole notion that the 'care system' is 'failing' can be understood, in part, as part of an *ideological* project which *needs to* reveal failure so as to provide a rationale for the privatization agenda.

## Parents and young people: examining the excluding and filtering processes

From the period reaching back into the Major years, a dominant strand within policy, protocol and practice has stressed the importance of social workers and associated professionals working 'in partnership' with the parents of children and young people (DoH 1995). Within the discourse focused on SWP, however, the parents of children 'looked after' are rendered largely irrelevant or requiring replacement. Indeed, birth parents are entirely absent in the official literature on SWP until the brief references are made to them in the annexes of the working group report (Le Grand 2007a). Indeed, as ADSS has observed, the Green Paper, for example, 'omits to attach sufficient importance to the continuing role of birth parents in the life of children in care. Bearing in mind that most children in care should and do go home, the emphasis should be on empowering birth parents rather than on taking on their role to a disempowering extent' (ADSS, LGA and Confed 2007: 2). Le Grand and Pettigrew, for example, have maintained:

> Social workers need to have the authority to make decisions and see them implemented. This means giving the capacity to secure, on behalf of a looked after child, high quality health and education, regular family and peer contact (if appropriate) and choice of appropriate placement to the responsible worker. *In short, they need to be a caring, responsible 'parent'.*
>
> (Le Grand and Pettigrew, 2006 emphasis added)

Elsewhere, explicit references to 'services users' make it plain that this construct does *not* include parents: for example, Le Grand (2007a: 39) specifically refers to 'service users (i.e. children in care)' and in this way 'birth parents' are effectively deleted. Furthermore, this can, perhaps, be interpreted as being rather contemptuous of parents (despite the fact that parents entirely hold or share 'parental responsibility' with the local authority 'looking after' their children).

The presentation of the views of children and young people in care, on the SWP plan, is more complex because a core motif which characterizes the entire *Care Matters* endeavour is that the views of this group are vital and much sought after.

It is maintained, for example that there were responses from 1376 children and young people to the consultation exercise (DfES 2007b: 5). Indeed, it is estimated that the government 'gained the views of over 10% of the care population directly' (DfES 2007c: 5). However, there are also puzzling 'silences' and elisions which suggest that SWP is being introduced 'behind the backs' of children and young people. The *Young People's Guide to the Care Matters Green Paper* (DfES 2006g) simply omits any mention of evolving the SWP model (and fails to mention the plan to send some 'looked after' young people to private boarding schools). Not surprisingly, therefore, the document summarizing young people's responses similarly does not refer to SWP (DfES 2007c). Perhaps rather disingenuously (given they were not asked to comment on the issue in the 'guide' prepared for them), it is then confided that most 'children did not comment on the idea' of SWP 'specifically' (DfES 2007b: 13). However, those 'young people who were consulted', on SWP, 'were initially confused by the concept, then sceptical about if they would make any difference' (DfES 2007b: 13).

Certainly children and young people do appear to be concerned about confidentiality being eroded: 'Young people in particular were concerned about confidentiality. They felt that the more people were aware of the child or young person's background, the more likely it was that they would be stigmatised or bullied' (DfES 2007b: 7). Similarly, it was reported by the DfES that children 'were concerned that information would be shared about them without there permission' (DfES 2007b: 7: see also Munro 2001). However, by the time the White Paper was published, these fears had been filtered from the discourse, despite SWP potentially leading to more people and organizations accessing children and young people's personal information and data.

## Conclusion

Historically, of course, the 'looked after' system is, in part, a 'legacy of minimum standards and minimum objectives that was inherited from the Poor Law' (Parker et al. 1991: 74). It remains important, therefore, not to reify existing organizational forms and to fall into the trap of arguing that such structures and practices (even now, of course, retaining traces of the ethos of the poor law and its modalities of operation) should be merely 'retained' and 'defended'. However, it appears that the SWP plan is rooted in a particular perception of 'transformation', one which pivots on the core insight that services can only be improved by injecting more marketization, more commodification and more competition. Furthermore, following Bourdieu (2001), this could be regarded as part of a wider conservative 'restoration' which is incessantly seeking to create more ideological and material spaces for capital accumulation.

This chapter has tried, therefore, to illuminate the key elements contained within the SWP model and has gone on to identify how this particular project is being orchestrated. At present, this model remains vulnerable to critique not only in terms of the three key issues mentioned earlier, but also because a good deal of the associated official literature tends, for example, to skim over some fairly complex legal questions. Behind the hostility towards 'bureaucracy' is also a profoundly anti-democratic intent. Moreover, the glib notion that that SWP can provide structures to house and nurture '*independent* professionals, making *professional* decisions' is manifestly unconvincing given that these social workers are likely to be constrained (perhaps albeit on occasions in deceptively subtle ways) by the requirement to generate financial profits (Le Grand 2007a: 23, emphases added). Perhaps more fundamentally, this chapter – like the rest of this book – suggests that some of the problems caused, in part, by neoliberalism cannot be solved by neoliberalism.

**Reflection and talk box 8**

What is your view of the plan to set up Social Work Practices (SWP)?

The 'independent' experts promoting SWP appear keen on constructing the debate in a very specific manner. What is the significance of the words and terms featured in Table 8.1?

How is local authority social work constructed by the primary definers of the SWP plan?

Is it legitimate for financial profits to be accrued by SWP?

Why do the idea of 'partnership' and the commitment to working in 'partnership' with birth parents appear to be downgraded in the discourse focused on SWP?

Is the notion that local authority social work services are 'failing' children convincing?

How carefully are the views and opinions of children and young people, who are 'looked after', being gathered on the plan to establish SWP?

Discuss how the notion of 'liberation' features in the dominant discourse on SWP?

How helpful are some of the insights of Gramsci and Boltanski and Chiapello in understanding how the drive to install SWP is being orchestrated?

For those within Children's Services, and beyond, intent on trying to prevent the establishment of SWP, what is the best way to mount a campaign? Where are the 'weak points' in the arguments of those pressing for SWP?

# 9 Conclusion

The book has aspired to provide to a series of 'signposts' which direct readers to engage in further debates about the way that Children's Services are being 'transformed' in England and, perhaps, elsewhere. Central here, it has been maintained, has been the confining neoliberal rationality which is influencing the nature of the changes under way. This is not, of course, to argue that the *entire* project of organizational, thematic and professional 'reform' is entirely and unambiguously rooted in neoliberalism. Nonetheless, neoliberalism has served – often implicitly – to provide the dominant, or hegemonic, core for the 'transformation' of Children's Services and associated sectors and spheres.

Some have asserted that New Labour's neoliberalism is 'an uncomfortable and strained construction rather than an essential political character' (Clarke et al. 2007: 146). However, since Blair's ascendancy to the leadership of the party, New Labour has become increasingly comfortable with the neoliberal agenda. As mentioned earlier, what Stuart Hall (2003) referred to as, the 'subaltern programme, of a more social-democratic kind, running alongside' has become more and more subdued, increasingly marginal and marginalized. This has been coupled – beginning with the period of Neil Kinnock's leadership (1983–92) – to a purging of leftist oppositional tendencies and the welcoming into the party of former Conservative MPs. Related to this, party democracy has been hollowed out with, for example, party conferences being reduced to 'rallies', largely orchestrated for television, in support of the leadership. Unsurprisingly, and partly related to many members' disgust, anger and sadness about the Iraq and Afghanistan debacles, this has led to the party's membership beginning to drain away.

None of this is, of course, to suggest, that the return to government of the Conservative Party is preferable. Indeed, given the emphasis that David Cameron, the Conservative Party Leader is placing on the role of philanthropy and charity in providing what are now public services, it is clear that the Opposition's own vision of 'transformation' is even more socially retrogressive (see, for example, 'Cameron wants charities paid market rate for public services', *Guardian*, 4 June 2008: 11). Whatever the fortunes of the Conservative Party, philanthropic endeavour and charity could, however, become more significant in the provision of services for children. Indeed, in some areas of Europe, such as the Republic of Ireland, private – and more specifically US – philanthropic foundations appear to be fulfilling a more central role, not only in terms of providing funding for particular projects, but also in seeking to orientate and influence the methodologies of research undertaken which examine services for children.

## Future(s)

In Chapter 2 it was suggested that the economic crisis, which began in 2007–08, could be prompting a 'financial regime change' (Ware 2008) and that there is now evidence of a movement away from neoliberalism. In England, for example, the Banking (Special Provisions) Act 2008 has provided the government with the power to acquire failing banks and this legislation has been used to bring about the part-nationalization of a number of banks and financial institutions; a move that would have been viewed as outlandish and an example of 'loony leftism' only months previously. In September 2008 when the financial crisis seemed to deepen – as stock markets around the world began to falter and plummet and a number of banking, mortgage and insurance companies failed – even the outgoing Bush administration was prompted to intervene decisively and to pass the Emergency Economic Stabilisation Act 2008: a measure which provided for greater government intervention and which seemed to run entirely counter to the rhetoric of neoliberalism. Indeed, these emergency measures, introduced in North America, Europe and elsewhere appeared to indicate something of a Keynesian resurgence. However, at the time of writing, it is clearly impossible to predict the way events will unfold. For example, New Labour policies seem far from unidirectional: while seeming intent on using the power of the state to intervene to try to deal with a crisis in capital liquidity, the government can still produce neoliberal proposals for the partial privatization of the post office and envisage the 'contracting out' social fund loans, subjected also to interest rate charges for the very poorest (Department for Work and Pensions 2008b). It does, however, appear likely that Children's Services in England, and further afield, will come under additional pressures because more children and their families, themselves likely to face additional stresses, are likely to need assistance (see also 'Councils expect social problems from recession', *Guardian*, 19 December 2008: 13; 'Slump will bring home violence', *Guardian*, 20 December 2008: 8). The International Labour Organization (ILO), for example, has predicted that a least 20 million jobs will be lost by the end of 2009 bringing global unemployment above 200 million for the first time.

This book has argued that the 'big picture' cannot be detached from what is taking place *within* Children's Services. That is, there is no partition around that sector which safeguards it – and those working in it – from other omnipresent and dominant economic and social tendencies and trajectories. Although this book has primarily focused on critical readings of policy documents, one aspect of the 'transformation' of Children's Services – which is difficult to overemphasize – is the sheer 'messiness' and unevenness of the process 'out there' in the world of practice. Despite the various branding initiatives which seek to render the process of change as organized, rational and coherent, it remains incomplete, contested and prone to be imagined and enacted in a multiplicity of ways by a range of different actors. This is because the CfC programme must engage with – and even comprise – ingrained expectations, ways of *understanding* and *doing* work with children and their families which may be averse to neoliberal 'common sense' (Garrett 2008a; forthcoming). Clearly, these embedded ways of comprehending and undertaking work within Children's Services need not be unambiguously progressive and may be rooted in a defence of professional privilege within particular fields (Bourdieu and Wacquant 2004). However, again highlighting the complexity of the 'transformation', the ingrained expectations of particular fields, such as social work, may also be grounded in a set of values and code of ethics which are potentially oppositional to neoliberalism. Perhaps the key point is that new political or policy imperatives 'do not arrive in empty spaces – they arrive in the middle of already crowded and contested spaces where other discourses jostle for dominance' (Clarke et al. 2007: 50). In this context, therefore, it remains important to understand that those seeking to promote neoliberal approaches are intent on a 'long war' and on ensuring change takes place and become embedded over many years, even decades. That is, as mentioned in Chapter 3, the aspiration is to try to create, within each individual worker and new entrant to the field, a new sense of professional milieu or habitus within Children's Services (see also Bourdieu and Wacquant 2004). Nonetheless, workers across the sector cannot be relied upon merely to 'translate', what have largely been, neoliberal plans – unambiguously – into neoliberal practices.

The New Labour administration has, of course, been keen to emphasize its expenditure on Children's Services. For example, the public is advised that investments 'in public services for education funding per pupil has doubled since 1997'. Coupled to this, a further '£21 billion invested in early years and childcare has funded the creation of over 1,700 Sure Start Children's Centres across the country. £680 million has been committed to Extended Schools over 2006–8 to provide activities, study aids and parenting and family support' (Social Exclusion Task Force 2008: 5). Nevertheless, the government appears to be failing to reach its own 'targets' to reduce the numbers of children who are poor. Moreover, in October 2008, the Audit Commission reported that the Children's Trusts, created by the government, have been 'confused and confusing'. Five years after the publication of ECM, there was 'little evidence of better outcomes for children and young people'. Professionals were, it seemed, 'working together' but this was 'often through informal arrangements outside the trust framework. Trusts get in the way: a third of directors . . . say the purpose of the trusts is "unclear", and the uncertainty is hampering their efforts to deliver better services' (Audit Commission 2008). The main findings were:

- Children's trusts have little if any oversight of budgets and money for Children's Services.
- The relationship between trusts and other local partnerships is unclear.
- Children's trusts are unsure whether they are strategic planning bodies or concerned with the detail of service delivery.

- In going ahead with trusts, the government seemed to have ignored the results of its own pilot study.
- There is little evidence that mainstream money has been redirected by children's trusts.

Indeed, these findings illustrate the fact that spending patterns – and the lauding of 'new' initiatives and programmes – often fail to reveal (and may even conceal) some of the more significant aspects of the changes under way. For this book, therefore, key questions have included: how is the private sector beginning to play a more substantial role? How is the case for 'transformation' being made and orchestrated? Which groups are operating as the primary definers, providing a critique of the 'the way things are' and mapping the 'way things should be'? What fields are they located in? What are their patterns of association, political and professional adherences? What, moreover, are some of the new patterns of control and regulation that are emerging? What are the new surveillance practices which are now evolving which are being directed at both the users of services and the providers of services?

## Architects of 'transformation'

Chapter 6, for example, focused on how leading New Labour politicians are obviously key definers of the 'change agenda'; in this instance, in relation to how 'ASBO politics' has been constructed in England. However, perhaps one of the key themes which have emerged is that academics, as well as politicians, are playing a key role in articulating 'change' and in providing an 'expert' and (contentiously) 'independent' foundation for neoliberal policy departures. This was apparent in, for example, Chapter 7 and the examination of the so-called 'sinbins' and – more substantially – in the following chapter which commented on the way in which the plan to privatize social work services for 'looked after children' is being promulgated and promoted.

More fundamentally, underpinning the analysis in this book has been an understanding that the diffusion of neoliberal ideas is not the result of the machinations of 'faceless, structural forces' (Peck 2004: 399). Rather, structurally positioned agents are immensely important in terms of how they seek to formulate and promote such ideas and establish a new 'common sense'. Part of this project, as suggested particularly in Chapters 7 and 8, strategically pivots on the need to eliminate counter-perspectives or untidy elements which do not *fit* within the grand vision of change or 'transformation'. Thus, the discourse on the plan to establish SWP seeks to place *beyond* the terrain of legitimate debate what many might still regard as fundamental and highly contentious aspects of the proposal. Here we could include, for example, questions relating to how the SWP plan deepens the tendency to commodify children in public care; how it fragments services for children and dilutes the democratic control of services. As argued earlier, there also appears to be a failure to thoroughly and rigorously encompass the views of children and young people themselves and their parents. More generally, within the discourse on the 'transformation' of Children's Services there is, as indicated in

Table 8.1, a move to castigate existing services which are provided in the public or local authority sector. Furthermore, important here is the central idea that – for practitioners – 'creative' work now lies beyond what is presented as a discredited and moribund public sector.

## Lifting the heart: ('creative') social work is elsewhere

As observed earlier, research has developed over the past 25 years which has illuminated how many social workers, for example, have become disenchanted with their work because it often appears dictated by centrally devised assessment schedules, a lack of time, little meaningful contact with the users of services and, more generally, poor working conditions. An emergent tendency in some of the research literature focusing on the 'transformation' of Children Services, seemingly heeding the critique and re-framing it, maintains that these problems can be solved by, what might be termed, a 'privatization fix'. That is, as Table 8.1 again makes clear, an important emergent idea in that it is possible to create zones of autonomy for professional enrichment and fulfilment within the private sector. Indeed, this appears to be one of the main ideas being deployed to try to galvanize workers, enlist them and win them over to a neoliberal vision of change.

The former prime minister Tony Blair (2006d) confided that one of the problems was that his 'poetic vision' of public sector 'reform' had to be 'articulated in the most technical prose [because the] vocabulary of public service reform is not designed to lift the heart'. While not seeking to emphasize discourse at the expense of material reality, this comment again serves to emphasize the government's preoccupation and 'way with words'. Blair's understanding also gels – in complex ways – with the new cultural and public policy focus on promoting 'happiness' and individual well-being (Ferguson 2008). In short, the discursive *presentation* of neoliberal approaches – its new 'spirit' (Boltanski and Chiapello 2005) – is becoming more central and there appears to be a new emphasis, as is clear from the official discourse on SWP, on highlighting how 'transformation' can fulfil practitioners and make professional lives more complete and emotionally rewarding. Similarly, an account of an IFSP project, argues that these projects provide staff with 'an opportunity to engage in the kind of creative practice that proceduralisation, bureaucracy and managerialism have made impossible to achieve in the mainstream social work arenas'. Within such projects – all of which are not outside the public sector – there is the opportunity for greater 'flexibility', 'creativity' and 'imagination' (Parr 2008: 11). Seemingly operating in what David Cameron has referred to as a 'post-bureaucratic age', these new zones (either within IFSPs or the envisaged SWP), will, it appears, be nurturing and protective bubbles effortlessly sustaining 'creative' practice (see 'Cameron wants charities paid market rate for public services', *Guardian*, 4 June 2008: 11; see also BASW, 2008).

None of this is to suggest, of course, that those working within Children's Services are easily duped or fooled by the rhetoric of 'transformation' (see, for example, Mooney and Law 2007). Nonetheless, how the 'reform' programme is be assembled and amplified remains important because it illuminates how those promoting neoliberal change have constantly to adapt and reposition themselves to generate and sustain a measure of consent for their blueprints. This in turn is, however, likely to give way to further disenchantment as there will be a failure, save for an elite few, to deliver on neoliberalism's promises.

Although much of this book has focused on how Children's Services are being subjected to processes of neoliberalization, it is also important to stress – although this is not an independent dynamic – the state's new 'watchfulness' and how technologies are increasingly being deployed to conduct surveillance of the 'risky' and the *potentially* risky (Pollack, 2008). Within Children's Services, as highlighted in Chapter 5, this is reflected in the envisaged deployment of new systems of dataveillance, such as the much criticized CPd and the CAF/eCAF (see also Table 5.1). Within the associated, emerging paradigms what was formerly regarded as 'private' or 'personal' information held on the users of services is now more frequently apt to be 'shared' with the significance of discourses and practices pivoting on protecting confidentiality eroded.

In late 2008, however, it was the ability of Children's Services adequately to safeguard vulnerable and endangered children which became a subject of national and international interest. In what follows, therefore, the aim is to provide an initial interpretation of some of the key themes which emerged and which were highlighted, particularly by the media.

## 'Baby P'

'Baby P', a 17-month-old boy, died on 3 August 2007 from severe injuries inflicted while he was in the care of his mother, her 'boyfriend' – who was, it appears, 'hidden' from social workers and other professionals – and Jason Owen, a lodger in the household. On 11 November 2008 at the Old Bailey two men were found guilty of causing or allowing the death of a child or vulnerable person. The mother had already pleaded guilty to the same charge. Importantly, for Children's Services, 'Baby P' had been subject to a child protection plan from 22 December 2006, following concerns that he had been abused and neglected. He was still subject to this plan when he died (Ofsted, Healthcare Commission, HMC 2008).

After the convictions in November, and into the following month, the case of 'Baby P' dominated the media, even displacing news of the evolving economic crisis and being a major feature of 'Prime Minister's questions' in the House of Commons ('Editorial – learning the lessons, again', *Guardian*, 13 November 2008: 34.) Indeed, on occasions, it appeared that the tragedy, and the sheer scale of media attention which it was being afforded, was serving as a signifier for a disparate mix of anxieties and projects. Perhaps rather crudely, it might even be argued that the 'Baby P' case – with its stock of stereotypical characters, and, seemingly, easily identifiable 'villains' – was also providing a refuge from the new and unpredictable politics of fear and uncertainty prompted by the global economic crisis.[1] On the weekend, following the convictions, for example, the *Independent on Sunday* gave over its front page and nine inside pages to the 'story'. Elsewhere, a 'Justice for Baby P' campaign was established on the social networking Internet site, Facebook:

this envisaged and planned for a petition and a protest march on Parliament; it also drew attention to the composition of a special song and proposed the wearing of blue ribbons as a mark of remembrance for the dead child. The imagery associated with the media presentation of the case was also striking and emotive. The day following the convictions, for example, four photographs featuring five soiled and bloodstained items of clothing belonging to the child were printed in a number of newspapers (see '50 injuries, 60 visits – failures that led to the death of Baby P', *Guardian*, 12 November 2008: 1). Four computer-generated images of a damaged baby's head were also published by *Guardian* and other newspapers ('Sixty missed chances to save baby used as punchbag', *Guardian*, 12 November 2008: 4–5). Furthermore, a number of 'crime-scene' body-map illustrations of the child, with various identified injuries, were produced in some newspapers.

The key, internationally circulated, iconic image of the child which appeared on television, the Internet and in newspapers was published in *Guardian* on 15 November 2008.[2] Here the child, with blonde hair and blue eyes was photographed gazing and reaching upwards while stood on a black-and-white chequer-board kitchen surface. Indeed, the child almost seems to be positioned like a piece on a chessboard to be moved around by players (various individuals, organizations and social forces) seeking to utilize his death to achieve specific hegemonic readings of the tragedy ('Eight in 10 seriously harmed children "missed" by agencies', *Guardian*, 15 November 2008: 1). What can be identified, therefore, as some of the main themes emerging from the tragedy which impinge on the 'transformation' of Children's Services? This is an important question because beneath the often hysterical response to the death it is possible identify a largely retrogressive politics.

### Hounding and intimidating public sector professionals

Perhaps, one of the main key themes to emerge was the 'targeting' of individual public sector professionals for allegedly failing to protect the child. In some respects this was similar to what occurred following the death of Victoria Climbié. For example, early in 2008, the Care Standards Tribunal, while deliberating on the case of the child's former Haringey social worker, Lisa Arthurworrey, confided that to 'blame everything on Ms. Arthurworrey is . . . to make her a scapegoat for the failings of a number of people'. However, it then went on to casually assert that there was 'no doubt that Ms. Arthurworrey was seen as *a monster* by many people as a result of Victoria's death' (Care Standards Tribunal 2008: 20, 13, emphasis added). With the 'Baby P' case, this type of demonization was once again apparent ('Social worker chiefs call for end to demonization of their colleagues', *Guardian*, 13 November: 15; see also Toynbee 2008). Two days after the convictions the *Sun*, for example, set out to 'name and shame' four Haringey workers and the paediatrician who failed adequately to examine the child. The newspaper called on 'our army of outraged readers to join our crusade' to have these workers 'kicked out of their jobs': it also provided a telephone number for people to ring if they knew five individuals – Sharon Shoesmith, Gillie Christou, Maria Ward, Sylvia Henry, all employed by Haringey Council, and Dr Sarah Al-Zayyat. Meanwhile, one upmarket broadsheet took to referring to the Haringey staff and councillors subject to public criticism as the 'Haringey Eight'.[3]

Perhaps not entirely surprisingly, given this type of press coverage, it was reported that threats had been made that one of Shoesmith's two daughters would be killed. One typewritten letter, mailed to her home address in London, contained a photograph of the sacked director, taken from the *Sun*, with the words 'a Christmas box – your daughter will be in' attached. Other communications, which Shoesmith received, suggested that she should kill herself. She also received emails entitled '100 Ways to Commit Suicide' and e-cards with pictures of 'Baby P' containing messages such as 'forever on your conscience'. Furthermore, her aged mother and former mother-in-law were pursued by reporters asking what they felt about Shoesmith 'being responsible for the death of a baby'. As the year drew to a close, the police were reported to have reinforced her doors and windows and offered her protection ('Sacked head of council children's services receives death threats', *Guardian*, 2 December 2008: 5).

### 'Inadequate' 'underclass' parents

In terms of the presentation of those responsible for 'causing or allowing the death', the notion of 'evil' was frequently mentioned in the press. For example, a letter writer to the *Guardian*, on 3 December 2008, compared those responsible for causing or allowing the death of 'Baby P' to Ian Brady, one of the infamous 'Moors murderers'.[4] In this context, the 'boyfriend' of the mother of 'Baby P' was, according to the police, 'sadistic' and 'fascinated' by pain. He was also 'said to have tortured guinea pigs as a child and tormented frogs by breaking their legs'. Moreover, he was 'a keen collector of Nazi memorabilia' ('Sixty missed chances to save baby used as punchbag', *Guardian*, 12 November 2008: 5).

The 'boyfriend' may well have possessed these types of characteristics and have had these fixations. However, it would seem that explanations which dwelt on the notion of 'evil' provide a far from adequate explanation of the tragedy. What is, perhaps, of more interest, given some of the core preoccupations of this book, is how a number of keywords and phrases, associated with the regulatory social agenda of neoliberalism, were regurgitated and deployed in the press. Here, moreover, it was the 'quality press' and not the tabloids which seemed to take the lead. In the *Guardian*, for example, Simon Jenkins (2008b: 37) connected the death of the child to 'problem families'. It was, however, the 'underclass' construct which appeared to be more frequently used. The weekend after the convictions, for example, the *Observer* argued that the 'fate' of 'Baby P' had 'focused the spotlight once again on child protection services and loopholes in the net designed to protect the most vulnerable children, *as well as broader questions of how to reach an underclass of inadequate parents* raising children in volatile circumstances' ('Put more children at risk into care', the *Observer*, 16 November 2008: 2, emphasis added). These were, it was asserted, 'families that were straight out of *nightmares . . .* an *underclass . . .* untouched by the affluence of modern Britain' ('Why children are left to die beyond help's reach', the *Observer*, 16 November 2008: 18).

Indeed, it could be argued that the New Labour's 'ASBO politics', with its so-called 'neighbours from hell' (Home Office 2007), provided the discursive foundation for such press accounts of the child's death and these 'broader questions'. In addition, a number of articles attempted to forge a connection between the cases of 'Baby P' and that of Shannon Matthews and her mother, Karen.[5] In the *Observer*, it was maintained that the case of 'Baby P' 'ran in parallel to that of Shannon, a more horrific shadow . . . It has subsequently been proved that as with the mother of Baby P, Karen Matthews was well known to social services but no sustained action was taken to save her children from her' ('She "loved Shannon to bits": but she had her kidnapped. Inside the dark, dangerous world of Karen Matthews', *Observer*, 7 December 2008: 29–32). The same article then went on to argue that it 'was easy to present her as a representative of a feckless *underclass*, a broken society, a generation of parents only concerned for their own childish emotions' (ibid.: 31, emphasis added).

The newspaper presentation of Karen Matthews, frequently fused to that of 'Baby P', was characterized by, what can be termed, a certain class loathing and contempt. This was, perhaps, most apparent in an article by columnist, Sophie Heawood, published in the *Independent on Sunday* in mid-November 2008. Here she argued:

> It's what seems to be an *underclass*, a level of British society that is not just struggling with poverty – this is way beyond being poor – but often getting by with *subnormal intelligence* levels, living in a world *with no professional aspirations* whatsoever, for generations, where criminality is normality, with people who seem to have not just fallen through the net of literacy or personal improvement, but missed out on education or social development altogether.
>
> (Heawood 2008: 42, emphases added)

Her solution to these problems was that her readers should 'join a mentoring scheme to befriend a struggling child . . . And how about mentoring adults? Could we create more real-life schemes, and not just TV shows, where people like Karen Matthews can get to know people from less troubled backgrounds? It's the entrenchment of the *underclass* that keeps people there' (Heawood 2008: 43, emphasis added).

Following the death of 'Baby P', a number of other ideas were discussed which drew attention to how the tragedy – seemingly a reflection of a wider societal crisis – could be explained. For the former Conservative Party leader, Iain Duncan Smith (2008), the case of 'Baby P' was a sign of the 'broken society' which he, and David Cameron, was seeking to fix. He – along with a number of other signatories – also had a letter published in the *Guardian*, on 1 December 2008, imploring that the Prime Minister seize 'the opportunity of initiating a long-term inquiry to examine how we can stop some of today's children becoming the abusing parents of tomorrow'. This apparent request for earlier and more substantial interventions into the lives of children and their families was also supported by the Shadow Secretary for Work and Pensions, Chris Grayling, who called for out of work parents to have their home lives and prospects investigated in the context of Conservative Party plans to 'tackle underclass Britain' (' "Never-worked" families face

Tory scrutiny', *Observer*, 7 December 2008: 5). In the *Guardian*, columnist Jenni Russell (2008: 42) also endeavoured to connect the case of 'Baby P' to more encompassing welfare issues, by championing New Labour's controversial 'willingness to challenge lifetime dependency' in its welfare to work reforms (see also Department for Work and Pensions 2008a).

### *The joint area review: opening up space for debate on 'transformation'?*

The joint area review (JAR) of Haringey Children's Services, with particular reference to the question of 'safeguarding' was undertaken by Ofsted, the Healthcare Commission and HM Inspectorate of Constabulary: it was published on 1 December 2008.[6] The 'summary judgement' of the inspection 'identified a number of serious concerns in relation to safeguarding of children and young people in Haringey'. Thus, for the JAR, the 'contribution of local services to improving outcomes for children and young people at risk or requiring safeguarding' was 'inadequate and needs urgent and sustained attention' (Ofsted, Healthcare Commission, HM Inspectorate of Constabulary 2008: 3). Although the short report was frequently couched in the language of arid managerialism, its message was clear. However, the report and the debate which it subsequently generated has appeared to prise open some space for more progressive debates on the 'transformation' of Children' Services.

First, a by-product of the JAR was that attention also began to focus on the role of Ofsted itself. For example, the organization – its maxim 'raising standards, improving lives' – had previously approved of services for children within the borough and had maintained that thorough 'quality assurance systems are in place' ('Haringey issues apology after "anguish" of Baby P case', *Guardian*, 14 November 2008: 4; 'Ofsted accused of complacency on child protection', *Guardian*, 11 December: 4).[7] The JAR, however, subsequently argued that there was 'too much reliance on quantitative data to measure social care, health, and police performance, without sufficiently robust analysis of the underlying quality of service provision and practice' (Ofsted, Healthcare Commission, HM Inspectorate of Constabulary 2008: 4). Clearly, such a remark had a more general resonance as well as being likely to rebound on Ofsted, which had also tended to rely heavily an quantitative measures.

Second, the JAR brought into a wider public domain a theme which had, perhaps, previously largely been confined to the field of social work and academic journals associated with social work and social policy: what this book has referred to as social work's 'e-turn' (see also Garrett 2005). The JAR reported that in Haringey, some 'allocations of cases within social care services' were even 'made electronically and without discussion with social workers'. Moreover, the 'existing social care electronic recording system operated by the council lacks sufficient flexibility and, although this impedes effective practice by social workers, there has been insufficient priority given to resolving this issue by managers (Ofsted, Healthcare Commission, HM Inspectorate of Constabulary 2008: 7, 14). In the *Guardian*, for example, Simon Jenkins maintained that the 'belief has long been bred in the bone of the children's minister, Ed Balls, that any computer can solve the world's ills at the click of a mouse. It is a dangerous lie' (Jenkins 2008b: 37). Furthermore, research, conducted by Sue White and her colleagues on the amount of time social workers were being compelled to spend in front of computer screens began to receive wider coverage (White et al. 2008; see also Munro 2008). In this context, it was reported that a Liberal Democrat MP, John Hemmings, was calling for an independent inquiry into the ICS (Child protection stifled by £30m computer system – report', *Guardian*, 19 November 2008: 7). Furthermore, UNISON (2008a: 8–9) questioned if this troubled and controversial system was 'fit for purpose'.

Third, there were indications that more sensible debate might be beginning to evolve on what could and could not be achieved by public sector professionals working within Children Services. For example, when Ed Balls claimed that a 'Baby P' case would not 'happen again', he was responded to by the chairperson of the Society of Local Authority Chief Executives and Senior Managers (SOLACE) who maintained in 'our view good people making good judgments in good systems can still not be enough to prevent some parents harming or killing their children' ('Balls "was irresponsible" to promise Baby P case will not happen again', *Guardian*, 12 December 2008: 17). In a similar vein, stressing that it was not possible to entirely eliminate the risks posed to children, the president of ADSS asserted that while the 'case is clearly an individual tragedy, it is not a symptom of a broken child-protection system . . . This work is complex and difficult and sadly we cannot eliminate risk or the miscalculation of risk. Not every tragedy can be prevented but we must continue to strive to do so' ('50 injuries, 60 visits – failures that led to the death of Baby P', *Guardian*, 12 November 2008: 4). In short, Children's Services could not, like private sector corporations inflating their 'products', claim that 'things could never go wrong'.

Fourth, a comparative picture of child deaths began to emerge with, for example, some of the work of academics undertaking comparative research entering into the media presentation of the issue. It was pointed out that children in England and Wales are, in fact, less at risk than in most developed countries: the 'baby murder rate is highest in the US and only Greece, Italy, Spain and Sweden have lower rates than England and Wales' ('Urgent inquiry into childcare ordered', *Guardian*, 13 November 2008: 14). Moreover, as Polly Toynbee (2008), noted in the *Guardian*, the numbers of children killed has fallen steadily: down 50 per cent in England and Wales since the 1970s. In America, however, which as suggested in Chapter 3 is so frequently a template for New Labour's 'transformation' of Children's Services, child murders have risen 17 per cent since the 1970s.

Fifth, attention was drawn to the how neoliberal policies – reflected in unfilled vacancies, a high turnover of staff and the dependence on agency staff – was impacting on the ability of workers within Children's Services to deliver an effective service. Thus, the JAR sensibly concluded that this

> high turnover of qualified social workers in some social care teams has resulted in heavy reliance on agency staff, who make up 51 of 121 established social worker posts. This results in lack of continuity for children and their families and of care planning. Action has been taken to

attract staff, including an increase in pay scales and a graduate trainee scheme.

(Ofsted, Healthcare Commission, HM Inspectorate of Constabulary 2008: 13)

Related to this, BASW revealed that nationally about '11% of posts were vacant, rising to 30% in some of the most stressful urban communities' ('Social worker chiefs call for end to demonization of their colleagues', *Guardian*, 13 November 2008: 15).[8]

However, it has been the trade union, UNISON (2008b), which has provided the most cogent response to the crisis within Children's Services, by producing a ten-point plan for protecting vulnerable children (see Table 9.1).

**Table 9.1** UNISON's ten-point plan for protecting vulnerable children

*Co-working on all child protection visits*: child protection visits to be done by two practitioners.

*More social workers and support staff*: an urgent action plan to fill vacancies and to review staffing levels across all social work teams.

*National caseload management standards*: enforced through the inspection process and regularly audited by the council leadership, with sanctions against employers who breach the Code of Practice for Social Care Employers.

*More resources*: a planned programme of investment in children and families' social work.

*Cull of bureaucracy*: a root and branch zero-based review of all bureaucracy and consideration of similar measures to those used to cut red tape in schools.

*Re-establish homecare services for children and families*: homecare workers to act as 'the eyes and ears' of social services.

*Complete overhaul of the Integrated Children's System (ICS)*: to create a system that is fit for purpose and commands the confidence of social workers. Immediate remedial measures by councils, where the system is impeding effective, efficient work.

*Review of legal processes*: There is widespread concern about the impact of the recent hike in court fees that local authorities must pay. There should be a review of the decision on fee levels and of the Child and Family Court Advisory Support Service's funding and capacity to ensure that resource constraints are not influencing legal proceedings and outcomes.

*Better support and more reflective practice*: Social workers should have at least two years post-qualifying experience before being allocated child protection cases. There should be consistent, high quality supervision that is both supportive and challenging.

*Measures to rebuild morale, confidence and status of social workers*: Redress the devastating impact on morale through a sustained campaign to promote positive public awareness about what social work achieves.

## Another 'transformation' is possible

Perhaps this ten-point emergency plan reveals that there are other competing visions of change within Children's Services. More generally, this book,
although critical of many of New Labour's plans to 'transform' services for
children and their families, remains – as signalled at the outset – impatient
with accounts of change which nostalgically yearn for a bygone 'golden'
past. Indeed, part of the foregoing analysis has maintained that many of the
solutions to social problems, posited by the New Labour administration, are
intensely backward looking.

Fredric Jameson (2000: 225–6) urges his readers to 'do the impossible,
namely to try and think positively *and* negatively all at once; to achieve . . . a
type of thinking that would be capable of grasping the demonstrably baleful
features of capitalism along with its extraordinary and liberating dynamism
simultaneously'. Although this book has – largely as a counterweight to the
more numerous, more upbeat, accounts of the 'reform agenda' – concentrated
on the more 'baleful' aspects of the 'transformation' of Children's Services,
the dialectical approach, proposed by Jameson, might aid an understanding
of – and resistance to – some of the more damaging changes now under way.

The ability of those located with Children's Services to resist neoliberal
inflected 'transformations' is, however, likely to depend on the ability of
such workers to make linkages with other workers in other sectors and with the
users of services (Mooney and Law 2007). Making, and sustaining, connections with the various social movements committed to continuing to oppose
the faltering neoliberal project is also vital.

# Appendix A

In Nottinghamshire our Children's Services have achieved excellent standards of performance against national indicators. We are committed to continuous improvements through investment both in services and in staff development.

## Social Workers Field Work Teams

£18,012 - £28,320 pa Ref: ESC/332/JE    Location: Various

If you are qualified or about to qualify there are opportunities to join one of our Localities in Reception/Assessment or Children's Services teams. You will be joining a vibrant and motivated staff group where you are encouraged to develop new skills and be innovative in your practice. We have invested in the work environment and in new technology. We offer opportunities to develop your career, competitive salaries and six extra days' annual leave.

## Family Resource Workers
### Family Resource Team

(Two Posts)
£18,012 - £25,911
Ref: ESC/334/JE    Location: Geding & Mansfield

Full-time experienced child care workers are required to work with children aged 8 years to 18 years. Significant experience of working with families in crisis is necessary.

## Team Manager Children's Services Team

(Part-time/Jobshare)
£30,594 - £34,413 pa Ref: ESC/333/JE    Location: Mansfield

You will need the essential management skills to lead a team of qualified and unqualified staff in the delivery of responsive and high quality services to all children together with our partners. You will be part of a management team that is committed to improving services, developing staff and embracing new ways of working. Experience in all aspects of statutory child care work is essential.

Interviews for this post to be held on 14 June 2004.

Application forms/Job Descriptions available from Employee Services Centre by:

e-mail: jobs@nottscc.gov.uk stating Job Title & Ref No. and your name, address & postcode.

Alternatively, please telephone 0845 3304218 or apply in writing to: Employee Services Centre, County Hall, West Bridgford, Nottingham NG2 7QP.

For more information, please contact Barbara Booth on Tel: 01623 433233. e-mail: barbara.booth@nottscc.gov.uk

Or visit our website: www.nottinghamshire.gov.uk/ workingforchildrensservices

Closing date: 4 June 2004.

Equality in Services & Employment

Nottinghamshire
County Council
Social Services

# Notes

## Chapter 1

1  In this book, 'England' is not simply a substitute term for 'United Kingdom'. Policy on Children's Services in Scotland, Wales and Northern Ireland, although frequently dominated discursively by the same preoccupations, has not always mirrored that in England. This book focuses on England, but Chapter 7, for example – in the context of a discussion on 'intensive family support' projects (IFSPs) – refers to developments in Scotland.

2  In her review into the status of social care services, published in April 2007, Dame Denise Platt (Chair of the Commission for Social Care) drew attention to a criticism of the *British Journal of Social Work* with its 'small readership' and articles that are 'tortuously theoretical and get nowhere' (Platt 2007: 17). This could, of course, be interpreted as a question of subjective preference or taste. However, it might also be argued that this criticism, from a primary definer of the purpose and intent of social work and social care, was actually targeted at the journal's willingness to engage with often abstract theoretical and political questions.

3  'Baby P', a 17-month-old boy, died on 3 August 2007 from severe injuries which were inflicted while he was in the care of his mother, her partner and a lodger in the household, Jason Owen. On 11 November 2008 at the Old Bailey two men were found guilty of causing or allowing the death of a child or vulnerable person. The mother had already pleaded guilty to the same charge. 'Baby P' had been subject to a child protection plan from 22 December 2006, following concerns that he had been abused and neglected. He was still subject to this plan when he died.

4  In June 2007 Gordon Brown succeeded Tony Blair as Prime Minister and it could be argued that there is now a greater willingness to refer to 'Labour', or even the 'Labour Party'. Throughout this book, however, 'New Labour' is referred to because the analysis developed in what follows indicates that the current government does not, despite the more 'interventionist' emergency response to the so-called 'credit crunch' in 2008, diverge in any significant way from the politics of New Labour (see also Garrett 2008a). This was reflected, in late 2008, with the announcement of plans to partly privatize the postal service ('Brown faces Labour revolt on post plans', *Guardian*, 17 December 2008: 14–16). Simon Jenkins (2008a) has argued that the 'banks have not been "nationalised", just deluged with money . . . [T]his is not socialism in our time, just public money hurled at the face of capitalism'. Furthermore, 'to the extent that the New Labour "project" has had intellectual shape, it has been provided by Brown rather than Blair . . . Probably more than Blair, Brown

represents the pure form of New Labour' (McKibbin 2007: 17–18; see also Lancaster 2008).

5 Providing further evidence of attentiveness to the discursive construction of the plan to 'transform' Children's Services, New Labour has been intent on trying to manage public concerns about the database. The name given to this element of the project has, therefore, frequently changed. For example, at different times the official literature referred to 'information hubs', 'information sharing and assessment' systems, the Children's Index, or simply the 'Index'. Now, however, the preferred designation is ContactPoint. The acronym used throughout this book is, however, CPd which embraces the core fact that the system remains a 'database'; a feature of the system the government has been keen, over time, to erase.

## Chapter 2

1 'Neoconservatism' is a related 'ism' which has also generated global opposition. This is 'entirely consistent with the neoliberal agenda of elite governance, mistrust of democracy, and the maintenance of market freedoms. But it veers away from the principles of pure neoliberalism and has reshaped neoliberal practices in two fundamental respects: first, in its concern for order as an answer to the chaos of individual interests, and second, in its concern for overweening morality as the necessary social glue to keep the body politic secure in the face of external and internal dangers' (Harvey 2005: 82). This and the following chapter draws on my 'How to be modern: New Labour's neoliberal modernity and the *Change for Children* programme', *British Journal of Social Work*, 38(2): 270–89, 2008. I am grateful to Oxford Journals for permitting me to have recourse to this article.

2 Notions such as 'reinventing government' and the argument that governments should be intent on 'steering not rowing' are entirely consistent with the process of neoliberal reconfiguration (Osborne and Gaebler 1992). Jan Nederveen Pieterse – in his observations on what he terms the evolution of 'Neoliberal Empire', a formation that twins practices of empire with those of neoliberalism – has commented on some of the tension between small-government ideology and big-government reality in the USA. This tension is now especially apparent given that big 'government now returns in the form of a huge homeland security department, military and intelligence expansion, new surveillance and security systems, propaganda policies and government support for industries at risk' (Nederveen Pieterse 2004: 124). These remarks encourage us to see anti-'big government' politics, with greater clarity, as anti-welfare politics.

3 It is also important to recognize that the 'state is not a "thing" reducible to fixed, static boundaries but an active and creative process of institution-building and intervention' (Coleman and Sim 2005: 104). The neoliberal state has, in fact, multiple identities and multiple boundaries. So, to extend and complicate Bourdieu's metaphor, the state may be less a 'battlefield' site and more an expansive terrain on which occurs a series of seemingly discrete and unconnected skirmishes. A more detailed account of the work of Bourdieu can be found in Garrett (2007a; 2007b)

4 Importantly, though, class is not a stable, fixed social patterning. Thus, while 'neoliberalization may have been about the restoration of class power, it has not necessarily meant the restoration of economic power to the same people' (Harvey 2005: 31).

5 Chris Harman (2008) has produced an interesting argument which maintains that there is a tendency to place too great an emphasis on 'precariousness', 'insecurity' and so on. From an entirely different political position, Giddens tends to reframe 'risk' as the creation of new 'opportunities' within the market: 'Active risk taking is recognized as inherent in entrepreneurial activity, but the same applies to the labour force.

Deciding to go to work and give up benefits, or taking a job in a particular industry are risk-infused activities – but such risk taking is often beneficial both to the individual and to the wider society' (Giddens 1998: 116).

6  It might also be argued that the current fixation with 'what works' and 'evidence-based practice' is partly derived from the penal estate (Martinson 1974).

7  In may be better to refer to 'Third *Ways*' because similar policies have been pursued in other jurisdictions: for example, Germany, Australia, and the USA. Giddens (2001) has argued that there is a 'global' debate on the 'Third Way'. Finlayson (2003) has produced an interesting contribution on the 'Third Way' in England and illuminated how the concept was derived from other than neoliberal sources.

8  What is more, Gordon Brown's own political vocabulary is strikingly similar to that of Giddens (and Blair). For example, Brown (2007) believes that public services can 'make the difference' by becoming 'social innovators . . . taking risks . . . standing up to entrenched interests . . . [able to] to move beyond old, dull and all-too-familiar "one size fits all" solutions'.

9  For example, one senior government minister, in his review of *Over to You*, has asserted that 'New Labour has been good at paying teachers and nurses and police, not good enough at making them feel like *real entrepreneurs*' (Miliband 2007: 24, emphasis added). Indeed, the government is intent on reforming and improving welfare services 'through the embedding of business culture' (Farnsworth 2006: 818).

10 Gramsci's key ideas are to be found in the Prison Notebooks, comprising 33 exercise books, written between 8 February 1929 and June 1935 'when a severe setback in his health prevented him from continuing his study' (Martin 1998: 40). Readers new to Gramsci can find English translations of his writings in Bellamy (1994), Forgacs (1988) and Hoare and Nowell Smith (2005). Elsewhere, I have written on Gramsci and social work (Garrett 2008c; forthcoming).

## Chapter 3

1  This chapter is not concerned with emerging macro forms of *organizational* governance within Children's Services (for example, Children's Trusts and Local Safeguarding Boards). This section of the book also reworks some of the material previously featured in 'New England and New Labour: retracing American templates for the *Change for Children* programme?', *Journal of Comparative Social Welfare*, 23(1): 31–46, 2007. I am grateful to Taylor and Francis for granting me permission to refer to this piece.

2  It was reported that Sharon Shoesmith, the head of Children's Services in Haringey who was sacked in December 2008 on account of her role in the 'Baby P' case, was scheduled to be a key speaker at conference on improving child protection, in January 2009. Perhaps reflecting New Labour's orientation on these themes, almost to the point of caricature, the title of her paper was to have been: 'Breaking down silos: inspiring ownership and sharing responsibility for measuring impacts and outcomes across partnerships' ('Why children are left to die beyond help's reach', *Observer*, 16 November 2008: 18–19.

3  'Vulgate' refers to an ancient Latin version of the Scriptures made by St Jerome and others in the fourth century.

4  The 'welfare reform legislation of 1996' refers to the Personal Responsibility and Work Reconciliation Act (PRWORA) 1996. Jamie Peck (2001), specifically focusing on the various workfare programmes constructed following the enactment of this legislation, has provided an authoritative guide to the evolution of these 'reforms'. Mimi Abramovitz (2006: 337), noting the drop in welfare caseloads, maintains if welfare 'reform' genuinely 'set out to improve the lives of women, something has gone

dangerously awry'. Surveying the impact of PRWORA, she concludes that it should be seen as part of a neoliberal agenda that has three main goals: work enforcement, marriage promotion and the creation of a smaller welfare state. In relation to the third dimension she observes that the 'inept response to Hurricane Katrina further high-lights what happens when the government sheds responsibility for general welfare ... As with the low-lying flooded neighbourhoods in New Orleans, the poor, women, and persons-of-colour are disproportionately represented among the victims of governmental aloofness about poverty' (Abramovitz 2006: 347).

5  The government has maintained, for example, that a 'child with conduct disorder at age 10 will cost the public purse around £70,000 by age 28 – up to ten times more than a child with no behavioural problems' (Chief Secretary to the Treasury 2003: 14).

6  In this context, Caroline Elkins (2005) has produced a fascinating recent study of British 'counter-insurgency' in Kenya in the 1950s and early 1960s. What is particu-larly striking is how the vocabulary associated with this endeavour is still so prevalent in a contemporary, 'home' and civilian context: for example, the references to 'screening', 'targeting', 'reception centres', the 'hard core', and so on. See also the comments of the social welfare adviser, to the colonial secretary in 1951, on the role that social work potentially fulfils in helping to achieve cultural hegemony: 'Social work in civilised countries became the safeguard of society. Without it hardship would, as it had in the past, lead to brigandage and even revolution' (in Elkins 2005: 108).

7  Sure Start Local Programmes (SSLPs) were set up between 1999 and 2003 in the 'most disadvantaged' areas of the country. However, SSLPs became 'children's centres' and there are now 2,500 centres open. The New Labour administration has maintained that 'Sure Start was never an event. It is a journey'. However, it has stated that the most recent National Evaluation of Sure Start (NESS), drawing on fieldwork under-taken between April 2005 and July 2007, revealed a 'significant improvement' on the previous 2005 interim report. For example, children in SSLP areas exhibited 'more positive social behaviour' and 'greater independence/self-regulation' (see DCSF 2008b). There is a manifesto commitment that by 2010 there will be 3500 Sure Start Children's Centres. In a related development, it was reported, in April 2008, that Nottingham was to become an 'early intervention city, a laboratory for testing some successful US anti-poverty schemes' (Wintour 2008).

8  The CtC is also being deployed in other European locations. Boutellier (2001), for example, has reported that CtC has been operated in the Netherlands where the 'high-risk profile of a CtC community is determined, among other things, on the basis of a survey among school pupils' (Boutellier 2001: 373).

## Chapter 4

1  All references to the Laming Report will simply provide, for the sake of brevity, the relevant paragraph number. The chapter will also make use of some of the material initially featured in 'Protecting children in a globalised world: 'race' and place in the Laming Report on the death of Victoria Climbié', *Journal of Social Work*, 6(3): 315–36, 2006. I am grateful to Sage for granting me permission to have recourse to and rework some of this material.

2  Although it will not be provided in what follows, it is possible, in fact, to refer to and plot the *geography* of the Climbié tragedy.

3  Two journalists, visiting Berthe and Francis prior to the parents' journey to London to the Inquiry, commented: 'Their [Berthe and Francis'] hopes rested on Victoria and the reasons can be seen all around Abidjan. In the dirty streets, little girls sell fruit and vegetables for money. In tiny backstreet sheds, other children toil away in crude

smelting works where aluminium roofs are melted down to make pots' (Israel and McVeigh 2001). Perhaps, this brief description illuminates the fact that neoliberalism, impoverishment and economic exploitation – and what we have seen David Harvey refer to as 'accumulation by dispossession' – were likely to be factors constraining these parents' choices.

4  What was significant in the early social work encounters with Victoria and her aunt, in Ealing, was the fact that no adequate attempts were made to liaise with welfare services in France. However, if enquiries had been 'vigorously pursued in France' this may have resulted in 'information coming to light' about Victoria being 'known' to French social services and that her 'school in Paris had registered . . . a Child at Risk Emergency Notification with the French education authorities' in February 1999 because of the repeated absences from school (para. 4.71). Indeed, at 'no stage had Ealing Social Services attempted to verify independently any aspect of Kouao's life before her arrival in England' (para. 4.166; see also para. 6.440–1).

5  Related to this point, the way in which the migratory movement of people is often described may also fuel this 'animosity' toward individual migrants, even serving to promote 'xeno-racism' (Fekete 2001). Thus, these spatial displacements are often likened to an 'environmental catastrophe' and with words such as 'mass', 'horde', 'horde' and 'swarm' being deployed (Fekete 2001: 27). In this context, it should also be noted that it was an asylum-seeking minicab driver who acted decisively and took Victoria to hospital prior to her death (Weir 2003).

6  See, for example, 'South African minister attacks poaching of staff', *Community Care*, 31 May–6 June 2001: 8; 'UK recruitment agency sets up shop in Pretoria', *Community Care*, 14–20 June 2001: 5; 'UK "helping to strip Africa of health staff" ', *Guardian*, 27 May 2005: 9. In 2005 it was reported that there 'has been an 82 per cent increase in the number of overseas social workers entering the UK' according to research commissioned by the DoH. Between April 2003 and May 2004 'numbers rose from 1,390 to 2,524 – the largest increase recorded to date' (see 'Biggest ever rise in overseas staff', *Community Care*, 10–16 February 2005: 14).

7  The Care Standards Tribunal (2008: para. 71) has correctly observed that the 'role played by the medical profession in the tragedy has, as far as we are aware, never been analysed in the same detail as the role of the social workers. However, we do not accept that they are totally absolved from any responsibility'.

## Chapter 5

1  Some of the material featured in this chapter is derived from and radically reworks previously published pieces: 'The electronic eye: emerging surveillant practices in social work with children and families', *European Journal of Social Work*, 7(1): 57–71 which was published in 2004: also two articles which appeared the following year; 'Social work's "electronic turn": notes on the deployment of information and communication technologies in social work with children and families', *Critical Social Policy*, 25(4): 529–54; 'New Labour's new electronic "telephone directory": the Children Act 2004 and plans for databases on all children in England and Wales', *Social Work and Social Sciences Review*, 12(1): 5–22. I am grateful to Taylor and Francis, Sage and Whiting & Birch for giving me permission to refer to my work again.

2  Liberty, the civil and human rights organization, recently called London the 'snooping capital of the world' and the UK has the highest density of closed circuit television (CCTV) cameras anywhere in the world (Robinson, O. 2003).

3  Boyne (2000: 292), in fact, has referred to what he perceives as the 'relative calm with which contemporary developments of surveillance powers have been received'. Numerous 'reality TV' shows, such as *Big Brother*, may have domesticated certain

modes of surveillance, such as CCTV (see in this context Bauman 2002: ch. 2; Wayne 2003; McGrath 2004). Cindy Katz (2008) has produced insights into how, in the USA, notions of 'risk' and childhood are impacting on how parents are resorting to privately purchased surveillance technologies.

4  Forty per cent of black males are profiled on the database are on the National DNA Database. It has also been reported that nearly 1.5 million 10- to 18-year-olds will have been entered by 2009 (see 'DNA register "labels children criminal" ', *Observer*, 9 March 2008: 4). The director of forensic services at New Scotland Yard and spokesman for ACPO has argued that all school children at risk of becoming criminal should be entered onto the National DNA Database (Graef 2008).

5  Table 5.1 is partly derived from information produced by the Information Commissioner's Office in November 2006 (ICO 2006b). It does not purport to be exhaustive.

6  Telford and Wrekin Council, under the auspices of an IRT scheme, operated, it appears a system of 'traffic lights' as opposed to 'flags'. Ruddy (2004) contains a short account on a CPd pilot developed and deployed by East Sussex Council.

7  All future references to the contributions in the House of Lords' Committee Stage debate of the Children Bill in May 2004 will simply provide the name of the contributor and the relevant column (col.) in the House of Lords' Hansard.

8  See '333,000 users to have access to database of English children', *Guardian*, 18 June 2007: 12; 'Lost in the post – 25 million at risk after discs go missing', *Guardian*, 21 November 2007: 1; 'Personal details of millions of learner drivers lost by contractor in Iowa', *Guardian*, 18 December 2007: 4.

9  See 'ID contractor denounced over data lose', *Guardian* 23 August 2008.

10  See 'Security fears prompt call for the scrapping of children's database', *Guardian*, 6 December 2007: 10. Given the loss of data stored by the government, fears have also now been expressed about the security of the CAF/eCAF system as well as the CPd.

11  The website is located at http://www.everychildmatters.gov.uk

12  Taylorism refers to the production techniques devised by Frederick W. Taylor (1856–1915). Donna Baines (2004b: 277) has observed that within social work in Canada, 'Taylorization has taken place, in part, through the integration of computer packages that increase the pace and volume of work, the gathering of statistics, the monitoring of worker productivity through E-supervision. Some models of E-supervision involve the use of computer-based packages that remind workers of pre-set time limits for certain parts of the job (for example the completion of intake and assessments), the order in which these tasks must be completed and when workers must seek supervisory approval before moving on. The computer package does not permit workers to complete tasks in other than the prescribed order. Failure to complete the tasks on time is reported electronically to the supervisor.' In this context, the Joint Area Review of Haringey Children's Services, following the death of 'Baby P' revealed that some 'allocations of cases within social care services are made electronically and without discussion with social workers' (Ofsted, Healthcare Commission, HMC 2008: 14).

# Chapter 6

1  Stuart Hall et al. (1978), in their classic study of the 'mugging' phenomenon, direct us to identify the discursive origins of keywords and terms: to seek out how they are *put to work*, politically deployed to create, or trigger, certain meanings or associations and enter into popular usage. Indeed, it could be argued that 'anti-social behaviour' – like 'mugging' in a different way during a different period – connotes a 'whole complex of social themes' (Hall et al. 1978: 19). An earlier version of this chapter was published, in 2007, as 'Making "anti-social behaviour": a fragment on the evolution

of "ASBO politics" in Britain', *British Journal of Social Work*, 37(5): 839–56. I am grate-ful to Oxford Journals for giving me permission to have recourse to my work again.

2  In early 2008, the New Labour Housing Minister, Caroline Flint, located the council estate at the forefront of the government's 'modernizing' policy agenda with the suggestion unemployed tenants should be compelled to sign 'commitment contracts' which highlighted their desire to find work: 'It would be a big change of culture from the time when the council handed over someone the keys and forgot about them for 30 years. The question that we should ask of new tenants is what commitment they will make to improve their skills, find work, and take the support that is available to them' (in Fabian Society 2008). The proposed cultural shift is, of course, entirely in tune with the neoliberal politics which characterises New Labour's evolving approach to governance.

3  When it was suggested that Blair and his cabinet were influenced by Richard Sennett's (2004) *Respect: The Formation of Character in an Age of Inequality*, Sennett disappointed New Labour by asserting that 'Mr Blair, I fear has shown no respect for public sector workers, with all his targets, surveillance and testing. Indeed, his predicament is that he has lost respect of society', ('Blair believes his agenda is a moral certainty', *Guardian*, 18 May 2005: 13). In a subsequent interview, however, Sennett was to provide a more favourable response to New Labour's plans (see 'With respect', *Guardian*, 14 January 2006).

4  Sir Ian Blair, when the Commissioner of the Metropolitan Police, subsequently argued that children at risk of joining teenage gangs could be taken into care (see 'Met chief: stop gangs by taking children into care', *Guardian*, 3 March 2007: 1).

5  Sheffield Hallam University, for example, provides a 'Postgraduate Certificate Anti-Social Behaviour Law and Strategies' programme.

6  There are also indications that Jack Straw (the New Labour administration's first Home Secretary, 1997–2001) attempted to deploy his personal experience to support tougher measures. When 'his parents divorced he and his mother moved to a council estate where, as a grammar school boy, he stood out. His mother was plagued by a difficult next door neighbour, and when mutual accusations came to court the teen-age Straw had to give evidence on behalf of his mother, who was cleared of assault, while the neighbour was bound over to keep the peace' (Burney 2005: 19). Frank Field, the MP for Birkenhead, also played a role in promoting locating 'anti-social behaviour' at the core of New Labour politics. His revealingly titled *Neighbours From Hell* called for policies that would enable the 'decent majority' to 'repel the advance of . . . scarcely disguised semi-barbarian forces' (Field 2003: 6).

7  This tactic of laying emphasis on the 'authenticity' derived from 'experience' and the 'real world' has also been apparent in the USA in attempts made to defend 'tougher' approaches to minor infractions of the law: 'What particularly galls police about these critiques is that ivory tower academics – many of whom have never sat in a patrol car, walked or bicycled a beat, lived in or visited regularly troubled violent neighbourhoods, or collected any relevant data of their own "on the ground" – cloak themselves in the mantle of the empirical "scientist" and produce "findings" . . . Police don't have time for these virtual-reality theories; they do their own work in the real world' (Bratton and Kelling 2006; see also Garrett 2007c).

8  See also the Foreword by the Prime Minister in the Prime Minister's Strategy Unit (2007). 'Terrorism' and ASBOs was explicitly conjoined when Lord Carlile raised the prospect of introducing 'terror asbos', in his third annual report on the operation of the control orders which place 'terror' suspects under virtual house arrest. Carlile was of the opinion that 'TASBOs' could be used as an alternative to control orders in some 'low level' cases (see 'Asbo proposal for terror suspects', *Guardian*, 19 February 2006: 14).

9 There also exists a wider European dimension to this tendency to blur issues related to crime and (in) security. In 2000, for example, the Commission of the European Communities (CEC 2000) provided common guidelines and proposals for the prevention of crime throughout the European Union. In the context of this chapter's thematic preoccupation, the definition of 'crime' is significant in that it was maintained that the 'concept . . . covers separate realities'. These were said to include '*anti-social conduct, which without necessarily being a criminal offence*, can by its cumulative effect generate a climate of tension and insecurity' (CEC 2000: 6, emphasis added). That is – paradoxically – a crime (in the form 'anti-social conduct') could be committed *without* there having being a 'criminal offence'. Other documents emerging from the EU have served to render elastic notions as to what constitutes 'crime' with the Council of the EU, for example, maintaining that crime prevention 'covers all measures that are intended to reduce or otherwise contribute to reducing crime and citizens' *feeling of insecurity*' (Council of the European Union 2001: 4, emphasis added).

10 Sadie Parr, in an evaluation of an IFSP, without a core residential unit, has maintained that such projects have to contend with 'the *competing priorities* of the (child centred) ECM strategy and the (community-focused) Respect agenda' (Parr 2008: 10–11, emphasis added). However, this is highly problematic notion because the foundational concept that the child's welfare is 'paramount', in the Children Act 1989 (s. 1), suggests that their can be no 'competing priorities' of equal weight or force.

## Chapter 7

1 More recently, these projects have been referred to as 'Family Intervention Projects' (see Home Office 2007). In April 2007 there were 53 and 11 of these either have, or are envisaged as having, 'core' residential units. An earlier version of this chapter was presented as a paper at the world conference of the International Federation of Social Workers held in Munich, 30 July–3 August 2006. This was then published, the following year as 'Sinbin solutions: the "pioneer" projects for "problem families" and the forgetfulness of social policy research', in *Critical Social Policy*, 27(2): 203–30. I am grateful to Sage for permission to refer to my work again. Readers are also directed to the exchange which resulted following the publication of my initial article (see Garrett 2007d; Nixon 2007).

2 *Shameless*, an awarding winning television series screened by Channel 4 since January 2004, is focused on a what would seem to be a stereotypical, fictional 'problem family' living on a Manchester council estate. The series emphasizes the roguish, drunken and chaotic character of the family, yet it – primarily – invites the audience to recognize the coping ability of the family and its communal warmth. Given the popularity of the series, it might be argued that this reflects a certain public ambivalence about the 'problem family'.

3 Dillane et al. (2001: 7), in their Executive Summary, state that 59 per cent of 'active cases' were deemed successful.

4 Some evidence suggests that the 'problem family' can be interpreted as part of matrix of ideas partly preoccupied with Irish people in Britain. In the early 1950s, for example, Spinley (1953) provided an account of 'one of the worst slums in London'. She went onto describe a district which was 'notorious . . . for vice and delinquency . . . a major prostitution area' and the 'blackest spot in the city for juvenile delinquency'. In this area, she asserted 'a large proportion of the inhabitants are Irish; social workers say: "The Irish land here, and while the respectable soon move away, the ignorant and the shiftless stay"' (Spinley 1953: 40; see also Garrett 2004).

5  Hall (1960: 166) maintained that 'anti-social families are families unwilling or unable to accept social aid voluntarily, as distinct from the "social weak", who show some willingness to co-operate.'
6  Table 7.1 is derived from Dillane et al. (2001) and Nixon et al. (2006). The latter research team investigated all but the Dundee Families Project. As noted above, additional 'trailblazer' projects are now in the process of being set up (Respect Task Force 2006: 22; see also NCH 2006; Parr 2008).
7  The NCH also concedes, rather blandly that 'racial harassment may be a component of the range of difficulties being expressed by potential consumers' (NCH Action for Children Scotland 1995: 5).
8  This may also be one of the consequences of the emphasis now placed on 'multi-disciplinary working', particularly in engagements with children and their families. That is to say, a certain 'blurring' may occur and users of services may be left unclear who it is they are dealing with, and what their powers, entitlements and rights may be (see also Garrett 2003a: ch. 4). Nixon et al. (2006) fail, moreover, to comment on how families they interviewed could, perhaps, have been unclear precisely what the role of the research team was within the projects. Nonetheless, this apparent lack of clarity about roles, on the part of some respondents, may have influenced the comments they provided.
9  Indeed, there are specific paragraphs which illuminate a sense of edgy equivocation and self-censoring (Nixon et al. 2006: 51, para. 3 provides a fascinating example). Writing for a different audience, the researchers elsewhere appear to condemn media constructions of 'problem families' and 'anti-social families', yet, as this chapter suggests, they themselves are vulnerable to the charge that they are implicated in such constructions (see Parr and Nixon 2008).

## Chapter 8

1  In the Green Paper the envisaged model was referred to as 'Social Care Practices'. Subsequently, this was changed to 'Social Work Practices' (SWP). This chapter, for ease of reference, mostly refers to SWP, the current name for this envisaged model. Some of the discussion featured in this chapter was previously published in my article 'Social work practices: silences and elisions in the plan to 'transform' the lives of children 'looked after' in England which was published in *Child and Family Social Work*, 13(3): 311–18. I am grateful to Blackwell for giving me permission to refer to and rework some of this material.
2  The reference to children 'looked after' at risk of being 'left behind' periodically recurs in the literature associated with the *Care Matters* programme. Although not a focal concern of this chapter, this phrase hints at the impact of US policy-making on New Labour governments (see also Chapter 3). The No Child Left Behind Act of 2001 is controversial federal legislation introduced to improve the 'performance' of primary and secondary schools (see also Goldstein 2004).
3  This section of the Le Grand working group report implicitly seeks to erase parents. The sheer vagueness of the remarks relating to the 'formal transfer of responsibility' is, of course, also striking.
4  The staffing structure of SWP might also encompass students on placements and each of the practices could be 'linked with a local university to provide access to a library etc' (Le Grand 2007a: 31).
5  The notion that social workers come to work with 'a strong moral purpose, idealism, energy, enthusiasm and a commitment to rectifying injustice' is repeated mantra-like in the discourse pivoting on SWP. It appears initially in Pettigrew (2006) and is cut-and-pasted into a *Guardian* article by Le Grand and Pettigrew (2006). It then occurs in

the report of the 'independent' working group (Le Grand 2007a) and again in Le Grand (2007b). Other phrases are also apt to be recursive in the discursive presentation of those advocating SWP.

6 Their work is based on a detailed study of the evolution of management literature circulating throughout the private sector in France, but their reading and interpretation of this literature has a more general European resonance. Importantly, Boltanski and Chiapello (2005: 96) conclude, however, that the 'mobilizing capacity contained in the new spirit of capitalism as deployed in 1990s management literature seems to us poor'. It might also be argued that the arguments deployed in, for example, the literature associated with SWP are also unconvincing.

7 None of this is meant, of course, to imply that those seeking to defeat the plan to introduce SWP can only have recourse to the realm of the discursive (see, for example, Mooney and Law 2007).

8 Polly Neate and Alastair Pettigrew were also members of Conservative Party Commission on Social Workers (2007) which reported the same year as the Le Grand working party. Harriet Ward is the academic chiefly associated with the formulation and promotion of the 'looking after children' (LAC) system (Ward 1995). It remains difficult to overemphasize the significance of this technology of intervention given that it provided the foundation for further developments relating to the assessment of children and families. For example, LAC was immensely significant in terms of providing a systematic template for how to Taylorize the *work* in social work and to facilitate e-working. Significantly also, both LAC and SWP discourses find commonality in how each seeks to marginalize the parents of children and young people 'looked after'.

9 Le Grand was a senior adviser to the Blair administration from 2003 to 2005. He has also been, as Polly Toynbee (2006) reminded readers of the *Guardian*, the 'architect of the NHS payment-by-results market' (see also Le Grand 2007b). Perhaps, in this context, the remarks of Bourdieu in *Homo Academicus* remain apt. Here he criticized 'consecrated intellectuals': these were, for him, establishment figures, heavy with symbolic capital and a sense of their own worth, who are 'crowned with scholastic glory . . . the ultimate product of the dialectic of acclaim and recognition which drew into the system those most inclined to reproduce it without distortion' (Bourdieu 2003: 83).

10 Toynbee (2006: 37), criticizing the SWP idea in the *Guardian*, reports: 'Not long ago I found a venture capital investment offer from a company called Valley Care. They had bought 12 houses as homes for three children each, at £150,000 per property. The prospectus said the children each brought with them a fee of between £3,000 and £6,500 a week. Staff would be paid just £12–£15,000 a year – not highly qualified. So each home would make between £150,000 and £300,000 profit a year: the worse the children, the higher the profit.'

## Chapter 9

1 During the months of November and December 2008, a number of other cases involving Children's Services were also reported in the media. Two boys, Romario Mullings-Sewell (2 years) and Delayno Mullings-Sewell (3 months) were killed in Manchester and their mother was arrested on suspicion of murder. The children were said to be known to social services but not on the child protection register ('Doctor alerted police to "distressed" mother hours before child killings', *Guardian*, 14 November 2008: 14). A case in Sheffield, involving child sexual abuse taking place within a family over a number of years, was also reported ('Agencies face row over "unspeakable abuse" by father who raped and impregnated sisters', *Guardian*, 27 November 2008: 4).

2  In the *Guardian*, this image and the related news report was placed above a seemingly more significant report – 'Brown signals further rate cut as G20 leaders gather'. This told readers about the 'crisis meeting of the G20' seeking to put in place a collective response the 'global recession'.

3  According to the *Independent*, on 2 December 2008, the so-called 'Eight' were: Shoesmith, who had been identified by Capita – the private company that oversees the borough's schools – to be the director of Children's Services in Haringey in 2005; three social workers, Ward, Christou and Henry; Shoesmith's deputy, Cecilia Hitchen; Clive Preece, the service head for children and families; Haringey council leader, George Meehan; and Liz Santry, lead councillor for Children's Services in the borough. Shoesmith was subsequently sacked, on the authority of Ed Balls, the Secretary of State for Children, Schools and Families, with immediate effect on 8 December 2008 ('Baby P case director is sacked without payout', *Guardian*, 9 December 2008: 7). Both Meehan and Santry resigned their positions. Perhaps somewhat obscured by the media portrayal of the social workers involved were the comments of 'Baby P's father: 'I would . . . like to thank the social workers who have been involved since P's death. They have acted with professionalism and courtesy' ('Three told to expect "significant" jail time over baby's death', *Guardian*, 15 November 2008: 14). Not for the first time, following the deaths of children, the police appeared to have largely evaded the scrutiny of the media.

4  The 'Moors Murders' were committed by Ian Brady and Myra Hindley in the Manchester area of England between 1963 and 1965. Their five victims were children between the ages of 10 and 15 years.

5  Shannon Matthews, it was alleged had been kidnapped: later it was revealed that the child had been hidden by her mother, Karen, and an accomplice, Michael Dovovan. Karen Matthews was charged with child neglect and perverting the course of justice. In December 2008, she and Donovan were found guilty on charges of kidnapping, false imprisonment and perverting the course of justice. Following the verdict, Superintendent Andy Brennan described the troubled and pathetic Karen as 'pure evil'. An image of her, published in *Observer*, also appeared to resemble a familiar image of Myra Hindley ('She "loved Shannon to bits": but she had her kidnapped. Inside the dark, dangerous world of Karen Matthews', *Observer*, 7 December 2008: 29–32).

6  This swiftly completed JAR commenced on 13 November 2008 and was completed by 26 November 2008. Although not a central focus of the investigators and relegated to the appendix, the document revealed the poverty and hardship encountered by many of the borough's residents even prior to the current economic 'downturn': 'Long-term unemployment is twice the national rate and almost twice the London rate . . . Northumberland Park ward has the highest unemployment rate of all London wards at 16.7%, almost eight times the national rate. It is estimated that 21% of households in Haringey are living in unsuitable accommodation' (Ofsted, Healthcare Commission, HM Inspectorate of Constabulary 2008: 15).

7  Haringey Social Services also received a 'glowing joint review' just months before the death of Victoria Climbié (editorial 'Who inspects the reviews?', *Community Care*, 11–17 July 2002: 5; see also Garrett 2003a: 141–2).

8  Partly in response to this situation it was announced that the government was to set up a new taskforce to 'improve the quality and status of social workers in the wake of the Baby P scandal in Haringey'. Headed by Moira Gibb, the chief executive of Camden council, it is to be, according to the government, a 'nuts and bolts review' of social work practice ('Review aims to boost social workers' status and quality', *Guardian*, 8 December 2008: 4).

# References

Abramovitz, M. (2006) Welfare reform in the United States, *Critical Social Policy*, 26(2): 336–65.

Adorno, T.W. (2003) *Can One Live After Auschwitz: A Philosophical Reader*. Stanford, CA: Stanford University Press.

ADSS, LGA and Confed (2007) *Care Matter: Transforming the lives of Children in Care*. http://adass.org.uk/publications/conresp/2007/transforming.pdf

Allen, C. (2003) Desperately seeking fusion: on 'joined-up thinking', 'holistic practice' and the *new* economy of welfare professional power, *British Journal of Sociology*, 54(2): 287–306.

Allen, C. (2005) On the social relations of contract research production: power, positionality and epistemology in housing and urban research, *Housing Studies*, 20(6): 989–1007.

Association of Directors of Social Services (ADSS) (2002) *Tomorrow's Children: A Discussion Paper on UK Child Care Services in the Coming Decade*. London: ADSS.

Audit Commission (2008) Every Child Matters – are we there yet? Press release, 29 October.

Axford, N., Berry, V., Little, M. and Morpeth, L. (2006) Developing a common language in Children's Services through research-based inter-disciplinary training, *Social Work Education*, 25(2): 161–76.

Back, L., Keith, M., Khan, A., Shukra, K. and Solomos, J. (2002) The return of assimiliationism: race, multiculturalism and New Labour, *Sociological Research Online*, 7(2). http://.socresonline.org.uk/7/2/back.html

Baines, D. (2004a) Pro-market, non-market: the dual nature of organizational change in social services delivery, *Critical Social Policy*, 24(1): 5–29.

Baines, D. (2004b) Caring for nothing: work organization and unwaged labour in social services, *Work, Employment and Society*, 12(2): 267–95.

Bairstow, K. (1994/95) Liberation and regulation? Some paradoxes of empowerment, *Critical Social Policy*, 4: 34–47.

Barnett, A. (2000) Corporate populism and partyless democracy, *New Left Review*, 3: 80–9.

Barrett, M. (1992) Words and things: materialism and method in contemporary feminist analysis, in M. Barrett and A. Phillips (eds) *Destabilizing Theory: Contemporary Feminist Debates*. Cambridge: Polity Press.

Bauman, Z. (1991) *Modernity and the Holocaust*. Cambridge: Polity Press.

Bauman, Z. (2000a) Social issues of law and order, *British Journal of Criminology*, 40: 205–21.

Bauman, Z. (2000b) *Liquid Modernity*. Cambridge: Polity Press.

Bauman, Z. (2002) *Society Under Siege*. Cambridge: Polity Press.

Bauman, Z. (2004) *Wasted Lives: Modernity and its Outcasts*. London: Polity Press.

Bawden, A. (2006) Is sharing caring? *Education Guardian*, 12 December.

Beck, U. (2000) Zombie categories, in J. Rutherford (ed.) *The Art of Life*. London: Lawrence and Wishart.

Beckett, C. (2003) The language of siege: military metaphors in the spoken language of social work, *British Journal of Social Work*, 33: 625–39.

Bell, M. (2008) Put on ICS? *Community Care*, 5 June: 18–20.

Bellamy, R. (ed.) (1994) *Gramsci: Pre-Prison Writings*. Cambridge: Cambridge University Press.

Bellamy Foster, J. (1998) Introduction, in H. Braverman, *Labour and Monopoly Capitalism: The Degradation of Work in the Twentieth Century – 25th Anniversary Edition*. New York: Monthly Review Press.

Bennett, T., Grossberg, L. and Morris, M. (2005) *New Keywords: A Revised Vocabulary of Culture and Society*. Oxford: Blackwell.

Bentley, N. (2007) Speech in NCVCCO Children's Services Debate, 8 January. London: CBI.

Bhattacharyya, G., Gabriel, J. and Small, S. (2001) *Race and Power: Global Racism in the twenty-first century*. London: Routledge.

Bigo, D. (2006) Security, exception, ban and surveillance, in D. Lyon (ed.) *Theorizing Surveillance*. Cullompton: Willan.

Birnbaum, N. (2004) Missing in action: the New Deal legacy in American politics, *Soundings*, 28: 167–84.

Blacker, C.P. (ed.) (1952) *Problem Families: Five Enquiries*. London: Eugenics Society.

Blair, T. (1999) Beveridge revisited: a welfare state for the 21st century, in R. Walker (ed.) *Ending Child poverty: Popular Welfare in the 21st Century*. Bristol: Policy Press.

Blair, T. (2003) Prime Minister's speech to Congress, 18 July. www.number-10.gov.uk/output/Page4220.asp

Blair, T. (2005) We are the change-makers. Speech by Prime Minister Tony Blair to the Labour Party Conference, Brighton, 27 September.

Blair, T. (2006a) Time for a proper debate on law and order, 23 June. www.number-10.gov.uk/output/Page9737.asp

Blair, T. (2006b) PM targets eradication of anti-social behaviour, 10 January. www.number-10.gov.uk/output/Page8898.asp

Blair, T. (2006c) Interview with BBC on social exclusion, 31 August. www.pm.gov.uk/output/Page10023.asp

Blair, T. (2006d) Our sovereign value – Fairness, 5 September. www.number-10.gov.uk/output/Page10037.asp

Blair, T. (2007) Our nation's future – the role of work, 30 March www.number-10.gov.uk/output/Page11405.asp

Blears, H. (2004) *The Politics of Decency*. London: Mutuo.

Boltanski, L. and Chiapello, E. (2005) *The New Spirit of Capitalism*. London: Verso.

Bourdieu, P. (1991) *Language and Symbolic Power*. Cambridge: Polity Press.

Bourdieu, P. (2000) *Pascalian Meditations*. Cambridge: Polity Press.

Bourdieu, P. (2001) *Acts of Resistance: Against the New Myths of Our Time*. Cambridge: Polity Press.

Bourdieu, P. (2002) Social space and symbolic power, in M. Haugaard (ed.) *Power: A Reader*. Manchester: Manchester University Press.

Bourdieu, P. (2003) *Homo Academicus*. Cambridge: Polity Press.

Bourdieu, P. and Accardo, A., Balazas, G., Beaud, S., Bonvin, F., Bourdieu, E., Bourgois, P., Broccolichi, S., Champagne, P., Christin, R., Faguer, J.P., Garcia, S., Lenoir, R.,

Oeuvrard, F., Pialoux, M., Pinto, L., Podalydes, D., Sayad, A., Soulie, C. and Wacquant, J.D. (2002) *The Weight of the World: Social Suffering in Contemporary Society*. Cambridge: Polity Press.

Bourdieu, P. and Wacquant, L. (1999) On the cunning of imperialist reason. *Theory, Culture & Society*, 16(1): 41–59.

Bourdieu, P. and Wacquant, L. (2001) NewLiberalSpeak: notes on the new planetary vulgate, *Radical Philosophy*, 105: 2–6.

Bourdieu, P. and Wacquant, L.J.D. (2004) *An Invitation to Reflexive Sociology*. Cambridge: Polity Press.

Boutellier, H. (2001) The convergence of social policy and criminal justice, *European Journal of Criminal Policy and Research*, 9: 361–80

Boyne, R. (2000) Post-panopticism, *Economy and Society*, 29(2): 285–307.

Bratton, W. and Kelling, G. (2006) There are no cracks in the broken windows, *National Review Online*, 28 February. www.nationalreview.com/comment/bratton_kelling200602281015.asp

Braziel, J.A. and Mannur, A. (eds) (2003) *Theorizing Diaspora*. Oxford: Blackwell.

Brenner, N. and Theodore, N. (eds) (2002) *Spaces of Neoliberalism*. Oxford: Blackwell.

British Association for Adoption and Fostering (BAAF) (2004) *Information, Referral and Tracking – the Professional Basis for Informed Judgement: Extract from BAAF's Response to Every Child Matters*. London: BAAF.

British Association of Social Workers (BASW) (2003) *Briefing on Asylum and Immigration (Treatment of Claimants etc) Bill*. www.basw.co.uk/articles.php?articleId=157

British Association of Social Workers (BASW) (2004) *Notice to Members: Asylum and Immigration (Treatment of Claimants etc) Bill 2004*. www.basw.co.uk/articles.php?articleId=179

British Association of Social Workers (BASW) (2007) *Care Matters: Transforming the Lives of Children and Young People in Care – Consultation Response Form*. www.basw.co.uk/Default.aspx?tabid=54&articleID=539

British Association of Social Workers (BASW) (2008) *Outcome of Motions from BASW AGM – 30 April 2008*. www.basw.co.uk/default.aspx?tabid=53&articleID=757

Brown, A.D. (2003) Authoritative sensemaking in a public inquiry report, *Organization Studies*, 25(1): 95–112.

Brown, A.P. (2004) Anti-social behaviour, crime control and social control, *Howard Journal of Criminal Justice*, 43(2): 203–12.

Brown, G. (2006) How to embrace change, *Newsweek*, 12 July. www.msnbc.msn.com/id/13121948/site/newsweek/

Brown, G. (2007) Speech to Labour Party Conference. http://news.bbc.co.uk/2/hi/uk_news/politics/7010664.stm

Burney, E. (2002) Talking tough, acting coy: what happened to the Anti-social Behaviour Order? *The Howard Journal of Criminal Justice*, 41(5): 469–84.

Burney, E. (2005) *Making People Behave: Anti-social Behaviour, Politics and Policy*. Cullompton: Willan.

Butler, J. (2004) *Precarious Life*. London: Verso.

Cabinet Office (1998) *Our Information Age: The Government's Vision*. London: Cabinet Office.

Cabinet Office (1999) *Modernising Government*. London: Cabinet Office.

Cabinet Office (2000) *E-government: A Strategic Framework for Public Services in the Information Age*. London: Stationery Office.

Calder, M. C. (2004) Out of the frying pan into the fire? A critical analysis of the integrated children's system. *Child Care in Practice*, 10(3): 225–40.

Callinicos, A. (2006) *Universities in a Neoliberal World*. London: Bookmarks.

Cameron, D. (2008) Extremism, individual rights and the rule of law in Britain. Speech given on 26 February. www.conservatives.com/tile.do?def=news.story. page&obj_id=142585&speeches=1

Cammack, P. (2004) Giddens's way with words, in S. Hale, W. Leggett and L. Martell (eds) *The Third Way and Beyond: Criticisms, Futures, Alternatives*. Manchester: Manchester University Press.

Care Standards Tribunal (2008) LA v General Social Care Council. www.carestandardstribunal.gov.uk/Judgments/j890/LA%20-%20(Decision)%20020608.doc

Carey, M. (2007) White-collar proletariat? Braverman, the deskilling/upskilling of social work and the paradoxical life of the agency care manager, *Journal of Social Work*, 7(1): 93–114.

Carvel, J. (2004) All eyes on the child, *Guardian Society, Children's Services Supplement*, 19 May: 2–3.

Castells, M. (2000) Materials for the exploration of the network society, *British Journal of Sociology*, 51(1): 5–24.

Central Information Technology Unit (CITU) (1996) *Governing Direct: A Prospectus of the Electronic Delivery of Government Services*. London: CITU and Office of Public Service.

Chand, A. (2003) 'Race' and the Laming Report on Victoria Climbié: lessons for inter-professional policy and practice, *Journal of Integrated Care*, 11(4): 28–38.

Chand, A. (2008) Every child matters? A critical review of child welfare reforms in the context of minority ethnic children and families, *Child Abuse Review*, 17: 6–22.

Channer, Y. and Parton, N. (1990) Racism, cultural relativism and child protection, in The Violence Against Children Study Group, *Taking Child Abuse Seriously*. London: Unwin Hyman.

Charlesworth, S.J. (2000) *A Phenomenology of Working class Experience*. Cambridge: Cambridge University Press.

Chief Secretary to the Treasury (2003) *Every Child Matters*. London: HMSO, Cm 5860. www.dfes.gov.uk/everychildmatters/

Children's Workforce Development Council (2008) *The State of the Children's Social Care Workforce 2008: Summary Report*. Leeds: CWDC.

Clarke, J. (2004) *Changing Welfare, Changing States*. London: Sage.

Clarke, J. (2005) New Labour's citizens: activated, empowered, responsibilized, abandoned. *Critical Social Policy*, 25(4): 447–63.

Clarke, J., Newman, J., Smith, N., Vidler, E. and Westmarland, L. (2007) *Creating Citizen-Consumers: Changing Publics and Changing Public Services*. London: Sage.

Cleaver, H., Barnes, J., Bliss, D. and Cleaver, D. (2004) *Developing Identification, Referral and Tracking Systems: An Evaluation of the Processes Undertaken by Trailblazer Authorities: Interim Report*. London: Department of Education and Skills.

Cleaver, H., Walker, S., Scott, J., Cleaver, D., Rose, W., Ward, H. and Pithouse, A. (2008) *The Integrated Children's System: Enhancing Social Work and Inter-Agency Practice*. London: Jessica Kingsley.

Cohen, P. (2004) A place to think? Some reflections on the idea of the university in the age of the 'knowledge economy', *New Formations*, 53: 12–28.

Coleman, N. and Harris, J. (2008) Calling social work, *British Journal of Social Work*, 38(3): 580–99.

Coleman, R. and Sim, J. (2005) Contemporary statecraft and the 'punitive obsession': a critique of the new penology, in J. Pratt, D. Brown, M. Brown, S. Hallsworth and W. Morrison (eds) *The New Punitiveness: Trends, Theories and Perspectives*. Cullompton: Willan.

Commission of the European Communities (CEC) (2000) *The Prevention of Crime in the*

*European Union: Reflection on Common Guidelines and Proposals for Community Financial Support*. 29 November, COM 786.

Committee on Local Authority and Allied Personal Services (1968) *Report of the Committee on Local Authority and Allied Personal Social Services*. London: HMSO.

Confederation of British Industry (CBI) (2006a) Making Every Child Matter, *Transforming Public Services Brief*, November.

Confederation of British Industry (CBI) (2006b) *Children first: The Power of Choice in Children's Services*. London: CBI.

Conservative Party Commission on Social Workers (2007) *No More Blame Game – The Future for Children's Social Workers*. www.fassit.co.uk/leaflets/No%20More%20Blame%20Game%20-%20The%20Future%20for%20Children's%20Social%20Workers.pdf

Cooper, A. (2005) Surface and depth in the Victoria Climbié inquiry report, *Child and Family Social Work*, 10: 1–9.

Council of the European Union (2001) *Council Decision Setting up a European Crime Prevention Network*. 26 April, 7794/01.

Cunningham, S. and Tomlinson, J. (2005) Starve them out: does every child matter? A commentary on Section 9 of the Asylum and Immigration Act (Treatment of Claimants, etc) Act 2004, *Critical Social Policy*, 25(2): 253–75.

Cushman, M. (2004) Why database projects fail to support professionals. Paper presented at Tracking Children: A Road to Danger in the Children Bill seminar, London School of Economic, 6 April.

Daly, M. (2008) Wither EU social policy? An account and assessment of developments in the Lisbon social inclusion process, *Journal of Social Policy*, 37(1): 1–21.

Davis, A. and Garrett, P. M. (2004) Progressive practice for tough times: social work, poverty and division in the 21st century, in M. Lymbery and S. Butler (eds) *Social Work Ideals and Practice Realities*. London: Palgrave.

Davis, M. (2006) *Planet of Slums*. London: Verso.

Deacon, A. (2000) Learning from the US? The influence of American ideas upon 'new labour' thinking on welfare reform, *Policy & Politics*, 28(1): 5–18.

Department for Children, Schools and Families (DCSF) (2006) Hughes announces chairs of care working groups. Press release, 28 November.

Department for Children, Schools and Families (DCSF) (2007) *The Children's Plan: Building Brighter Futures*. London, TSO.

Department for Children, Schools and Families (DCSF) (2008a) *Building Brighter Futures: Next Steps for the Children's Workforce*. Nottingham: DCSF Publications.

Department for Children, Schools and Families (DCSF) (2008b) Sure Start shows positive impact on lives of children and families – but ministers say more to do. Press release, 4 March.

Department for Children, Schools and Families (DCSF) (2008c) Government intensifies drive to tackle anti-social behaviour in young people by stepping in early. Press release, 18 March.

Department for Communities and Local Government (DCLG) (2006) *Anti-social Behaviour Intensive Family Support Projects*. London: Department for Communities and Local Government.

Department for Communities and Local Government (DCLG) (2008a) *Digital Inclusion: An Analysis of Social Disadvantage and the Information Society*. London: Department for Communities and Local Government.

Department for Communities and Local Government (DCLG) (2008b) *Technology Futures and Digital Inclusion*. London: Department for Communities and Local Government.

Department for Communities and Local Government (DCLG) (2008c) *Understanding Digital Exclusion*. London: Department for Communities and Local Government.

Department for Education and Skills (DfES) (2004) *Every Child Matters: Change for Children.* www.dfes.gov.uk/

Department for Education and Skills (DfES) (2005a) *Learning from Information Sharing and Assessment Trailblazer.* http://www.dfes.gov.uk/

Department for Education and Skills (DfES) (2005b) *Information Sharing Index – Lewisham.* London: Stationery Office.

Department for Education and Skills (DfES) (2005c) *Fact Sheet: Information Sharing (IS) Index.* London: Stationery Office.

Department for Education and Skills (DfES) (2005d) Better Services for Children as Government Acts on Lord Laming Recommendation. Press release, 8 December.

Department for Education and Skills (DfES) (2005e) *Common Assessment Framework for Children and Young People: Guide for Service Managers and Practitioners.* London: Stationery Office.

Department for Education and Skills (DfES) (2005f) *Fact Sheet: Lead Professional.* London: Stationery Office.

Department for Education and Skills (DfES) (2005g) *Common Core of Skills and Knowledge for the Children's Workforce.* London: Stationery Office.

Department for Education and Skills (DfES) (2005h) *Multi-agency Working: Glossary.* London: Stationery Office.

Department for Education and Skills (DfES) (2006a) *Children's Workforce Strategy: Building a World-class Workforce for Children, Young People and Families.* London: Stationery Office.

Department for Education and Skills (DfES) (2006b) *Multi-agency Working: Toolkit for Practitioners.* London: Stationery Office.

Department for Education and Skills (DfES) (2006c) *The Lead Professional: Practitioners' Guide.* London: Stationery Office.

Department for Education and Skills (DfES) (2006d) *The Lead Professional: Managers' Guide.* London: Stationery Office.

Department for Education and Skills (DfES) (2006e) Options for Excellence: review of the social care workforce. Press release, 27 January.

Department for Education and Skills (DfES) (2006f) Pathfinder project to look at boarding provision for vulnerable children and young people. Press release, 6 November.

Department for Education and Skills (DfES) (2006g) *Young People's Guide to the Care Matters Green Paper.* Newcastle Upon Tyne: Office of the Children's Rights Director.

Department for Education and Skills (DfES) (2007a) *Care Matters: Time for Change.* London: Department for Education and Skills.

Department for Education and Skills (DfES) (2007b) *Care Matters: Consultation Responses.* London: Department for Education and Skills.

Department for Education and Skills (DfES) (2007c) *Care Matters: Young People's Responses.* London: Department for Education and Skills.

Department for Work and Pensions (2008a) *No One Written Off: Reforming Welfare to Reward Responsibility.* Norwich: TSO.

Department for Work and Pensions (2008b) *The Social Fund: A New Approach* www.dwp.gov.uk/consultations/2008/social-fund-new-approach.pdf

Department of Health (DoH) (1995) *The Challenge of Partnership in Child Protection.* London: HMSO.

Department of Health (DoH) (1998) *Quality Protects: Framework for Action.* London: HMSO.

Department of Health (DoH) (1999a) *Adoption Now: Messages for the Research.* Chichester: Wiley.

Department of Health (DoH) (1999b) Tide is turning on adoption. Press release, 18 October.

Department of Health (DoH) (2000a) *Adoption: the future.* London: HMSO. Cm 5017.

Department of Health (DoH) (2000b) Prime Minister announces action to overhaul adoption process. Press release, 7 July.

Department of Health (DoH) (2002) New social work degree will focus on practical training. Press release, 22 May.

Department of Health (DoH) (2004) Children's charter for health and social care unveiled today. Press release, 15 September.

Department of Health, Department for Education and Employment, Home Office (2000) *Framework for the Assessment of Children in Need and their Families.* London: Stationery Office.

Department of the Environment (1995) *Anti-Social Behaviour on Council Estates: A Consultation Paper on Probationary Tenancies.* London: Department of the Environment.

Dillane, J., Hill, M., Bannister, J. and Scott, S. (2001) *Evaluation of the Dundee Families Project.* Glasgow: Dundee City Council, Scottish Executive, NCH Scotland.

Dolowitz, D.P. with Hulme, R., Nellis, M. and O'Neill, F. (eds) (2000) *Policy Transfer and British Social Policy.* Buckingham: Open University.

Dowty, T. (2004) What type of help families need and what help is available now? Paper presented at the Tracking Children: A Road to Danger in the Children Bill seminar, London School of Economic, 6 April.

Dudley Edwards, R. (2005) Blunkett is torn apart by the media hounds, *Sunday Independent,* 6 November.

Dumenil, G. and Levy, D. (2004) *Capital Resurgent: Roots of the Neoliberal Revolution.* Cambridge, MA: Harvard University Press.

Duncan Smith, I. (2008) The legacy of broken lives, *Guardian,* 13 November.

Dyer-Witheford, N. (1999) *Cyber-Marx: Cycles and Circuits of Struggle in High-Technology Capitalism.* Urbana and Chicago, IL: University of Illinois Press.

Elkins, C. (2005) *Imperial Reckoning: The Untold Story of Britain's Gulag in Kenya.* New York: Holt.

Elmer, G. (2004) *Profiling Machines.* Cambridge, MA: MIT.

Elmer. G. and Opel, A. (2006) Pre-empting panoptic surveillance: surviving the inevitable war on terror, in D. Lyon (ed.) *Theorizing Surveillance.* Cullompton: Willan.

Evans, R.J. (2001) Social outsiders in German history, in R. Gellately and N. Stoltzfus (eds) *Social Outcasts in Nazi Germany.* Princeton, NJ: Princeton University Press.

Fabian Society (2008) Flint: We must break link between council housing and worklessness. Press release, 5 February. http://fabians.org.uk/events/socialhousing-conference-08/speech

Fairclough, N. (2000) *New Labour, New Language?* London: Routledge.

Farnsworth, K. (2006) Capital to the rescue. *Critical Social Policy,* 26(4): 817–43.

Fekete, L. (2001) The emergence of xeno-racism, *Race & Class,* 43(2): 23–40.

Felstead, A., Jewson, N. and Walters (2005) *Changing Places of Work.* Houndsmill: Macmillan.

Ferguson, H. (2001) Social work, individualization and life politics, *British Journal of Social Work,* 31: 41–55.

Ferguson, H. (2003) In defence (and celebration) of individualization and life politics for social work, *British Journal of Social Work,* 33(5): 699–707.

Ferguson, H. (2004) *Protecting Children in Time: Child Abuse, Child Protection and the Consequences of Modernity.* Houndsmill: Palgrave.

Ferguson, I. (2008) Neoliberalism, happiness and wellbeing, *International Socialism,* 117: 123–43,

Ferguson, I. and Lavallette, M. (2004) Beyond power discourse: alienation and social work, *British Journal of Social Work*, 34: 297–312.

Field, F. (2003) *Neighbours From Hell*. London: Politico's Publishing.

Finlayson, A. (2003) *Making Sense of New Labour*. London: Lawrence and Wishart.

Flint, J. (2003) Housing and ethnopolitics: constructing identities of active consumption and responsible community, *Economy and Society*, 32(3): 611–29.

Flint, J. (2004a) Reconfiguring agency and responsibility in the governance of social housing in Scotland, *Urban Studies*, 41(1): 151–72.

Flint, J. (2004b) The responsible tenant: housing governance and the politics of behaviour, *Housing Studies*, 19(6): 893–909.

Foley, P. and Rixon, A. (eds) (2008) *Changing Children's Services*. Bristol: Policy Press in association with the Open University.

Foord, M. and Young, F. (2006) Housing managers are from Mars, social workers are from Venus: anti-social behaviour, 'respect' and interprofessional working – reconciling the irreconcilable, in A. Dearing, T. Newburn and P. Somerville (eds) *Supporting Safer Communities – Housing, Crime and Neighbourhoods*. London: Chartered Institute for Housing.

Foot, M. (2005) A triumph of hearsay and hysteria, *Guardian*, 5 April.

Forgacs, D. (ed.) (1988) *A Gramsci Reader*. London: Lawrence and Wishart.

Foucault, M. (1980) The eye of power, in C. Gordon (ed.) *Power/Knowledge*. Brighton: Harvester.

Foundation for Information Policy Research (2006) *Children's Databases – Safety and Privacy: A Report for the Information Commissioner*. www.fipr.org/childrens_databases.pdf

France, A. and Crow, I. (2005) Using the 'risk factor paradigm' in prevention: lessons from the evaluation of communities that care. *Children & Society*, 19(2): 172–84.

France, A. and Utting, D. (2005) The paradigm of 'risk and protection-focused prevention' and its impact on services for children and families, *Children & Society*, 19(2): 77–90.

Franko Aas, K. (2005) The ad and the form: punitiveness and technological culture, in J. Pratt, D. Brown, M. Brown, S. Hallsworth and W. Morrison (eds) *The New Punitiveness: Trends, Theories and Perspectives*. Cullompton: Willan.

Fraser, N. (1997) *Justice Interruptus: Critical Reflections on the Post-Socialist Condition*. London: Routledge.

Fraser, N. and Gordon, L. (1997) A genealogy of 'dependency': tracing a keyword in the U.S. welfare state, in N. Fraser, *Justice Interruptus: Critical Reflections on the Post-Socialist Condition*. London: Routledge.

Freeman, R. (1999) Recursive politics: prevention, modernity and social systems, *Children & Society*, 13(4): 232–41.

Friedman, J. (2000) Americans again, or the new age of imperial reason, *Theory, Culture & Society*, 17(1): 139–46.

Furedi, F. (2004) *Therapy Culture*. London: Routledge.

Garland, D. (2001) *The Culture of Control: Crime and Social Order in Contemporary Society*. Oxford: Oxford University Press.

Garrett, P.M. (1999) Producing the moral citizen: the 'looking after children' system and the regulation of children and young people in public care, *Critical Social Policy*, 19(3): 291–312.

Garrett, P.M. (2000) The hidden history of the PFIs: the repatriation of unmarried mothers and their children from England to Ireland in the 1950s and 1960s, *Immigrants and Minorities*, 19(3): 25–44.

Garrett, P.M. (2002a) Social work and the 'just society': diversity, difference and the sequestration of poverty', *The Journal of Social Work*, 2(2): 187–210.

Garrett, P.M. (2002b) Yes minister: reviewing the 'looking after children' experience and identifying the messages for social work research. *British Journal of Social Work*, 32: 831–46.

Garrett, P.M. (2003a) *Remaking Social Work with Children and Families: A Critical Discussion on the 'Modernisation' of Social Care*. London: Routledge.

Garrett, P.M. (2003b) The trouble with Harry: why the 'new agenda of life politics' fails to convince, *British Journal of Social Work*, 33(3): 381–97.

Garrett, P.M. (2004) *Social Work and Irish People in Britain: Historical and Contemporary Responses to Irish Children and Families*. Bristol: Policy Press.

Garrett, P.M. (2005) Social work's 'electronic turn': notes on the deployment of information and communication technologies in social work with children and families, *Critical Social Policy*, 25(4): 529–54.

Garrett, P.M. (2007a) Making social work more Bourdieusian: why the social professions should critically engage with the work of Pierre Bourdieu, *European Journal of Social Work*, 10(2): 225–43.

Garrett, P.M. (2007b) The relevance of Bourdieu for social work: a reflection on obstacles and omissions, *Journal of Social Work*, 7(3): 357–81.

Garrett, P.M. (2007c) Learning from the 'Trojan horse'? The arrival of 'anti-social behaviour orders' in Ireland, *European Journal of Social Work*, 10(4): 497–511.

Garrett, P.M. (2007d) 'Sinbin' research and the 'lives of others', *Critical Social Policy*, 27(4): 560–65.

Garrett, P.M. (2008a) Helping Labour to win again? Anthony Giddens' programme for the new prime minister, *Critical Social Policy*, 28(2): 235–46.

Garrett, P.M. (2008b) Questioning Habermasian social work: a note on some alternative theoretical resources, *British Journal of Social Work*, advanced electronic access from 17 March. http://bjsw.oxfordjournals.org/

Garrett, P.M. (2008c) Thinking with the Sardinian: Antonio Gramsci and social work, *European Journal of Social Work*, 11(3): 237–50.

Garrett, P. M. (2009) Marx and 'modernization': reading *Capital* as social critique and inspiration for social resistance to neoliberalization, *Journal of Social Work*, 9(2): 199–221.

Garrett, P. M. (forthcoming) The 'whalebone' in the (social work) 'corset'? Notes on Antonio Gramsci and Social Work Educators, *Social Work Education*.

Gellately, R. and Stoltzfus, N. (eds) (2001) *Social Outcasts in Nazi Germany*. Princeton, NJ: Princeton University Press.

General and Municipal Boilermakers Union (GMB) (2005) GMB Congress demands end to electronic tagging of workers 'battery farm' workplaces. Press release, 6 June. www.gmb.org.uk/Templates/Internal.asp?/NodalID=91861

Geoghegan, L. and Lever, J. with McGimpsey, I. (2004) *ICT for Social Welfare*. Bristol: Policy Press.

Giddens, A. (1998) *The Third Way: The Renewal of Social Democracy*. Cambridge: Polity Press.

Giddens, A. (ed.) (2001) *The Global Third Way Debate*. Cambridge: Polity Press.

Giddens, A. (2003) Introduction – neoprogressivism: a new agenda for social democracy, in A. Giddens (ed.) *The Progressive Manifesto*. Cambridge: Polity Press.

Giddens, A. (2007) *Over to You, Mr Brown: How Labour Can Win Again*. Cambridge: Polity Press.

Giddens, A. (2008) New Labour in very alive, *Guardian*, 1 December.

Gilbert, J. (2004) The second wave: the specificity of New Labour neo-liberalism, *Soundings*, 26: 25–46.

Gilling, D. (2007) *Crime Reduction and Community Safety*. Cullompton: Willan.

Gilroy, P. (2005) Melancholia or conviviality: the politics of belonging in Britain, *Soundings*, 29: 35–47.

Glass, N. (1999) Sure Start: the Development of an early intervention programme in the United Kingdom, *Children & Society*, 13(4): 257–64.

Golding, P. (2000) Forthcoming features: information and communications technology and the sociology of the future, *Sociology*, 34(1): 165–84.

Goldstein, R.A. (2004) Who needs the government to police us when we can do it ourselves? The new panopticon in teaching, *Cultural Studies/Critical Methodologies*, 4(3): 320–8.

Goodman, S. and Speer, S.A. (2007) Category use in the construction of asylum seekers, *Critical Discourse Studies*, 4(2): 165–85.

Graef, R. (2008) The usual suspects, *Guardian*, 21 March.

Graham, S. (2006) Surveillance, urbanization and the US revolution in military affairs, in D. Lyon, D. (ed.) *Theorizing Surveillance*. Cullompton: Willan.

Gray, J. (2003), Blair in thrall to the myth of a monolithic modernity, *Guardian*, 19 April.

Gregory, M. and Holloway, M. (2005) Language and the shaping of social work, *British Journal of Social Work*, 35: 37–53.

Gregg, P. (2008) *Realising Potential: A Vision for Personalised Conditionality and Support*. London: Department for Work and Pensions.

Grint, K. and Woolgar, S. (1997) *The Machine at Work*. Cambridge: Polity Press.

Guillari, S. and Shaw, M. (2005) Supporting or controlling? New Labour's housing strategy for teenage parents, *Critical Social Policy*, 25(3): 402–17.

Guru, S. (2008) Social Work and the 'War on Terror', *British Journal of Social Work*, advanced electronic access from 22 September. http://bjsw.oxfordjournals.org/

Hall, P. (1960) *The Social Services of Modern England*. 5th edn. London: Routledge and Kegan Paul.

Hall, S. (1993) Thatcherism today, *New Statesman and Society*, 26 November. 14–17.

Hall, S. (2003) New Labour's double-shuffle, *Soundings*, 24: 10–25.

Hall, S. and Jacques, M. (1989) *New Times: The Changing Face of Politics in the 1990s*. London: Lawrence and Wishart.

Hall, S., Critcher, C., Jefferson, T., Clarke, J. and Roberts, B. (1978) *Policing the Crisis: Mugging, the State and Law and Order*. Houndsmill: Macmillan Education.

Hare, I. (2004) Defining social work for the 21st century: the International Federation of Social Workers' revised definition of social work, *International Social Work*, 47(3): 407–27.

Harlow, E. (2004) Why don't women want to be social workers anymore? New managerialism, postfeminism and the shortage of social workers in Social Services Departments in England and Wales, *European Journal of Social Work*, 7(2): 167–79.

Harlow, E. and Webb, S.A. (eds) (2003) *Information and Communication Technologies in the Welfare Services*. London: Jessica Kingsley.

Harman, C. (2008) Theorising neoliberalism, *International Socialism*, 117: 25–49.

Harris, J. (1998) Scientific management, bureau-professionalism, new managerialism: the Labour process of state social work, *British Journal of Social Work*, 28: 839–62.

Harvey, D. (2005) *A Brief History of Neoliberalism*. Oxford: Oxford University Press.

Hauss, G. and Ziegler, B. (2008) City welfare in the sway of eugenics: a Swiss case study, *British Journal of Social Work*, advanced access from 10 April. http://bjsw.oxfordjournals.org/

Hawkins, D.J., Catalano, R.F. and Arthur, M.W. (2002) Promoting science-based prevention in communities, *Addictive Behaviours*, 27: 951–76.

Hawkins, L., Fook, J. and Ryan, M. (2001) Social workers' use of the language of social justice, *British Journal of Social Work*, 31: 1–13.

Haworth, A. and Manzi, T. (1999) Managing the 'underclass': interpreting the moral discourse of housing management, *Urban Studies*, 36(1): 153–65.

Haylett, C. (2001) Modernisation, welfare and 'third way' politics: limits in 'thirds'?, *Transactions of the Institute of British Geographers*, 26(1): 43–56.

Heawood, S. (2008) The world around Baby P is wrong: why are we afraid to say so. *Independent on Sunday*, 16 November.

Heffernan, K. (2006) Social work, new public management and the language of 'service user', *British Journal of Social Work*, 36: 139–47.

Heron, G. (2004) Evidencing anti-racism in student assignments: where has all the racism gone? *Qualitative Social Work*, 3(3): 277–95.

Hill, A. (2007) How problem families learn self-respect, *Observer*, 30 September.

Hillyard, P., Sim, J., Tombs, S. and Whyte, D. (2004) Leaving a 'stain upon the silence': contemporary criminology and the politics of dissent, *British Journal of Criminology*, 44: 369–90.

Hine, J. (2005) Early multiple intervention: a view from on track, *Children & Society*, 19(2): 117–30.

Hoare, Q. and Nowell Smith, G. (eds) (2005) *Antonio Gramsci: Selections from Prison Notebooks*. London: Lawrence and Wishart.

Hobsbawm, E. (2008) The £500bn question, *Guardian*, 9 October.

Hogan, C. and Murphey, D. (2002) *Outcomes: Reframing Responsibility for Well-being*. Baltimore, MD: Annie E. Casey Foundation.

Holman, B. (2003) Curran leads attack on antisocial behaviour, *Zero 2 Nineteen*, 29 July.

Home Office (1998) *Fairer, Faster, Firmer*. London: Home Office.

Home Office (2002) *Entitlement Cards and Identity Fraud: A Consultation Paper*. London: Home Office.

Home Office (2003a) *Respect and Responsibility: Taking a Stand Against Anti-Social Behaviour*. London: Home Office.

Home Office (2003b) *Together – Tackling Anti-Social Behaviour*. London: Home Office.

Home Office (2007) Innovative new help to tackle 'neighbours from hell'. Press release, 11 April. www.respect.gov.uk/article.aspx?id=9072

Home Office (2008) *Youth Crime Action Plan 2008*. London: Home Office.

Home Office Border and Immigration Agency (2008) *Introducing Compulsory Identity Cards for Foreign Nationals*. London: Home Office.

House of Lords and House of Commons Joint Committee on Human Rights (JCHR) (2004) *Children Bill: Nineteenth Report of the Session 2003–4*. London: Stationery Office.

Howard League for Penal Reform (2008) Prison suicide leaps by 37% in 2007. Press release, 2 January.

Howe, D. (1994) Modernity, postmodernity and social work, *British Journal of Social Work*, 24(5): 513–32.

Hudson, J. (2000) E-galitarianism? The information society and New Labour's repositioning of welfare, *Critical Social Policy*, 23(2): 268–91.

Hudson, J. (2002) Digitising the structures of government: the UK's information age government agenda, *Policy & Politics*, 30(4): 515–31.

Hughes, B. (2005) Information sharing announcement speech. Department for Education and Skills. Press release, 8 December.

Hughes, B. (2007) Children's Workforce Development Council speech. Department for Education and Skills. Press release, 27 March.

Humphries, B. (2004) An unacceptable role for social work: implementing immigration policy, *British Journal of Social Work*, 34(1): 93–107.

Hunt, J. (2004) Roaring trade on the e-market, *Society Guardian, e-public supplement*, 25 February.

Hutton, J. (2006) Welfare reform: 10 years on, 10 years ahead. Department for

Work and Pension. Press release, 18 December. www.dwp.gov.uk/aboutus/2006/18-12-06.asp

Iarskaia-Smirnova, E. and Romanoz, P. (2002) A salary is not important here: the professionalization of social work in contemporary Russia, *Social Policy & Administration*, 36(2): 123–41.

Information Commissioner's Office (ICO) (2006a) *A Report on the Surveillance Society: For the Information Commissioner by the Surveillance Studies Network*. www.ico.gov.uk/upload/documents/library/data_protection/practical_application/surveillance_society_full_report_2006.pdf

Information Commissioner's Office (ICO) (2006b) Protecting Children's Personal Information: ICO Issues Paper, 22 November. www.ico.gov.uk/upload/documents/pressreleases/2006/protecting_childrens_personal_information.pdf

Irwin, G. (2008) Inequality and recession in the US and Britain, *Soundings*, 38: 117–30.

Israel, S. and McVeigh, T. (2001) What happened to Victoria will happen to someone else, *Observer*, 23 September. www.guardian.co.uk/uk/2001/sep/23/news.theobserver

Ives, P. (2004) *Language and Hegemony in Gramsci*. London: Pluto.

Jacquemin, M. (2004) Children's domestic work in Abidjan, *Côte d' Ivoire Childhood*, 11(3): 383–97.

Jacquemin, M. (2006) Can the language of rights get hold of complex realities of child domestic work? *Childhood*, 13(3): 389–408.

Jacques, M. (2008) Northern Rock's rescue is part of a geopolitical sea change, *Guardian*, 18 January.

James, A.L. and James, A. (2001) Tightening the net: children, community and control, *British Journal of Sociology*, 52(2): 211–28.

Jameson, F. (2000) Postmodernism or the cultural logic of late capitalism, in M. Hardt and K. Weeks (eds), *The Jameson Reader*. Oxford: Blackwell.

Jameson, F. (2002) The dialectics of disaster, *South Atlantic Quarterly*, 101(2): 197–305.

Jenkins, S. (2008a) The end of capitalism? No, just another burst bubble, *Guardian*, 15 October.

Jenkins, S. (2008b) Officialdom cannot hammer straight the crooked timber of mankind, *Guardian*, 14 November.

Johnson, R. (2004) Masculinities on a new frontier? Bush, Blair and the war on terror, *Soundings*, 28: 75–87.

Jones, C. (2001) Voices from the front line: state social workers and New Labour, *British Journal of Social Work*, 31: 547–62.

Jones, T. and Newburn, T. (2004) The convergence of US and UK crime control policy: exploring substance and process, in T. Newburn and R. Sparks (eds) *Criminal Justice and Political Cultures*. Cullompton: Willan.

Jordan, B. (2001) Tough love: social work, social exclusion and the third way, *British Journal of Social Work*, 31(4): 527–46.

Joseph, J. (2006) *Marxism and Social Theory*. Houndsmill: Palgrave Macmillan.

Katz, C. (2008) Childhood and the culture of management. Paper presented at Marginalized *Youth*, International Conference, University of Bielefeld, Germany, 31 January–2 February.

Kelling, G.L. and Coles, C.M. (1996) *Fixing Broken Windows: Restoring Order and Reducing Crime in Our Communities*. New York: Free Press.

Kendall, L. and Harper, L. (2002) *From Welfare to Wellbeing: The Future of Social Care*. London: IPPR.

Khan, S. (2003) Bombay calling . . ., *Observer*, 7 December.

King, D. and Wickham-Jones, M. (1999) From Clinton to Blair: the Democratic (Party) origins of welfare to work, *Political Quarterly*, 70(1): 62–75.

Klein, N. (2007) *The Shock Doctrine: The Rise of Disaster Capitalism*. London: Allen Lane.

Knight, T. and Caveney, S. (1998) Assessment and action records: will they promote good parenting? *British Journal of Social Work*, 28(1): 29–43.

Kunstreich, T. (2003) Social welfare in Nazi Germany, *Journal of Progressive Human Services*, 14(2): 23–53.

Labour Party (1996) *Protecting Our Communities: Labour's Plans for Tackling Criminal, Anti-social Behaviour in Neighbourhoods*. London: Labour Party.

Ladipo, D. (2001) The rise of America's prison-industrial complex, *New Left Review*, 7: 109–24.

Laming, Lord (2009) *The Protection of Children in England. A Progress Report*. London: Stationery Office.

Lancaster, J. (2008) Cityphobia, *London Review of Books*, 30(20): 3–6.

Law, A. and Mooney, G. (2007) Strenuous welfarism: restructuring the welfare labour process, in G. Mooney and A. Law (eds) *New Labour/Hard Labour: Restructuring and Resistance Inside of the Welfare Industry*. Bristol: Policy Press.

Le Grand, J. (2007a) *Consistent Care Matters: Exploring the Potential of Social Work Practices*. London: Department for Education and Skills.

Le Grand, J. (2007b) *The Other Invisible Hand: Delivering Public Services through Choice and Competition*. Princeton, NJ: Princeton University Press.

Le Grand, J. and Pettigrew, A. (2006) Childcare would be better as a business, *Society Guardian*, 4 October. www.guardian.co.uk/society/2006/oct/04/childrensservices.comment

Leggett, W. (2005) *After New Labour: Social Theory and Centre Left Politics*. Basingstoke: Palgrave.

Levitas, R. (1996) The concept of social exclusion and the new Durkheimian hegemony, *Critical Social Policy*, 16(1): 5–21.

Lewis, G. and Neal, S. (2005) Introduction: contemporary political contexts, changing terrains and revisited discourses, *Ethnic and Racial Studies*, 28(3): 423–44.

Ling, T. (2002) Delivering joined-up government in the UK: dimensions, issues and problems, *Public Administration*, 80(4): 615–42.

Little, M., Axford, N. and Morpeth, L. (2003) Children's Services in the UK 1997–2003: problems, developments and challenges for the future, *Children & Society*, 17(3), 205–14.

London Borough of Brent (1985) *A Child in Trust: The Report of the Panel of Inquiry into the Circumstances Surrounding the Death of Jasmine Beckford*. London: Borough of Brent.

London Borough of Greenwich (1987) *A Child in Mind: Protection of Children in a Responsible Society. The Report of the Commission of Inquiry into the Circumstances Surrounding the Death of Kimberley Carlile*. London: London Borough of Greenwich.

London Borough of Lambeth (1987) *Whose Child? The Report of the Public Inquiry into the Death of Tyra Henry*. London: Borough of Lambeth.

Lorenz, W. (2005) Social work and a new social order – challenging neo-liberalism's erosion of solidarity, *Social Work & Society*, 3(1): 93–101. http://socwork.net/Lorenz2005.pdf

Lyon, D. (2001a) *Surveillance Society: Monitoring Everyday Life*. Buckingham: Open University Press.

Lyon, D. (2001b) Surveillance after September 11, *Sociological Research Online*, 6(3). www.socresonline.org.uk/6/3/lyon.html.

Lyon, D. (2003) *Surveillance after September 11*. Cambridge: Polity Press.

Lyon, D. (ed.) (2006) *Theorizing Surveillance*. Cullompton: Willan.

Mackintosh, M., Raghuram, P. and Henry, L. (2006) A perverse subsidy: African trained nurses and doctors in the NHS, *Soundings*, 34: 103–14.

Macnicol, J. (1987) In pursuit of the underclass, *Journal of Social Policy*, 16(3): 293–318.

Macpherson, Sir William of Cluny (1999) *The Stephen Lawrence Inquiry*. London: Stationery Office.

Malloch, M.S. and Stanley, E. (2005) The detention of asylum seekers in the UK, *Punishment & Society*, 7(1): 58–71.

Manovich, L. (2001) *The Language of the New Media*. Cambridge, MA: MIT Press.

Martin, J. (1998) *Gramsci's Political Analysis*. Houndsmill: Macmillan.

Martinson, R. (1974) What works? – questions and answers about prison reform. *Public Interest*, 35: 22–54.

Marx, K. (1990) *Capital*. Vol. 1. London: Penguin.

Mason, P., Morris, K. and Smith, P. (2005) A complex solution to a complicated problem? Early messages from the national evaluation of the Children's Fund Prevention Programme, *Children & Society*, 19: 131–43.

Mathiason, N. (2007) Children's homes hit by buyout fears, *Observer*, 14 October. http://society.guardian.co.uk/children/story/0,,2191473,00.html

Matthews, R., Easton, H., Briggs, D. and Pease, K. (2007) *Assessing the Use and Impact of Anti-Social Behaviour Orders*. Bristol: Policy Press.

Mautner, G. (2005) The entrepreneurial university, *Critical Discourse Studies*, 2(2): 95–120.

May, C. (2002) *The Information Society*. Cambridge: Polity Press.

McGhee, D. (2005) *Intolerant Britain? Hate, Citizenship and Difference*. Maidenhead: Open University Press.

McGrath, J.E. (2004) *Loving Big Brother*. London: Routledge.

McKibbin, R. (2007) Pure New Labour, *London Review of Books*, 29(19): 17–19.

McLaughlin, H. (2008) What's in a name: 'client', 'patient', 'customer', 'consumer', 'expert by experience', 'service user' – what's next?', *British Journal of Social Work*, advanced electronic access from 21 February. http://bjsw.oxfordjournals.org/

McLaughlin, K. (2007) Regulation and risk in social work: the General Social Care Council and the Social Care Register in context, *British Journal of Social Work*, 37(7): 1263–77.

McLaughlin, K. (2008) *Social Work, Politics and Society*. Bristol: Policy Press.

Miliband, D. (2007) Out with the old, in with the new, *Observer*, 25 March.

Millie, A., Jacobson, J., McDonald, E. and Hough, M. (2005) *Anti-social Behaviour Strategies*. Bristol: Policy Press.

Ministry for Justice (2008) Lord Goldsmith recommends new emphasis on the common bond of citizenship. Press release, 11 March.

Mitchell, D. (1996) Back in circulation, *Community Care*, 6–12 April.

Modood, T. (2005) A defence of multiculturalism, *Soundings*, 29: 62–72.

Mooney, G. and Law, A. (eds) (2007) *New Labour/Hard Labour: Restructuring and Resistance Inside of the Welfare Industry*. Bristol: Policy Press.

Muncie, J. (2004) Youth justice: globalisation and multi-modal governance, in T. Newburn and R. Sparks (eds) *Criminal Justice and Political Cultures*. Cullompton: Willan.

Muncie, J., Hughes, G. and McLaughlin, E. (eds) (2002) *Youth Justice: Critical Readings*. London: Sage.

Munck, R. (2005) Neoliberalism and politics, and the politics of neoliberalism, in A. Saad-Filho and D. Johnston (eds) *Neoliberalism: A Critical Reader*. London: Pluto.

Munro, E. (2001) Empowering children, *Child and Family Social Work*, 6: 129–37.

Munro, E. (2008) Lessons learnt, boxes ticked, families ignored, *Independent on Sunday*, 16 November.

National Children's Homes (NCH) (2006) Anti-social behaviour: supporting families and communities in Kirklees. Press release, 6 March.

National Children's Home (NCH) Action for Children Scotland (1995) Dundee Housing Project. Unpublished.

National Statistics (2004) Why is the UK population growing? Press release, 24 June.

Nederveen Pieterse, J. (2004) Neoliberal empire, *Theory, Culture & Society*, 21(3), 119–40.

Needham, C. (2004) Customer-focused government, *Soundings*, 26: 73–86.

Nellis, M. (2005) Electronic monitoring, satellite tracking, and the new punitiveness in England and Wales, in J. Pratt, D. Brown, M. Brown, S. Hallsworth and W. Morrison (eds) *The New Punitiveness: Trends, Theories and Perspectives*. Cullompton: Willan.

Neocleous, M. (1999) Radical conservatism, or the conservatism of radicals: Giddens, Blair and the politics of reaction, *Radical Philosophy*, 93: 24–35.

Neocleous, M. (2007) Whatever happened to martial law? Detainees and the logic of emergency, *Radical Philosophy*, May/June: 13–23.

Newburn, T. (2002) Atlantic crossings: 'policy transfer' and crime control in the USA and Britain, *Punishment & Society*, 4(2): 165–94.

Newburn, T. and Sparks, R. (2004) Criminal Justice and political cultures, in T. Newburn and R. Sparks (eds) *Criminal Justice and Political Cultures*. Cullompton: Willan.

Newman, J. (2001) *Modernising Governance: New Labour, Policy and Society*. London: Sage.

Nixon, J. (2007) Deconstructing 'problem' researchers and 'problem families' *Critical Social Policy*, 27(4): 546–57.

Nixon, J., Hunter, C., Parr, S., Myers, S., Whittle, S. and Sanderson, D. (2006) *Interim Evaluation of Rehabilitation Projects for Families at Risk of Losing their Homes as a Result of Anti-social Behaviour*. London: Office of the Deputy Prime Minister

Office for Standards in Education (Ofsted) (2007) *Making ContactPoint Work*. www.ico.gov.uk/upload/documents/pressreleases/2006/ protecting_childrens_personal_information.pdf

Office for Standards in Education (Ofsted), Healthcare Commission, Her Majesty's Inspectorate of Constabulary (2008) *Joint area review: Haringey Children's Services Authority Area*. www.ofsted.gov.uk/oxcare_providers/la_download/(id)/4657/(as)/ JAR/jar_2008_309_fr.pdf

Office of the EU Commissioner for Human Rights (OEUCHR) (2005) *Report by Mr. Alvaro Gil-Robles, Commissioner for Human Rights, on His Visit to the United Kingdom, 4th–12th November 2004*. Strasbourg: Council of Europe.

Osborne, D. and Gaebler, T.A. (1992) *Reinventing Government: How the Entrepreneurial Spirit is Transforming the Public Sector*. Reading, MA: Addison Wesley.

Owen, J. (2000) We will not be tagged, *Community Care*, 19–25 October, special supplement, *Leaping the Digital Divide: Making IT Happen*: 19.

PA Consulting Group (2004) ID Cards – Home Secretary announces private sector partner. Press release, 24 May. www.paconsulting.com/news/press_release/2004/ pr_20040524_id_cards.htm

Papps, P. (1998) Anti-social behaviour strategies – individualistic or holistic? *Housing Studies*, 23(5): 639–56.

Parker, R., Ward, H., Jackson, S., Aldgate, J. and Wedge, P. (1991) *Looking After Children: Assessing Outcomes in Child Care*. London: HMSO.

Parr, S. (2008) Family intervention projects: a site of social work practice, *British Journal of Social Work*, advanced electronic access from 23 April. http://bjsw.oxfordjour nals.org/

Parr, S. and Nixon, J. (2008) Rationalising family intervention projects, in P. Squires (ed.) *ASBO Nation*. Bristol: Policy Press.

Parton, N. (2006a) *Safeguarding Childhood: Early Intervention and Surveillance in a Late Modern Society*. Houndsmill: Palgrave.

Parton, N. (2006b) Changes in the form of knowledge in social work: from the 'social' to the 'informational'? *British Journal of Social Work*, 38(2): 253–69.

Payne, L. (2003) Anti-social behaviour. *Children & Society*, 17: 321–4.

Peck, J. (2001) *Workfare States*. London: Guilford Press.

Peck, J. (2004) Geography and public policy: constructions of neoliberalism, *Progress in Human Geography*, 28(3): 392–405.

Penna, S. (2005) The Children Act 2004: child protection and social surveillance, *Journal of Social Welfare and Family Law*, 27(2): 143–57.

Performance and Innovation Unit (PIU) (2000) *The Prime Minister's Review of Adoption: A Performance and Innovation Unit Report*. London: Stationery Office.

Performance and Innovation Unit (PIU) (2002) *Privacy and Data-sharing: The Way Forward for Public Services*. London: Cabinet Office.

Pettigrew, A. (2006) Whatever happened to social work? A professional perspective, in What Makes the Difference *Can the State be a good parent? Making the Difference for Looked After Children and Care Leavers*. London: WMTD/National Care Leaving Care Advisory Service.

Philp, A.F. and Timms, N. (1957) *The Problem of 'the Problem Family'*. London: Family Service Units.

Pileggi, M.S. and Patton, C. (2003) Bourdieu and cultural studies, *Cultural Studies*, 17(3/4): 313–25.

Pine, L. (1995) Hasude: The imprisonment of 'asocial' families in the Third Reich, *The Germany History Society*, 13(2): 182–98.

Pinkerton, J. (2006) Developing a global approach to the theory and practice of young people leaving care, *Child and Family Social Work*, 11: 191–8.

Pithouse, A. (2007) Early intervention in the round: a great idea but . . ., *British Journal of Social Work*, advanced electronic access from 4 October. http://bjsw.oxfordjournals.org/

Platt, D. (2007) *The Status of Social Care – A Review*. www.dh.gov.uk/en/Publicationsand-statistics/Publications/PublicationsPolicyAndGuidance/DH_074217.

Pollack, S. (2008) Labelling clients 'Risky': social work and the neoliberal welfare state, *British Journal of Social Work*, advanced electronic access from 30 May. http://bjsw.oxfordjournals.org/

Pratt, J., Brown, D., Brown, M., Hallsworth, S. and Morrison, W. (2005) Introduction, in J. Pratt, D. Brown, M. Brown, S. Hallsworth and W. Morrison (eds) *The New Punitiveness: Trends, Theories and Perspectives*. Cullompton: Willan.

Precht, D. (2003) Northampton On Track Project: some lessons from the first year's work, *Practice*, 15(1): 2–21.

Prideaux, S. (2005) *Not So New Labour: A Sociological Critique of New Labour's Policy and Practice*. Bristol: Policy Press.

Prime Minister's Strategy Unit (2007) *Building on Progress: Security, Crime and Justice*. London: HM Government.

Purnell, J. (2008) Ready to work, skilled for work. Speech at Unlocking Britain's Talent conference. 28 January. www.dwp.gov.uk/aboutus/2008/28-01-08

Rawles, S. (2008) Portraits of respect, *Society Guardian*, 26 March.

Reeves, R. (2007) *CoCo Companies: Work, Happiness and Employee Ownership*. London: Employee Ownership Association.

Renton, D. (2001) *Marx on Globalisation*. London: Lawrence and Wishart.

Respect Task Force (2006) *Respect Action Plan*. London: Home Office.

Robinson, A. (2006) Towards an intellectual reformation: the critique of common sense and the forgotten revolutionary project of Gramscian theory, in A. Bieler and A. Morton (eds) *Images of Gramsci*. London: Routledge.

Robinson, G. (2003) Technicality and indeterminacy in probation practice: a case study, *British Journal of Social Work*, 33(5): 593–610.

Robinson, O. (2003) Every breath you take, *Guardian, Office Hours*, 20 October.

Rodger, J.J. (2006) Antisocial families and the withholding of welfare support, *Critical Social Policy*, 26(1): 121–44.

Rose, N. (2000) Government and control, *British Journal of Criminology*, 40: 321–39.

Ruddy, L. (2004) The hub of action, *Community Care*, 9–15 September.

Runnymede Trust (2000) *The future of Multi-Ethnic Britain*. London: Profile Books.

Russell, J. (2008) We must dare to rethink the welfare that benefits no one, *Guardian*, 21 November.

Rustin, Margaret (2005) Conceptual analysis of critical moments in Victoria Climbié's life, *Child and Family Social Work*, 10: 11–19.

Rustin, Michael (2004) Learning from the Victoria Climbié Inquiry, *Journal of Social Work Practice*, 18(1): 9–19.

Rutherford, J. (2005) Commentary: how we live now, *Soundings*, 30: 9–17.

Sales, R. (2002) The deserving and undeserving? Refugees, asylum seekers and welfare in Britain, *Critical Social Policy*, 22(3): 456–79.

Sapey, B. (1997) Social work tomorrow: towards a critical understanding of technology in social work, *British Journal of Social Work*, 27: 803–14.

Sargent, S. (2003) Adoption and looked after children: a comparison of legal initiatives in the UK and USA, *Adoption & Fostering*, 27(2): 44–53.

Schuster, L. and Solomos, J. (2004) Race, immigration and asylum: New Labour's agenda and its consequences, *Ethnicities*, 4(2): 267–300.

Scott, P. (2004) Prospects for knowledge work: critical engagement or expert conscription? *New Formations*, 53: 28–41.

Scourfield, P. (2007) Are there reasons to be worried about the 'caretelisation' of residential care, *Critical Social Policy*, 27(2): 155–81.

Scraton, P. (ed.) (1987) *Law, Order and the Authoritarian State*, Milton Keynes: Open University Press.

Secretary of State for Education and Skills (2006) *Care Matters: Transforming the Lives of Children and Young People in Care*. London: HMSO.

Secretary of State for Health (1998) *Quality Protects: Transforming Children's Services – The Role and Responsibilities of Councillors*. London: Department of Health.

Secretary of State for Health and the Secretary of State for the Home Department (2003) *The Victoria Climbié Inquiry – Report of an Inquiry by Lord Laming*. London: HMSO, Cm 5730.

Selwyn, N. (2002) 'E-stablishing' an inclusive society? Technology, social exclusion and UK government policy making, *Journal of Social Policy*, 31(1): 1–20.

Sennett, R. (2004) *Respect: The Formation of Character in an Age of Inequality*. London: Penguin.

Simpkin, M. (1983) *Trapped Within Welfare: Surviving Social Work*. London: Macmillan.

Sivanandan, A. (2006) Attacks on multicultural Britain pave the way for enforced assimilation, *Guardian*, 13 September.

Skinner, G., Tonsager, A.M. and Hall, N. (2003) *Privacy and Data-Sharing: Survey of Public Awareness and Perceptions*. London: MORI.

Social Exclusion Task Force (2007) *Reaching Out: Think Family*. London: Cabinet Office.

Social Exclusion Task Force (2008) *Reaching Out: Improving the Life Chances of Families at Risk*. London: Cabinet Office.

Spinley, B.M. (1953) *The Deprived and the Privileged*. London: Routledge and Kegan Paul.

Squires, P. (2006) New Labour and the politics of antisocial behaviour, *Critical Social Policy*, 26(1): 144–69.

Squires, P. and Stephen, D.E. (2005) Rethinking ASBOs, *Critical Social Policy*, 25(4): 517–28.

Stabile, C.A. and Morooka, J. (2003) Between two evils, I refuse to choose the lesser evil, *Cultural Studies*, 17(3/4): 326–48.

Stallybrass, J. (1995) Empowering technology: the exploration of cyberspace, *New Left Review*, 211: 3–33.

Starkey, P. (2000) The feckless mother: women, poverty and social workers in wartime and post-war England, *Women's History Review*, 9(3): 539–59.

Stedman Jones, G. (1984) *Outcast London*. Harmondsworth: Penguin.

Stein, M. (2006) Wrong turn, *Guardian*, 6 December.

Straw, J. and Anderson, J. (1996) *Parenting*. London: Labour Party.

Swanson, J. (2000) Self help Clinton, Blair and the politics of personal responsibility, *Radical Philosophy*, 101: 29–39.

Taylor-Gooby, P. (2000) Blair's scars, *Critical Social Policy*, 20(3): 331–449.

Thompson, G. (2008) Are we all neoliberals now? 'Responsibility' and corporations, *Soundings*, 39: 67–75

Thomson, A. (2005) Old warhorse who lost his moral compass, *Sunday Independent*, 6 November.

Tisdall, E.K.M. (2006) Antisocial behaviour legislation meets children's services: challenging perspectives on children, parents and the state, *Critical Social Policy*, 26(1): 101–21.

Toynbee, P. (2006) We can't let children in care fall victim to privatisation, *Guardian*, 10 October.

Toynbee, P. (2008) This frenzy of hatred is a disaster for children at risk, *Guardian*, 18 November.

Tregeagle, S. and Darcy, M. (2007) Child welfare and information and communication's technology: today's challenge, *British Journal of Social Work*, advanced electronic access from 26 July. http://bjsw.oxfordjournals.org/

Tunstill, J., Allnock, D., Akhurst, S. and Garbers, C. (2005) Sure Start local programmes: implications of case study data from the national evaluation of Sure Start. *Children & Society*, 19(2): 158–71.

UNISON (2008a) *Progress Report on Safeguarding: UNISON Memorandum of Lord Laming*. London: UNISON. www.unison.org.uk/acrobat/B4364a.pdf

UNISON (2008b) *UNISON's 10-point Plan for Protecting Vulnerable Children*. www.unison.org.uk/localgov/pages_view.asp?did=7962

United Nations Development Programme (2005) *Human Development Report: International Cooperation at a Crossroads*. New York: Oxford University Press.

Van de Flier Davis, D. (1995) Capitalising on adoption, *Adoption & Fostering*, 19(2): 25–31.

VeriChip (2007) VeriChip Corporation Partners with Alzheimer's Community Care. Press release, 22 February. www.verichipcorp/news/1172151146

Wachsmann, N. (2001) From indefinite confinement to extermination, in R. Gellately and N. Stoltzfus (eds) *Social Outcasts in Nazi Germany*. Princeton, NJ: Princeton University Press.

Wacquant, L. (2001) The penalisation of poverty and the rise of neo-liberalism, *European Journal on Criminal Policy and Research*, 9: 401–12.

Wacquant, L. (2002) Slavery to mass incarceration, *New Left Review*, 13: 41–61.

Wacquant, L. (2005) The penal leap backward: incarceration in America from Nixon to Clinton, in J. Pratt, D. Brown, M. Brown, S. Hallsworth and W. Morrison (eds) *The New Punitiveness: Trends, Theories and Perspectives*. Cullompton: Willan.

Wade, R. (2008) Financial regime change, *New Left Review*, 53: 5–23.

Walker, R. (1999) The Americanization of British welfare: a case Study of policy transfer, *International Journal of Health Services*, 29(4): 679–97.

Walsh, C. (2002) Curfews: no more hanging around, *Youth Justice*, 2(2): 70–82.

Ward, H. (ed.) (1995) *Looking After Children: Research into Practice*. London: HMSO.

Waterworth, S. (2003) Temporal reference frameworks and nurses work organization, *Time & Society*, 12(1): 41–54.

Wayne, M. (2003) Surveillance and big brother. *Radical Philosophy*, 117: 34–43.

Webb, S.A. (2006) *Social Work in a Risk Society*. Houndsmill: Palgrave.

Weir, A. (2003) You mustn't presume, *Community Care*, 27 November–3 December: 34–6.

Welshman, J. (1999a) The social history of social work: the issue of the 'problem family' 1940–70, *British Journal of Social Work*, 29: 457–76.

Welshman, J. (1999b) Evacuation, hygiene, and social policy: the *Our Towns* report of 1943, *The Historical Journal*, 42(3): 781–807.

White, S., Hall, C. and Peckover, S. (2008) The descriptive tyranny of the Common Assessment Framework: technologies of categorization and professional practice in child welfare, *British Journal of Social Work*, advanced electronic access from 16 April. http://bjsw.oxfordjournals.org/

Williams, F. (2004) What matters is what works: why every child matters to New Labour. Commentary on the DfES Green Paper *Every Child Matters*, *Critical Social Policy*, 24(3): 406–27.

Williams, R. (1983) *Keywords: A Vocabulary of Culture and Society*. 2nd edn. New York: Oxford University Press. (First published in 1976.)

Winchester, R. (2003) Welcome to the machine, *Community Care*, 30 October–5 November: 26–8.

Winchester, R. (2004) Home truths, *Community Care*, 29 April–5 May: 30–1.

Wintour, P. (2008) Timely interventions, *Society Guardian*, 30 April.

Women's Group on Public Welfare (1943) *Our Towns – a Close Up: A Study Made in 1939–1942 with Certain Recommendations by the Hygiene Committee of the Women's Group on Public Welfare*. London: Oxford University.

Yuval-Davis, N., Anthias, F. and Kofman, E. (2005) Secure borders and safe haven and the gendered politics of belonging: beyond social cohesion, *Ethnic and Racial Studies*, 28(3): 513–35.

# Index

# 190   Index

# Related books from Open University Press
Purchase from www.openup.co.uk or order through your local bookseller

## SAFEGUARDING CHILDREN AND YOUNG PEOPLE
A Guide for Nurses and Midwifes

### Catherine Powell

While many nurses and midwives are in an ideal position to prevent, identify and respond to child maltreatment, they may not currently have a clear understanding of the theory, policy and practice of safeguarding children. This book, which has been written specifically for a nursing and midwifery audience, provides an accessible text that outlines and explores professional roles and responsibilities in the context of inter-agency working.

Importantly, it has chapters on:

- Child neglect
- Fabricated or induced illness
- Child death and child maltreatment
- Safeguarding vulnerable children

This groundbreaking book provides a much needed education, research, practice and evidence-based evaluation. The book also:

- Includes case examples and points for reflection
- Provides an analysis of children's rights and child protection
- Enables readers to understand and apply theory and policy to practice
- Outlines the roles and responsibilities of other agencies
- Helps readers develop skills to deal with sensitive and traumatic issues
- Addresses the importance of confidentiality and information sharing

Safeguarding Children and Young People is core reading for all nursing and midwifery students and practitioners. should consider and traps they should avoid when embarking on a social research project.

*Contents*
*Introduction: Why a safeguarding children guide for nurses and midwives? – Why every child matters – Child maltreatment – Safeguarding children: Professional roles and responsibilities – Safeguarding vulnerable children – Fabricated or induced illness – Child neglect – Child death and child maltreatment – Conclusion: Knowledge for practice.*

July 2007  256pp

ISBN–13: 978–0–335–22028–1  (ISBN–10: 0–335–22028–2) Paperback
ISBN–13: 978–0–335–22029–8  (ISBN–10: 0–335–22029–0) Hardback

# ADVOCACY FOR CHILDREN AND YOUNG PEOPLE

## Jane Boylan and Jane Dalrymple

*"A welcome contribution not only towards the development of advocacy policy and practice with children and young people across the UK and further afield . . . The authors . . . deftly combine . . . very pertinent theoretical perspectives with case studies and practical illustrations of how . . . discourses play out in the real world of children and young people's lives. In so doing the book provides a powerful and timely reminder to practitioners, policy makers and commissioners of the importance of critical reflective practice in understanding the dynamics at play."*

> Anne Crowley, Assistant Director (Policy and Research), Save the Children UK

*"This book is a serious read for anyone interested in the development of children's rights and advocacy. It has been thoroughly researched by two of the most highly respected commentators on the subject, and represents an authoritative and comprehensive guide. I would especially commend it to policy makers as providing a realistic account of what sometimes prevents good children's rights and advocacy practice, and for tackling very real and contentious issues such as 'best interest' principles getting in the way of giving full expression of children's own views."*

> Mike Lindsay, National Co-ordinator of Children's Rights Alliance for England

Presenting children and young people's advocacy as an exciting, radical and constantly developing way of working, Boylan and Dalrymple explore its controversial and challenging nature through a comprehensive examination of the theory and practice of advocacy. Readers are invited to consider advocacy as a powerful tool for promoting change in attitudes towards children and young people. The development of meaningful participation in decision making and systemic change in the provision of services for children and young people is identified as key to this process.

Key issues explored include:

- An historical overview of advocacy within professional practice
- The development of independent advocacy
- The contested nature of advocacy
- Children and young people's participation
- Forms and models for the provision of advocacy
- The relationship between advocacy and anti-oppressive practice

The authors draw on their own research and the experiences of young people, advocates and professionals working with children and young people to examine key messages and debates that have emerged. Case examples are used to illustrate advocacy dilemmas in a range of settings.

*Contents:*
*Acknowledgements - Foreword - Introduction - Charting the development of advocacy for children and young people - Childhood, children's rights and advocacy - The practice of advocacy: Participation, voice and resistance - What is advocacy and who defines it? - Forms of advocacy - Models for the provision of advocacy - Advocacy as a tool for anti-oppressive practice - The way forward: Optimism and notes of caution - References - Index.*

2009   160pp

978–0–335–22373–2 (Paperback)   978–0–335–22372–5 (Hardback)

# YOUNG PEOPLE AND SOCIAL CHANGE 2/E
New Perspectives

## Andy Furlong and Fred Cartmel

Reviews of the first edition:

*"Not only does the clarity of the authors' writing make the book very accessible, but their argument is also illustrated throughout with a broad range of empirical material . . . undoubtedly a strong contribution to the study of both contemporary youth and 'late-modern' society."*

*Youth Justice*

*"A very accessible, well-evidenced and important book . . . It succeeds in raising important questions in a new and powerful way."*

*Journal of Education and Work*

*"the book will be very popular with students and with academics. . . .. .The clarity of the organization, expression and argument is particularly commendable. I have no doubt that Young People and Social Change will rightly find its way onto the recommended reading lists of many in the field."*

*Professor Robert MacDonald, University of Teesside*

A welcome update to one of the most influential and authoritative books on young people in modern societies. With a fuller theoretical explanation and drawing on a comprehensive range of studies from Europe, North America, Australia and Japan, the second edition of *Young People and Social Change* is a valuable contribution to the field. The authors examine modern theoretical interpretations of social change in relation to young people and provide an overview of their experiences in a number of key contexts such as education, employment, the family, leisure, health, crime and politics.

Building on the success of the previous edition, the second edition offers an expanded theoretical approach and wider coverage of empirical data to take into account worldwide developments in the field. Drawing on a wealth of research evidence, the book highlights key differences between the experiences of young people in different countries in the developed world.

*Young People and Social Change* offers a wide-ranging and up-to-date introductory text for students in sociology of youth, sociology of education, social stratification and related fields.

*Contents*
*List of figures – The authors – Acknowledgements – Series editor's preface – The risk society – Change and continuity in education – Social change and labour market transitions – Changing patterns of dependency – Leisure and lifestyles – Health risks in late modernity – Crime and insecurity – Politics and participation – The epistemological fallacy of late modernity – Notes – References – Index.*

2006   208pp

978–0–335–21868–4 (Paperback)   978–0–335–21869–1 (Hardback)

**South Essex College**
Further & Higher Education, Southend Campus
Luker Road  Southend-on-Sea  Essex  SS1 1ND
Tel: 01702 220400  Fax: 01702 432320
Minicom: 01702 220642